West Bay, Bridport. No. 32

The
Bridport Railway

by
B.L. Jackson and M.J. Tattershall

THE OAKWOOD PRESS

Incorporating material first published as *The Bridport Branch* by the Oxford Publishing Co., 1976.

© Oakwood Press, B.L. Jackson & M.J. Tattershall 1998

British Library Cataloguing in Publication Data
A Record for this book is available from the British Library
ISBN 0 85361 520 9

Typeset by Oakwood Graphics.
Repro by Ford Graphics, Ringwood, Hants.
Printed by Alpha Print (Oxford), Witney, Oxon.

Above and opposite: Comic postcards taking a facetious look at railways were quite common, in particular on branch lines. Often the same picture sufficed for various locations, only the captions being changed to suit. *K. Bakes Collection*

Title page: Bridport signal box on 17th April, 1963. *C.L. Caddy*

Published by
The Oakwood Press (Usk)
P.O. Box 13, Usk, Mon., NP5 1YS.

Contents

	Foreword to First Edition	5
	Introduction	6
Chapter One	Early Railway Developments	7
Chapter Two	Construction	13
Chapter Three	The Broad Gauge Era	23
Chapter Four	The Final Years of Independence	39
Chapter Five	The Great Western Era	71
Chapter Six	The Route Described	111
	Goods Traffic	142
	Motive Power	147
	Rolling Stock	159
	Signalling and Train Working	163
	Working Methods	171
Chapter Seven	Nationalisation to Closure	175
Chapter Eight	Conclusion	209
Appendix One	Chronology	215
Appendix Two	Branch Line Staff	217
Appendix Three	Farewell to a Railway	221
	Acknowledgements	222
	Index	223

Joseph Gundry, first Chairman of the Bridport Railway Company, shown wearing the insignia of Provincial Grand Master of Dorset. *By permission of the Bridport Museum Service*

Foreword to First Edition

It gave me great pleasure when I was asked to write a foreword to the history of the Bridport branch.

There has been a long involvement of the Gundry family in the history of Bridport in general and in the branch line in particular. It was Joseph Gundry, my Great Grandfather of the Hyde, who was elected the Chairman of the Bridport Railway Company when it was formed in 1855, my Great Uncle Benjamin Pearkes Gundry also being a Director of the company, and it was these two who travelled on the engine on the first trial run along the line on 29th September, 1857.

The net and twine companies of Bridport, now incorporated in the firm of Bridport Gundry(Holdings) Ltd, were one of the best customers as regards goods traffic, thus the branch line was instrumental in bringing prosperity to the town.

It is also with regret that I write what is, in effect, a valediction to the line. It survived two threats of closure, and was saved by the narrowness of the West Dorset roads, but was finally closed on 5th May, 1975 after 120 years to the date, having been incorporated on 5th May, 1855.

Is it too much to hope that the line may be saved from oblivion and be preserved for the enjoyment of future generations; those who have happy memories of journeys on the Bridport branch will have nostalgic memories of the bluebells and wild flowers along the line in spring and summer, and the autumn tints on Powerstock Common. The puffing and huffing efforts of the engine as it ground its way up through Witherstone cutting, the clanging of milk churns being loaded at Toller. All these are things of the past, but is it beyond the wit of man that the line could become a nature trail before it becomes overgrown with brambles and rambling parasites, or a leisure area where the public could enjoy a walk through the countryside where wild life, such as deer, foxes and badgers could be seen in their natural environment?

My congratulations to both Mr Jackson and Mr Tattershall for completing the history of the Bridport branch before traces of it are obliterated and while records and memories are still available. It will be a valuable adjunct to the local archives and will be a help to future generations in assessing the initiative of their forebears.

Joseph Gundry
The Hyde
Bridport

21st October, 1976

Introduction

The Bridport branch was 9¼ miles long from Maiden Newton to Bridport station, and during its 118 years life span it saw many changes. It commenced as a private railway operated by the GWR on the ill-fated Broad Gauge. An extension to West Bay, it was hoped, would bring prosperity to both the railway company and the local community. Absorbed into the GWR, the line continued through two world wars and into a changing world in which the motor vehicle was eventually to dominate. The Bridport branch saw it all, and despite being proposed for closure in the 1963 Beeching plan it struggled on for a further 12 years, becoming Dorset's last passenger branch line to close.

Winding its way through the hills of West Dorset it was never the ideal route for a line to Bridport, but the geology of the land precluded most of the other proposed schemes from reaching the town. From Bridport the line ran up hill to the village of Powerstock where the station nestled under the shadow of Egardon Hill, then twisted and turned through wooded countryside where ancient Kings shot deer, and through the infamous Witherstone cutting to the next village of Toller, finally meeting the main line at Maiden Newton.

During its heyday the branch did good business connecting the small town of Bridport with the main line, and opening a gateway to Dorchester and Weymouth in the South, and northwards to London (Paddington), South Wales, the Midlands and North of England.

The quiet West Dorset countryside and the villages of Powerstock and Toller would be regularly awakened by the hiss of steam and later by the throb of diesel engines - as the branch trains called at their respective stations, making in years past the principal connection these places had with the outside world. But now all has gone and the railway will never return.

This book makes an attempt at tracing the history of the line from its inception through to closure. Every detail has been checked (where possible) with the documents still available. However, since the original edition of this work appeared 23 years ago many aids to research have been developed, in particular the preservation on microfilm of newspapers which has rendered them considerably easier to consult, and we hope this has enhanced the subject without destroying the character of the original work.

As well as a nostalgic look at the line from steam to diesel, the authors have attempted to give an insight into both railway history and railway working, together with a look at the involvement of the staff who operated the branch. The social and economic background against which the line traded and survived is also covered, and we hope the reader will enjoy this book as much as we have enjoyed researching the days when Bridport had a railway.

In the intervening years many former railwaymen and railway enthusiasts have taken their final journey, and it is to these good friends we dedicate this work.

B.L. Jackson
M.J. Tattershall

Chapter One

Early Railway Developments

Bridport is a small market town nestling between the hills of West Dorset, nine miles east of the Devon border and 15 miles west of Dorchester. The town has a population of about 6,000 and was granted Borough status by a Charter of 1253.

The main industry of the town was, and still is, the making of ropes, nets and twine, while 1½ miles away is Bridport harbour, now known as West Bay, which until the turn of the present century was an important part of the town as it supplied employment to a large number of the townspeople in the building of small sailing ships and fishing vessels.

Bridport has not changed much over the years and the character of the town remains much the same. It was served in the early days by rough roads and cart tracks to and from the surrounding districts. The only method of transport linking it with other places of importance was the daily coach service to Exeter, Taunton and Yeovil, that is, until the coming of the railway, the iron road that gave an unrivalled method of travel - which is where the story begins.

During the 1830s the railways had arrived. The world's first fully operational railway, carrying both passenger and goods traffic and worked by locomotives, had opened and proved to be an enormous success. As a direct result, railway companies sprang up all over the country. Between 1845 and 1846 there was a 'Railway Mania'; within a year no less than 272 railway Acts were passed through Parliament. Railway promotion was enjoying a boom, but so far the relatively small county of Dorset had been entirely neglected, although the major companies were gradually turning their attention to the area. Many of the lines were only paper proposals, and remained just that. It is, however, relevant to our story to mention some of them here.

The first scheme to appear in 1844 was the Wilts, Somerset and Weymouth Railway (WS&W), to construct a line from near Corsham in Wiltshire to Weymouth with branches from Yeovil to Sherborne, and from Maiden Newton to Bridport harbour. The Wilts, Somerset and Weymouth Company Act of Parliament was passed on the 30th June, 1845. During the same year the Great Western Railway (GWR) was proposing to construct a line to Falmouth in Cornwall. This was known as the Exeter Great Western Railway (EGWR) and was to be an extension of one of its existing lines that ended at Hungerford. It was to proceed via Westbury, Yeovil and Exeter - Bridport being served by a branch that was to run from Axminster.

A second scheme in the same year was a Bristol & Exeter Railway plan for a line from Durston (near Taunton) to Yeovil with a branch to Bridport and an extension from Yeovil to Weymouth, but in the event only the Durston-Yeovil branch was built.

At the same time the London & South Western Railway (LSWR) was planning its route to the West via Salisbury and Yeovil to Exeter. It also intended to serve the town of Bridport with a branch from Wayford (near Crewkerne) to join the WS&W's own proposed Bridport branch outside the town. Also during 1845 a coast line was surveyed by Captain Moorsom, Engineer of the Southampton and Dorchester Railway. His plan was for a line to Exeter as an extension of the Southampton and Dorchester. This new line, passing through Bridport, was known as the Exeter, Dorchester, Weymouth Junction Coast Railway, followed by the South Western & South Devon Coast Junction Railway, but only went as far as issuing a Prospectus.

There was also the proposed 'Exeter Yeovil and Dorchester Railway', with plans to construct a line from Exeter to Yeovil with a branch to Dorchester from Sutton Bingham.

A branch to Bridport was authorised in 1848, but the entire scheme foundered owing to the inability to raise capital.

There was great interest in a coast line, as joining the ports of the Bristol and English Channels was considered to be of great importance as the steamship was still in its infancy, and all goods sent by sea had the long and often dangerous passage around Land's End and along the Cornish coast. So, still in 1845, the Bristol and English Channels Direct Junction Railway was planned to join the port of Watchet (on the Bristol Channel) with Bridport. Not only did this link the Somerset & Dorset coasts at that time, but would have been the most direct route to South Wales via the Bristol Channel. This railway was to have used part of the Bristol and Exeter Railway to cross Somerset on its route to Bridport.

The Railway Mania swept Dorset like the rest of the country, and the final scheme to mention Bridport in that year was the Bristol and English Channels Connection Railway. There were plans to construct a harbour at Burnham and to build a line to serve both Bridport and Lyme Regis.

In 1847 the LSWR again sought powers for the construction of a line to Bridport, which included a junction at Wayford with a spur from a point four miles north of Axminster as well as a branch to Charmouth. To match this proposal the broad gauge EGWR also planned to take a line to Charmouth.

The year 1851 saw Castleman and Moorsom planning a revival of the 1845 Southampton and Dorchester scheme. It was to be under the name of the Dorchester and Exeter Coast Extension Railway. The new scheme left out Weymouth and took an easier route to the west of Bridport. Although this scheme was supported by the Board of Directors, it failed to gain the support of the shareholders.

At that stage the only railway that had succeeded in achieving its goal was the Southampton and Dorchester, having opened its line from Southampton to Dorchester on 1st June, 1847, to become Dorset's first railway. The Wilts Somerset & Weymouth, despite having received its Act of Parliament a month before the Southampton and Dorchester, was making very little progress, and all along the route there were many partly completed earthworks. Westbury was reached in September 1848 but, trapped in the aftermath of the Railway Mania, lack of funds delayed further progress. In March 1850 the Great Western took over the commitments and assets of the Wilts, Somerset & Weymouth Company, and Frome was reached in October. The Salisbury branch opened as far as Warminster on 1st September, 1851, but the following month it was reported that earthworks at Castle Cary had not progressed for three years, and nature was beginning to reclaim the land.

On 30th June, 1852 the GWR obtained an extension of time for completion of its WS&W line that was by now in severe financial difficulties. A local company called the Frome, Yeovil and Weymouth Railway was formed to try and raise the money required locally - this was a failure. The GWR had to proceed alone, and under these circumstances, powers for the Bridport and Sherborne branches were allowed to be forgotten.

The GWR was still interested in a line from Yeovil to Exeter of broad gauge construction, and in the 1852/3 session of Parliament promoted a Bill for the 'Devon and Dorset'. This line was to go westwards from Maiden Newton to join a previously intended route near Axminster. Bridport was to be served by a branch from Netherbury, a small village just north of the town. At this time the military authorities considered it important that there be a continuous line of railway along the south coast of England from Dover to Plymouth without break of gauge.

The South Western strongly opposed the Devon and Dorset scheme, although it did not renew its application to construct the projected line west of Dorchester. The South

Western Chairman had pledged, when the military had advocated a single gauge line along the coast, that the company would apply for powers to construct such a line. The Devon and Dorset scheme failed, and despite the pledge by the South Western when the Dorchester and Exeter Bill was submitted to the shareholders in the November of 1853 it was rejected. Again in 1854 the South Western deposited plans for a line from Dorchester to Bridport, a shortened version of the previous Exeter scheme known as the Dorchester and Bridport Railway. This scheme was not proceeded with.

During 1854 the people of Bridport were getting very dissatisfied with the outcome of the various railway schemes that had been drawn up. To date there had been 12 various deposited plans for a railway, but none had, or appeared likely to, come to fruition. The townspeople felt that the major companies were not to be relied upon, and that they must, if they wished to have a railway, build a line of their own.

On 28th September, 1854 a report was published by Henry J. Wylie, a Civil Engineer, on a survey he carried out on the proposed Bridport Railway. Henry Johnston Wylie was born in Edinburgh in July 1822. Following his education at Edinburgh Academy and Glasgow University he was apprenticed to George Marten of Glasgow. Later he went into partnership with James Peddie and commenced a number of public works including the Selkirk & Galashields Railway in 1856. The Bridport report opened with a whole page of deliberations and facts about railway schemes in Scotland; it also included the costs of these lines which made it quite obvious that Mr Wylie was quite an authority on Scottish railways. However, after this discourse Mr Wylie continued:

With reference to the Bridport district I have, after very considerable considerations, come to the conclusions that Maiden Newton is the point to which the railway from Bridport should be carried. By forming a junction at this point with the Wilts, Somerset and Weymouth Railway, communication is opened up with the whole railway system.

The report continued:

The Wilts, Somerset and Weymouth Railway being a branch of the Great Western system has been constructed on the broad gauge, and a line to join at Maiden Newton must necessarily be constructed on the same gauge. This is a disadvantage as regards cost, and, looking into the general character of the county, and the increased expense of this gauge, my opinion is that a line from Bridport will cost from £6,000 to £6,500 per mile, inclusive of all Parliamentary and other expenses. The length of the railway being constructed being 10 miles, and assuming the higher rate per mile, the whole capital required will only be £65,000.

Mr Wylie concluded his report:

The station at Bridport should, I think, be nearer the turnpike gate on the Beaminster road, as it will there suit both Bridport and Bradpole, and after passing the latter village, the line should be carried up the river Asker to Loders, and on in the direction of Poorstock, where there should be a station for the accommodation of that part of the district. The line should proceed by Poorstock Common to Toller Porcorum, and Toller Fratrum, on to Maiden Newton, where an easy junction can be made with the Wilts, Somerset and Weymouth Railway. Throughout the whole of this course there is no difficulty whatever, except the cutting at Poorstock Common, which will be heavy, and is indeed the principal cause of the increased expense of the line as compared with Scottish lines, which I have previously referred to, but with this exception the works are of an easy description; and there is nothing to prevent the line being opened in twelve months after the works shall have commenced.

As a direct result of the report a public notice was posted on the authority of Mr Edward Gill Flight, the Bridport Solicitor dealing with the legal aspects of the proposed railway. The notice read as follows:

The public are very respectfully informed that, in consequence of the civil engineer's favourable report on the practicability of a line of railway being completed from Bridport to Maiden Newton, for £65,000, the necessary steps are now in progress for applying to Parliament, in the ensuing session, for the requisite legislative powers. A full and detailed prospectus will shortly be published and in the meantime the undersigned will be glad to be favoured with any communications from parties interested in the undertaking so deeply affecting the prosperity of the town and district.

E.G. Flight, Solicitor, Bridport, 11th October, 1854

On the 16th October, 1854, Mr Flight received a communication as follows:

Sir,
We the undersigned residents of Bridport and its vicinity, deeply interested in the prosperity of the town and neighbourhood, having carefully read and considered the report of Mr Wylie on the practicability of the railway from Maiden Newton to Bridport, wish to express our sense of the great importance and advantages of this undertaking, based on such economical principles, and our hope of your complete success in carrying it through.
We remain, Sir
Yours respectfully

The correspondence was signed by 161 local persons, headed by the Mayor, and including Solicitors, Medical Practitioners, a Justice of the Peace, the Clergy and the Town Clerk.

This was truly a vote of confidence, with the result that on Friday 24th October, 1854 a committee meeting was held in the Council Chamber of the Town Hall, Bridport. The resolution, carried unanimously, was: 'That the line from Maiden Newton to Bridport be given the undivided and most hearty support of the Committee'.

Provisionally known as the Bridport and Maiden Newton Railway, an Act was put before Parliament. As all the other schemes for the area had been dropped, the Bill sailed through unopposed and received Royal Assent. Thus the Bridport Railway Company was incorporated on the 5th May, 1855.

The incorporated subscribers, who were in effect the first Directors of the company, consisted of Thomas Alexander Mitchell, Joseph Gundry, William Colfox, William Smith, John Hodder-Needall, Kirkman Daniel Hodgson, William Swatridge, Steven William Whetam, John Pike Stevens, Benjamin Pearkes Gundry, Thomas Legg and George Edmunds.

The share capital of the company was £65,000 divided into shares of £10 each, £2 10s. per share being the greatest amount that could be asked for in any one share call. The borrowing powers of the company by mortgage or bond was limited to £21,600, which could not be borrowed until all the share capital had been subscribed and half of it actually paid up.

Much of the Act is taken up with the necessary legal details covering mainly the Company Clauses Consolidation Act, the Land Clauses Consolidation Act, and the Railway Clauses Consolidation Act of 1845 (also part of the agreement between the Bridport Railway and the GWR, who were going to work the line for the local company).

On 11th May, 1855 the first meeting of the Directors was held at the residence of Mr Flight. At this meeting Joseph Gundry was elected Chairman, and Mr Flight the company Secretary. Mr Wylie was appointed as the company Engineer.

It was agreed that premises at 36 East Street, Bridport should be rented from Mr Flight as the company office, and today they are still used by local solicitors. In those far off days the rent paid by the railway company was £400 per year which appeared to be a lot of money, but did in fact include lighting, heating, a Boardroom and a general office. Mr Flight's appointment as Secretary was confirmed at a meeting on 9th July, 1855, at a salary of £200 per annum.

At that same meeting a decision was taken that was to cause many future problems for the Bridport company. Wylie, in his report on the system of permanent way to be adopted, was strongly in favour of the Macdonnell system, stating, 'My opinion is strongly in favour of the Macdonnell road, for although on the length of your line it will involve an outlay of, in round numbers, £1,050 more than the longitudinal sleeper road, it will prove in my opinion the more economical of the two'. The complete set of estimates for the permanent way for the branch was as follows:

	£	s.	d.
Barlow rail	16,926	5	0
Longitudinal sleepers	20,099	0	0
Cross sleepers	20,988	15	0
Macdonnell road	21,149	5	0

Unfortunately for the Bridport company the old adage, 'The dearest is not always the best' proved right!

Macdonnell rail had been introduced as a means of preventing the use of timber supports and sleepers which in those days were prone to rot away within a short period of time. Introduced by Mr J.J. Macdonnell in 1853, it cost £86 a mile more than timber road to lay, but the longevity of iron compared with timber was expected to give savings over a period of time. Briefly the system consisted of longitudinal rolled iron plates of various lengths up to 20 ft, the cross section of the plate being slightly curved and the top face of the plate having longitudinal ridges into which sat the bridge rail, a thin wooden strip acting as a packing piece between the two. The joints between the plates consisted of a short plate bolted under the main bearer plate, gauge was maintained by angle-iron cross ties bolted at 9 ft intervals to the bearer plates. During the short period of its life various minor modifications were made to the basic design in attempts to improve its performance, but the problems were to outweigh the advantages - as the Bridport company was to experience!

One of the original 'MacDonnell Plates' used on the Bridport branch. The bridge rail was placed in the clearly visible grooved section. Like many of these old plates, this one outlasted the branch, being used to cover a drainage pit.   *M.J. Tattershall*

BRIDPORT BRANCH GRADIENT CHART

Drawn by G.A. Pryer

West Bay Station - - - - - - - -
L
80
L
80
East Street Station - - - - - - - - - - - - -
153
Bridport Station - - - - - - - - - - - - - - - - -
L
360
130
62
L
52
Powerstock Station - - - - - - - - - - - - - - - - - -
L
75
50
270
85
130
Toller Station - - - - - -
200
L
150
190
L
100
Maiden Newton Station - - - - -

11 miles
10
9
8
7
6
5
4
3
2
1
0

Chapter Two

Construction

Work was at last about to start on a railway line to the town of Bridport and John Symonds of Symondsbury was appointed valuer and arbitrator for the company. It is recorded that he would receive a fee of 2 guineas per consultation, which were mainly over the purchase of land for the construction of the line. The contractor appointed to build the line was Kenneth Mathieson of Dunfermline, a 'Gentleman of unquestionable responsibility and extensive experience as a contractor, will contract to complete the works for a sum considerably below Mr Wylie's estimates'.

Mathieson was indeed a contractor of great experience. Born at Hopehill, Glasgow, in 1817 he was the son of an established contractor. Upon completing his education he was apprenticed as a mason, and then studied surveying before taking an appointment as surveyor to the Chester and Holyhead Railway. He later joined his father's business. He constructed at least eight railways in Scotland, plus two piers, a water works, and a reservoir, but it would appear that the Bridport branch was one of his few ventures south of the border. The first sod was cut at Loders by Joseph Gundry on the 19th June, 1855, a working base consisting of contractor's offices, carpenter's and smith's shops in brick and wooden buildings being established at that location. On the 3rd July, Mr Wylie, the Engineer, gave his first report to the company, which read as follows:

> The very short time that has elapsed since the works were commenced on your line does not enable one to report any great actual progress, but the contractors have now been proceeding with great vigour.
>
> The plant requisites for the construction of the line are now on the ground and in the course of the next week the cutting of the summit, which will be the heaviest part of the whole line, will begin.
>
> The working surveys, which now have been completed, have not brought to light any unforeseen difficulties, and as possession of nearly all the land in which the more difficult works are situated has already been obtained, I have every confidence that the whole line will be completed within the stipulated period.

By early August work was progressing well, over 200 men being employed. Construction had commenced in a field beyond the Beaminster road toll gate and proceeded northwards, the land being marked out with stakes for a considerable distance. Further along at Loders a stream was being diverted and an embankment had been raised to about 12 feet, the road having been lowered 10 feet to allow work on the overbridge to commence. Waggons drawn by horses were hauling material out of the cutting further along. At Witherstone Wood work had commenced on a cutting to be 50 to 60 feet deep.

At the October Board meeting it was brought to notice that Mr Mathieson the contractor, had taken out shares to the value of £10,000 in the Bridport Railway Company; upon hearing this the Board of Directors were resolved that they would not use the money or any part of it.

Work was proceeding well with the construction of the line. Towards the end of the year during excavations at Smokeham a human skeleton was discovered, which was later interred in Powerstock churchyard.

No sooner had work started on the line than a scheme by the LSWR to build a railway from Dorchester to Exeter via Bridport was again put forward. It also proved that not all shareholders were united in their cause, a letter published in the *Railway Times* during August 1855 and sent to the *Bridport News* by a shareholder reading as follows.

Sir,

Permit me to suggest to your readers, who are South Western Shareholders, the advantages, in point of time, economy and facility of arrangements that must result from adoption of the Bridport line as a link of the compulsory Exeter extension from Dorchester.

By means of a mixed gauge from Dorchester via Maiden Newton, Bridport and Stoke Cannon, there would be only 37 miles of railway to construct, that being the distance between Bridport and Stoke Cannon. Clearly the Great Western and the Bristol and Exeter have a strong interest in preventing the Yeovil line; and this would probably induce them, in conjunction with the Bridport, to enter into amicable terms with the South Western for working the space between Dorchester and Exeter with mixed gauge trains

The Bridport line will probably be finished in September 1856, as the works are rapidly progressing.

If any shareholder will contrast this scheme with the Yeovil project, he will at once discover the enormous saving of money that might thus be effected.

If you deem this communication worth inserting in your next paper, I shall have pleasure in furnishing you with data in a subsequent letter, showing in round numbers, the amount of estimated saving of money.

The saving of the line is obviously an important element in this plan for the consideration of the legislature and Government, more especially while we are at war, and when acceleration of the facilities of communication must be so all important to our National defences.

A Railway Shareholder
Bridport August 22. 1855.

A remonstrance signed by the Chairman of the Bridport Railway, Mr Joseph Gundry, was published in *The Times* on 3rd January, 1856.

This dealt with the matter at great length, mentioning the already approved Yeovil to Axminster line of the LSWR, and states as follows:

Under any circumstances it is impossible to imagine a clearer case of unnecessary competition with existing and authorised lines of railway. This competition is contemplated by a great and powerful company, at an expense to their shareholders of probably more than £170,000, thereby swamping an independent local company who has been driven to the necessity of making a railway for themselves, through the extraordinary conduct of the very parties who now would thus ruin that railway.

After at length describing the various reasons for not constructing a second railway to Bridport, it was mentioned that by laying a third rail, standard gauge traffic could be carried from Dorchester via Maiden Newton, the third rail being required as both the Great Western and Bridport Railway lines were laid to the broad gauge of 7 ft, whereas the LSWR was laid to the narrow gauge of 4 ft 8½ in.

Mr Gundry had sent letters to the Chairman and the Board of Directors of the LSWR in the November of 1855 stating that, although the Bridport company opposed the Dorchester to Bridport section of the proposed line, they were interested in allowing traffic from the section between Exeter and Bridport to use the Bridport Railway with a rail laid as far as Maiden Newton, and the Bridport company would assist in obtaining arrangements for the Great Western to convey the traffic to Dorchester. However, a reply from the Secretary of the LSWR stated that 'This company cannot entertain the question of a mixed gauge between Dorchester and Maiden Newton'.

With the granting of an application in Parliament for the construction of the LSWR line between Yeovil and Axminster in May of 1856, the coast scheme via Bridport was abandoned.

Meanwhile construction of the Bridport Railway was proceeding; in February of 1856 Wylie and Mathieson had a difference of opinion over the construction of the line. This was brought to the notice of the Board of Directors, who as a result appointed an independent referee to resolve the issue. On the 17th March Mr Wylie reported to the Directors on how work was progressing, carefully letting them know why work was behind schedule. He said:

> I am happy to be able to report to you that considerable and satisfactory progress has been made in the construction of your railway, the operations have until lately been confined to the portion of the line between Bridport and the summit at Witherstone, a distance of about five miles, and on this section all the masonry, with the exception of a few small drains, has been completed, a large portion of the fencing has been erected, and a considerable portion of the line has been formed, and requires little more than the ballasting and permanent way to complete it.

All sounded well, and so far it was a very favourable report, but Mr Wylie continued: 'The wet weather during the winter months has caused considerable loss of time but as the season advances the work will be carried on in a more uninterrupted manner, and will be pushed on with all expedition'.

Witherstone cutting was to be a great cause of trouble, as Mr Wylie tells the Directors: 'The only serious difficulties which have been met are the cut and embankment at the summit at Witherstone. In both of these, heavy slips have occurred but means are now being taken by alteration in the mode of working the cut which I have every reason to believe will be successful'. Although Witherstone was causing trouble he was able to say that work had started between the summit and Maiden Newton, and at the next general meeting he hoped to say with certainty when the line would be ready for opening.

The general statement of accounts was placed before the meeting and at this stage the company appeared to be financially sound, £29,627 15s. 10d. having been received and £24,578 3s. 6d. spent out.

In April the Directors were not satisfied with the engineering of the line and submitted that Mr Wylie himself or other competent person be stationed somewhere near so that he could conduct operations. Until Mr Wylie could assure the Directors that the progress was satisfactory, they were of the opinion that additional professional advice should be sought, and that Mr Wylie be informed of this forthwith. The Directors also declared that until the work was up-to-date, they would not pay the contractor his month's money; they also stipulated that every month Mr Wylie must issue a certificate of work completed, until this was received and found to be in order the contractor would not receive any money.

In May 1856 the company decided to build stations at Smokeham and Great Toller. The Board of Trade had a plan to build a new road at Toller and this station was postponed. In February 1857 Wylie was ordered to proceed with plans for a station at Smokeham, and Mr James Gerrard signed a contract in the July to build a structure at the cost of £260 10s. 0d. This station was named Poorstock until about 1862 when it was renamed Powerstock. At the time this station was being constructed a petition was received from the inhabitants of Loders asking for a station to be built near the village, but no action was ever taken towards its construction although the line ran along the outskirts of the village and was accessible at that point.

Returning to the events of 1856, the *Bridport News* of Saturday, 9th August brought the general public up-to-date, stating that they recorded with much satisfaction that the permanent way was laid in broad gauge width at the Bridport end of the line.

On the 6th September Mr Wylie again reported his progress to the Board, stating that up until the 28th August, 31,386 cubic yards of earth had been excavated, leaving only 74,834 cubic yards to remove. However, there was a snag, an extra 40,000 cubic yards had to be removed. Mr Wylie continued: 'The average rate of excavation for the past six months has been 34,000 cubic yards per month. At this rate the work would be completed by the end of the year and the line opened early in the spring'. There was also some outstanding work on four bridges and several other small items but these were not causing any concern and would be completed on time.

At a meeting held only three weeks later, Mr Wylie told the Board that the line would be ready and open by the 1st March, 1857. He had visited Witherstone cutting after a heavy storm and found that the works were none the worse for it and the embankments were solid. It appeared that they were at last winning.

The *Bridport News* for 1st November, 1856 reported, 'It is with great satisfaction we record that the works at Witherstone are making satisfactory progress. The embankment is now carried into the Powerstock Common, and we believe no further difficulties are anticipated at that part of the line. The progress on the whole of the line is satisfactory'.

Work had also commenced on the building of Bridport station, the contract being awarded to James Gerrard for £1,300. Back in December 1855 a plan for a station submitted by Wylie was rejected by the Board as being too expensive, as the cost then was not to exceed £1,000!

At the same time the finishing touches were being put to the Wilts & Somerset & Weymouth line which had opened to Yeovil in September 1856, the final section to Weymouth opening to traffic on 20th January, 1857. It was the vital link, without which the Bridport Railway would have been a branch to nowhere!

At last the main line was open to Dorchester albeit 10 years later than the rival LSWR. More importantly, the final section to Weymouth was ready, from where a large amount of traffic could be generated, in particular with the Channel Islands. There was, however, a near disaster within the first nine months of the line's opening. On Friday 11th September, 1857 a head-on collision on the single line between Maiden Newton and Evershot was narrowly averted, and the report in the *Dorset County Chronicle* made chilling reading.

It appeared that one of the up passenger trains from Weymouth had to meet and pass a down goods train at Maiden Newton station. On arrival of the passenger train the goods train had not come down, and Mr Aldrich the station master dispatched the train contrary to regulations. It proceeded towards the next station (Evershot) where it met the late running goods immediately on the approach to the station. The driver of the latter immediately, on seeing the impending disaster, backed his engine and thus avoided a collision It was stated that Mr Aldrich said that he had tried the telegraph to ascertain the whereabouts of the goods train, but could not get it to work.

When later inspected by the traffic manager for the district, the instruments were found to be in working order, Aldrich was suspended and later dismissed for irregular working of trains. He goes down in history as Maiden Newton's most transitory station master, his position being taken by William James who moved down the line from being station master at Evershot.

In the meanwhile problems were occurring with the construction work on the branch. An Engineer's report issued by Mr Wylie on the 6th March, 1857 cast gloom over the entire proceedings. According to Wylie in the previous September 'the line would be open for traffic on 1st March'. Instead the line was far from complete, the main problem being Witherstone cutting. The report read as follows:

> The very unfavourable weather which prevailed during the autumn and winter months has not only retarded the progress of the works generally, but rendered it necessary to stop altogether for some time. It has, therefore, been found impossible to finish the line so as to open on time as might have been the case had the weather proved favourable.

With one exception the embankments have stood the test of the winter remarkably well, and are now becoming remarkably consolidated while the slip that took place in the Whitley Bank is not of any serious consequence, but I regret to have to report that the symptoms of another slip have appeared in the Witherstone cutting. This occurred on the north side which has not previously shown movement towards the line, and will cause a considerable amount of extra excavation.

In some of the other clay cuttings, slips have taken place, but not to any great extent, and before the approach of another winter they will be thoroughly drained and rendered perfectly secure.

The masonry is nearly finished, there being only two small bridges and one small culvert to construct. The ballasting and the finishing of the line is being carried on from both ends towards Witherstone, so that soon after the cutting there is finished, which a short time of favourable weather will do now, the whole line will be ready for opening.

At this stage the combined cost of the land and the construction had far exceeded the original estimate. It was vital that the 400 shares that remained unsold be sold immediately, otherwise the property of the company would seriously deteriorate, but the sale of the outstanding shares would see the company through the unforeseen expenses that had occurred. It was announced 'The Directors had done all they could to sell the shares and it was now up to the shareholders themselves'. The Chairman agreed to take up some of the shares, and other Directors followed suit. The company was running out of funds and the future of the line was in jeopardy. On the 9th April, Mr Flight, the company Secretary, published an appeal for more money. He said: 'Owing to circumstances which the Directors could not have anticipated, the cost of the line will be considerably exceeded, and unless this can be effected the line must remain unfinished. A combined effort by the whole body of the shareholders will be sufficient to clear away the difficulty and danger'.

An appeal published by Mr Flight in the *Bridport News* on 18th April, 1857 reiterated the situation, stating that 'there are 440 shares left to be taken up, and these divided among the 220 shareholders would only add two shares to each shareholders present stake'. A novel idea was suggested in a letter to the paper the following week. Signed by 'A friend of the people', it suggested that Bridport Town Council impose a rate to purchase the shares, these being held in trust, the future dividends being used to improve the town, or if the finance could not be raised by a rate, sell Council property to raise the necessary funds! There were no replies to this premature scheme for municipal involvement in public transport!

A committee of shareholders was set up for the purpose of canvassing for further shares to be taken up. There followed throughout the month of crisis several other meetings of Directors. On 9th May they were told that 236 of the unappropriated shares had been taken as a result of the appeal.

At this time other small matters relative to the operation of the station were being taken care of. The Bridport Gas Company offered to supply gas to Bridport station at the cost of £60 providing the railway agreed to burn 16 lamps. This offer was not acceptable, and Mr Firman, who had the contract to supply lamps and naphtha to the GWR, was employed to illuminate both Bridport and Powerstock stations at the rate of 6s. 8d. per lamp per month. A stable was constructed at Bridport for the railway horses and four cottages just outside the terminus were repaired ready for occupation by the railway staff.

The Bridport company had entered into an agreement with the Great Western that when the line was complete the GWR would work it for two years with the following clauses:

The Bridport Railway Company to complete the line, and to keep in repair both the permanent way and the stations. The Great Western to supply the locomotives and all rolling stock and an efficient staff of servants.

A Select Committee consisting of an equal number of Directors of both companies to regulate the traffic carried and arrange the fares. The Great Western will first pay all the expenses of the working of the line and to hand over all the surplus receipts to the Bridport Company with several gentlemen of high standing to act as arbitrators in the case of dispute.

The agreement was debated for two hours at a Committee meeting before a decision was reached. Some of the Directors of the Bridport company thought that, as things stood, the Great Western had far too much control over the running of the line, and they were not very pleased with the arrangements. However, after a long debate the motion was carried and the seal of the two companies was affixed to the agreement.

On Wednesday 13th May, 1857 the first reported accident took place during the construction works, when George Whittaker sustained a compound fracture of his right leg after falling under ballast waggons.

On 22nd September, 1857 Mr Wylie reported to the Board that,

The works on the line are very nearly completed. The permanent way will be completed this week, which will allow an engine to run over the entire length from the junction at Maiden Newton to Bridport, and as soon as this is done a final notice for the opening to traffic will be given to the Board of Trade. The works are generally in a satisfactory condition.

The *Bridport News* on the 26th reported that, 'The last rails had been laid on the previous Thursday and it is expected that an experimental engine will run over the line next week'. In fact, this took place on Tuesday, the 29th, when an engine supplied by the GWR made trial runs over the line. The Chairman, several Directors, and a few other gentlemen travelled on the engine and in a truck attached to it. In a statement to the Board the next day the Chairman said he had much pleasure in informing them that they went most satisfactorily from the Bridport terminus to the Maiden Newton Junction, and that left no doubt that it would at once receive the sanction of the Government Inspector. They went over a considerable portion of the line at the rate of 40 mph and Mr Buckland, the locomotive superintendent for the GWR, said he had never tested a new line with so much satisfaction and pleasure. Under the circumstances they could relieve their minds of any doubts as to the line being sanctioned by the Government Inspector.

The Chairman and Officers of the Bridport company were in optimistic mood at the fifth half-yearly meeting on 30th September. Arrears on share calls only amounted to £378 15s. and there were only 80 shares left to be taken up. The Engineer, Wylie, reported that the permanent way would be completed within days, and the Board of Trade was duly informed.

Captain Tyler of the Board of Trade visited the line on Tuesday 6th October, and after a thorough inspection reported:

That the line is laid with 51 lb. bridge rails, on longitudinal rolled iron sleepers, weighing 60 lb. per lineal yard. The line requires ballast in certain places, and the fencing on the line is in a very poor state of repair and needs attention. There is a turntable at Bridport which is useless, unless there is one at Maiden Newton also, and two pairs of contractors shifting points near Witherstone that were used to transport clay to the spoil bank need to be removed.

Due to the fact the works were incomplete he could not recommend the opening of the line until these matters had received attention.

This was a blow after the optimistic opinion of their Engineer Mr Wylie, and the Chairman's remarks made shortly before. The mere fact of the line being laid with 51 lb. rails leaves one in doubt as to the strength of the work, as the original contract for the line specified that it be laid with rails weighing 90 lb. per yard, the contractor having to pay 3 per cent per ton to the makers of the permanent way as royalties for the patent. The line was laid with 'MacDonnell's patent permanent way', and at the time the Bristol and Exeter Railway had a section of line laid with the same type of track and found it to be very successful, and they were going to lay further sections of it.

The work required by Captain Tyler was at once put in hand, the *Bridport News* on the 16th October reporting a train running on the line:

It affords us great pleasure to be able to state that an engine, accompanied by a passenger carriage, containing ladies and gentlemen of this town, ran to and from Maiden Newton today. It also made a second trip to Smokeham taking about a quarter of an hour there and back. All expressed themselves highly gratified with the ride, the running of the carriage being remarkably free from oscillation and noise.

As the Board of Trade had yet to pass the line for public operation, it would appear that this train consisted of Directors, shareholders, and other interested parties.

Captain Tyler returned for a second time on 5th November, a thorough inspection of the line being made before bogie tank *Hesiod* and the inspection train consisting of two passenger coaches and four goods trucks - some of them loaded - arrived at Bridport station at 4 pm. The inspection party having alighted at the platform, the train backed onto a siding and the engine proceeded to the turntable where an attempt was made to turn it, but owing to some defect it was found impossible to do so. After taking water the engine returned the first class coach to the platform where, with lamps lit, it awaited the return of Captain Tyler who departed about 6 pm. Despite the incident with the turntable he found that all was in order. The offer of the Great Western to supply a tank locomotive until the turntable was completed at Maiden Newton overcame Captain Tyler's remarks on the subject at his earlier inspection and he passed the line as being acceptable to passenger traffic.

At last the Bridport Railway was completed, the line being opened on Thursday 12th November, 1857. The weather for the opening day was clear and fine, a noticeable difference to the routine of the town in the early morning being the non-departure of the daily coach from the Bull Hotel to Yeovil. By 8 am crowds had gathered at the station to see the first train depart at 8.15; it returned from Maiden Newton at 9 o'clock with the engine flying a flag at each corner. Mr Knight, the proprietor of the Bull Hotel, employed a two-horse omnibus to convey passengers between the hotel and the station, and all day people came and went by train, many watching the wonder of the age from the fields and bridges.

The *Bridport News* for Saturday 14th printed the following:

Bridport at last has a Railway. After disappointments without number, tedious delays, and various difficulties, trains are actually running from hence to almost all parts of the country, and bringing to our town not only numerous passengers, but also some of the necessities and comforts of life.

Thursday 17th November was declared a public holiday. Nearly all the shops were closed and a festive spirit swept through the town. As this was the day of the Yeovil Fair a great number of people decided to travel to the event by the railway services now provided; so many people turned up at the station to travel on the first train that Mr Daniel George Bingham, who had been appointed station master and manager, was

BRIDPORT RAILWAY.

OPENING

FROM

BRIDPORT TO MAIDEN NEWTON,

NOVEMBER 12th, 1857.

TIME BILL.

UP TRAINS from BRIDPORT.

FARES from BRIDPORT.			STATIONS.	WEEK DAYS.				
1st Class	2nd Class	3rd Class		1, 2, & 3 Class.	1 & 2 Class.	1 & 2 Class.	1 & 2 Class.	1 & 2 Class.
s. d.	s. d.	s. d.		A.M.	A.M.	P.M.	P.M.	P.M.
			BRIDPORT Dep.	8 15	9 25	12 45	3 50	6 15
1 0	0 8	0 3½	Powerstock ... „	8 25	...	...	...	6 25
2 4	1 6	0 9	MAIDEN NEWTON Arr.	8 45	9 50	1 10	4 15	6 45
				P.M.	P.M.			
29 4	21 6	12 5	London ... ... „	4 55	3 50	6 0	10 35	...
15 2	11 1	6 9½	Bristol ... ... „	12 15		4 15	7 55	9 40
3 9	2 7	1 4½	Dorchester ... „				4 35	7 28
5 0	3 6	1 11½	Weymouth ... „			20	4 50	7 45

DOWN TRAINS to BRIDPORT.

FARES from Maiden Newton.			STATIONS.	WEEK DAYS.				
1st Class	2nd Class	3rd Class		1 & 2 Class.	1, 2 & 3 Class.	1 & 2 Class.	1 & 2 Class.	1 & 2 Class.
s. d.	s. d.	s. d.		A.M.	A.M.	P.M.	P.M.	P.M.
2 8	2 0	1 2½	Weymouth .. Dep	8 10	8 10	12 45	...	6 10
1 5	1 1	0 7½	Dorchester ... „	8 30	8 30	1 0	...	6 30
						A.M.		
12 10	9 7	6 0½	Bristol ... „	...	6 35	11 15	1 20	3 30
							A.M.	
27 0	20 0	11 8	London „	...	...	9 15	11 0	1 0
						P.M.	P.M.	
...	...	...	MAIDEN NEWTON „	8 50	10 0	2 15	4 25	7 15
1 6	1 0	0 5½	Powerstock „	...	10 20	...	...	7 35
2 4	1 6	0 9	BRIDPORT Arr.	9 15	10 30	2 40	4 50	7 45

NO SUNDAY TRAINS AT PRESENT.

For further particulars see the Great Western's Company's Time Bills.

BRIDPORT: Printed by W. C. FROST, "Bridport News" Office.

Bridport Railway, opening timetable, 12th November, 1857.

unable to issue all the tickets by the departure time! This resulted in the branch train arriving half an hour late at Maiden Newton and in consequence missing its connection with the up main line train which had already departed. There not being another up train until 10.50 am, some passed the time admiring the scenery around the station whilst a large contingent proceeded to the Kings Arms, where liquid refreshment replaced exasperation with merriment, until the approach of the next train caused a dash back to the station where the multitude squeezed into the limited accommodation. The more fastidious later complained about their late arrival at Yeovil.

The first complaints about the railway appeared in the *Bridport News* on 19th November, and came from the farming community who resented the long wait at Maiden Newton when returning from Dorchester Market. However, either by accident or design, placed next to the letter was an advert for the Kings Arms where mine host 'Mr R. Bascombe begs to inform his friends and the public that his ESTABLISHMENT is replete with every comfort and convenience, arrangements having been made to meet the increasing TRAFFIC occasioned by the opening of the railway to Bridport'.

The previous week an advert had appeared offering tickets at 10s. 6d. each (including wine) for a dinner to celebrate the opening of the Bridport Railway to be held at the Bull Hotel, Bridport, on Tuesday 17th, with dinner on the table at 5 o'clock. 'A special train for the occasion at the usual fares will leave the Bridport station at 9.5 pm, in time to meet the down train at Maiden Newton for Dorchester and Weymouth'. This function was attended by 140 guests and among those who arrived on the first down train from London to Maiden Newton were several Directors and officials of the GWR. Two local members of Parliament, Mr T.A. Mitchell and Mr K.D. Hodgson, both Directors of the Bridport Railway Company, were driven into the town by a carriage drawn by two greys and preceded by the Bridport Band.

In a report of the occasion in the *Bridport News* the list of guests fails to mention the presence of Mr Wylie, the Engineer, or Mr Mathieson, the contractor. During the after-dinner speeches, Mr Gundry, the Chairman of the company, proposed the health of Mr Wylie: 'A gentleman whose assistance has been of more service than that of any other person'. Mr Reddie, the Assistant Engineer, briefly replied, but what he said was not recorded.

Of Mr Flight, Gundry said,

> I propose the health of the gentleman who was the sole originator of the scheme, and by whose energy and intelligence they were led to adopt it. Mr Flight has had many difficulties to encounter. It is very easy for a man to sit in a chair and devise schemes for public benefit, but it is far more difficult to put them into execution. Mr Flight had not only originated the scheme, but has seen it successfully carried out, and to him the honour was decidedly due.

It would appear that the wine flowed freely. Just about everything and everybody was toasted, so much so that towards the end Mr T.A. Mitchell MP thought they had forgotten the toast of the evening, and proposed success to the Bridport Railway! Much more praise was said of Mr Flight, to which he modestly replied.

Not to be outdone by the dinner for Directors and other officials, the navvies who had made the line possible had their own treat on Thursday 19th November with a feast of beef etc. and plenty of strong beer. As might have been expected with the abundance of ale, many of the men, in their own words, 'were quite glorious'.

A sale of contractor's equipment took place on Friday 20th November at Loders, where various items, including 25 young draught horses, 30 good earth wagons, 50 tons of contractor's rails, and a well-built dog cart went to the highest bidder, bringing to a close the building of Bridport's railway line.

BRIDPORT RAILWAY.

TIME BILL FOR DECEMBER, 1857.

UP TRAINS FROM BRIDPORT.

WEEK DAYS.

STATIONS.	1,2&3 Class.	1&2 Class.	1&2 Class.	1&2 Class.
	A.M.	A.M.	P.M.	P.M.
BRIDPORT .... Dep.	8 10	9 25	12 40	3 50
Poorstock .... ,,	8 20	..	12 50	..
MAIDEN NEWTON Arr.	8 45	9 50	1 10	4 15
Yeovil .... ,,	9 18	11 13	1 38	5 33
	P.M.	P.M.		
London .... ,,	4 55	3 50	6 0	10 35
Bristol .... ,,	12 15	2 30	4 15	7 55
	A.M.	A.M.		
Dorchester .... ,,	..	10 13	2 25	4 35
Weymouth .... ,,	..	10 30	2 40	4 50

DOWN TRAINS TO BRIDPORT.

WEEK DAYS.

STATIONS.	1,2&3 Class.	1&2 Class.	1&2 Class.	1&2 Class.
	A.M.	A.M.	P.M.	P.M.
Weymouth ...... Dep.	8 10	10 20	12 45	4 40
Dorchester ...... ,,	8 30	10 35	1 0	4 55
			A.M.	A.M.
Bristol ...... ,,	..	6 35	11 15	1 20
				A.M.
London ...... ,,	..	..	9 15	11 0
			P.M.	P.M.
Yeovil ...... ,,	8 50	9 20	1 40	3 50
MAIDEN NEWTON ,,	9 10	10 55	2 15	5 15
Poorstock ...... ,,	..	..	2 35	5 35
BRIDPORT ...... Arr.	9 20	11 20	2 45	5 55

NO SUNDAY TRAINS AT PRESENT. For further particulars see the Great Western Company's Time Bills.

Bridport Railway timetable for December 1857.

Chapter Three

The Broad Gauge Era

The daily service at the opening of the line was five trains each way on weekdays only, there being no Sunday service. By December this had been cut to four trains, the 6.15 pm up train and the return journey from Maiden Newton at 7.15 pm being cancelled. There were also slight alterations to the timings of the first train and the one at lunchtime. Although services were reduced soon after the opening and no trains ran on Sundays, by public request the company condescended to run a service on Christmas Day, there being three trains in each direction, the last one returning from Maiden Newton at the late hour of 8.30 pm. It was reported that about 180 persons left by the morning train, and a large number of people travelled to Bridport on the train which arrived at 12 o'clock.

On Boxing Day iron rails were placed across the line at Toller with the intention of derailing the train. A reward was offered for information leading to the apprehension of the culprit. On 8th January, 1858 the clerk at Bridport station reported that a large stone had been maliciously placed on the track. It would appear that vandalism and trespassing on the track is not just a present day complaint. A note in the diary of William Mabey, a local resident, records how small boys used to lay in between the rails and allow the train to pass over them.

One of the first special trains ran on Saturday 6th March, 1858. It was advertised to leave the station at 7.40 am to travel to Dorchester for the Assize Court. This was followed on 3rd April by the first excursion to London, leaving the station at 8.10 am on the Saturday morning and returning from Paddington on the following Tuesday afternoon at 2 pm, the first class fare being £1 0s. 8d. and second class 11s. 0d. This particular weekend was the Easter Holiday and there is little doubt that the company and the GWR were treating the idea of holiday travel quite seriously. On the Good Friday there were two trains each way on the branch to meet the main line trains that were operating a Sunday service.

On the surface all appeared to be well. At the sixth half-yearly ordinary general meeting held on 31st March, 1858 it was reported that from the opening of the railway until the end of January 1858, 9,688 passengers, 2,612 tons of goods and coal, plus many parcels had been conveyed over the line. There was, however, an ever-growing financial crisis, the editorial of the *Bridport News* stating, 'We sympathise with the Directors in their regret that their estimate for the construction of the line has been much exceeded by the cost. More money is required, no less a sum than £9,000'.

Mr Flight, also writing to the *Bridport News*, complained, 'Oblige me by informing your readers that those words were not used by me, and that words that I did use, are omitted from your report'.

There was also a considerable amount of claim and counter claim as to what was actually said at future meetings. At this point the authors, not wishing to escape their duty to record history accurately, have to point out that the many reports of future meetings have differing accounts of the situation. To use a modern phrase, 'creative accountancy' was often used, and certain other matters did not appear to be reported at meetings. Bearing in mind that minute books only tell what their compilers wanted recorded and the reports of meetings were actually taken to the newspaper office by one of the Board, a full picture was never painted.

An extraordinary meeting of the shareholders was held on 29th June, one of the main items for discussion being to effect a new working agreement with the GWR. This matter was delegated to several members of the Board.

GREAT CATTLE SHOW.

GREAT WESTERN RAILWAY,
EXCURSION TRAIN.

BRIDPORT TO LONDON.

ON TUESDAY, 8th DECEMBER, 1857, at 6 in the morning, calling at Poorstock Station. Returning to Bridport from the Paddington Station, London, on the following Thursday, leaving Paddington punctually at 3 in the Afternoon.

Fares from Bridport to London and back—

1st Class 21s. 2nd Class 14s. 3rd Class 10s.

It is requested that all Tickets be obtained at the Bridport Station before 3 p.m., on Monday, 7th December, 1857.

Tickets not transferable, and no luggage allowed except a carpet bag.

Advert for excursion train, to run on 8th December, 1857.

Bridport Railway timetable for Christmas 1857.

BRIDPORT RAILWAY,
In connection with the Great Western Railway.

ON
CHRISTMAS DAY, 1857,
THE PASSENGER TRAINS WILL RUN ONLY AS UNDERMENTIONED.

FROM BRIDPORT.				To BRIDPORT.			
STATIONS.	1, 2, & 3 Class.	1, 2, & 3 Class.	1, 2, & 3 Class.	STATIONS.	1, 2, & 3 Class.	1, 2, & 3 Class.	1, 2, & 3 Class.
	A.M.	P.M.	P.M.		A.M.	P.M.	P.M.
BRIDPORT ....Dep.	8 20	6 5	7 55	Weymouth ......Dep.	8 10	6 0	....
Poorstock .... ,,	8 30	6 15	8 5	Dorchester ...... ,,	8 30	6 20	....
MAIDEN NEWTON Arr.	8 50	6 35	8 25	London .... ,,	....	....	2 0*
Evershot .... ,,	9 10	6 49	....	Bristol .... ,,	7 0	....	5 10*
Yeovil .... ,,	9 35	7 10	....	Yeovil .... ,,	9 35	....	7 45
	P.M.			Evershot .... ,,	10 0	....	8 14
Bristol .... ,,	2 25	9 40	....	MAIDEN NEWTON ,,	10 12	6 40	8 30
London .... ,,	5 0	....	....	Poorstock .... ,,	10 35	7 0	8 50
	A.M.			BRIDPORT ....Arr.	10 45	7 10	9 0
Dorchester ...... ,,	10 30	....	8 45				
Weymouth ...... ,,	10 50	....	9 5				

Return Tickets available from Thursday 24th, to Monday 28th December, 1857, inclusive, except on the Sunday.

* These are 1st and 2nd Class only. A 3rd Class from London at 8 a.m.

When discussing the income from the line the Directors were cautious, and stated that, 'The traffic for so short a time cannot be taken as a fair test of what may be reasonably anticipated when the traffic shall have become more fully developed. The Directors hope more especially for an increase in the passenger traffic during the summer months'. This was followed by the publishing of the statement of accounts for the half year ending 24th February, 1858:

Receipts	£	s.	d.
Calls on shares with interest, including a £5 donation	64,279	5	4
Sale of timber and rent of cottages	34	14	0
Loans on Mortgages	21,600	0	0
Transfer fees	1	10	0
Total	85,915	9	4

Payments	£	s.	d.
Parliamentary	777	0	0
Excavating pits	72	18	0
Engineering	2,196	15	11
Purchase of land and compensation to tenants	10,523	11	10
Contractor	70,737	15	6
Stations	1,525	0	0
Surveyors and Solicitors charges and arbitration expenses	1,883	2	5
Stationery, printing, stamps and advertising	369	3	8
Interest on Mortgages	1,282	18	10
Secretary	550	0	0
Auditors	60	0	0
Miscellaneous expenses	577	12	1
Total	90,555	18	3
Balance due to Bankers	4,640	8	11

As there was now over £4,000 outstanding, the Directors appealed to the shareholders to each pay £1 17s. 6d. per share to pay off the deficit, although the Directors considered a further sum of £5,000 would be required to meet various liabilities, and preserve the balance in the hands of the Directors beyond the £4,000 due to their bankers for which the Directors had become responsible. Mr Gundry reminded the meeting that over £90,000 had already been spent on the construction of the line, and the cost of running it, without allowing for repair to the permanent way, which was 2s. 9½d. per mile. Mr Mathieson said 'The cost of working had been £439 and the receipts for the same period were £613 13s. 6d.'

The company funds were not helped by a burglary at Powerstock station on 14th April whilst the station master was at church. The intruder broke the kitchen window to gain entry, and no doubt expected to find a large amount of cash, but there was little at the station at this time and only between 1s. 0d. and 1s. 6d. was stolen.

Advertising was looked upon as a source of revenue. Messrs W. Frost, the local owners of the *Bridport News*, were given the advertising rights at Bridport station and were actively attempting to sell space on the waiting room walls and along the platform.

By July 1858, Mr Gundry had resigned his seat on the Board of Directors, and at an extraordinary meeting of shareholders held on the 22nd of the month, Thomas Legg was elected to the chair. It was a stormy meeting. They were there to consider a report by a committee set up in March to investigate the future working of the railway, two of the Directors, Mr Hodgson and Mr Mitchell, being involved in negotiations with the Great Western as to the working terms. Mr Mathieson said 'The Great Western ask a little more than the Bridport company could offer, and they offer a little less than the GWR would take, and the shareholders could leave the matter in the hands of Mr Hodgson and Mr Mitchell'.

The Bridport company had proposed to the GWR that they should work the line, incurring all expenses, management, maintenance of permanent way and renewals for a sum of 50 per cent of the gross receipts of the traffic carried, for a period of 21 years. The Bridport company applied to Parliament as early as possible for powers to raise Preference Capital to the extent of at least £15,000, but this power could not be obtained before the Spring of 1859. The GWR in the meantime advanced to the Bridport company the following sums: £1,000 for the payment of their interest on their debenture debit due in August and February, and £2,000 for the payment of pressing sundry liabilities. Such monies so advanced had to be repaid to the Great Western out of the first money raised by the proposed issue of Preference Shares. The Bridport company would have to be prepared to spend cash on repairing yet another slip to Witherstone cutting, and on the general improvement of the construction of the line to a sum not exceeding £4,000 of which £1,500 was to be laid out at Witherstone at once. A Mr Reader stood up at the meeting and said, 'I do not think that the results are satisfactory after the immense outlay which had been employed on the line'. He continued to say, 'They owe their present position to the ignorance of the people of Bridport as regards railway building, and I think they are to blame for not having a consulting engineer in the first place'. Mr Mathieson, the contractor for the line, referring to the remark made by Mr Reader, observed that the line was constructed with materials of a nature too light for the traffic, and the increased expenditure was in consequence of using those materials. He thought that if they had consulted an eminent engineer, and not trusted in themselves so much, they need not have been in the position in which they were now placed.

The main disagreement was that the GWR required 55 per cent of the gross receipts of the traffic, whilst the Bridport company accepted only 50 per cent to be a reasonable figure. However, it was agreed at the meeting that Mr Hodgson and Mr Mitchell be authorised to conclude the agreement with the Great Western over the future working of the line.

The Secretary read out a letter from a Mr Lane who had examined the line, and as a result the following items were named as being in need of immediate attention: concrete piers £600, cutting drains £1,800, side drains £800 to £1,000, alterations to the permanent way £2,700, ballast etc. £400, slips to embankments £300. The main expense in the area was at Witherstone cutting. Mr Lane also reported that the fencing was in need of urgent repair, but he was unable to state the cost of it. All these repairs and alterations to be made, and the line was barely a year old!

Mr Groves complained that the rate of carriage on the Great Western was higher than on the LSWR. He said that butter sent by him on the Great Western cost 5s. 0d. a ton more than the other company. He then went on to speak of the salary of the Secretary and the renting of the company offices. He remarked that £400 for the latter was an enormous sum, and he could not see how nine miles of railway could meet it. Mr Groves must have been a happy man when he read the *Bridport News* for the 7th August. It stated that as from the next week the rates of cartage of goods between Bridport and London would be materially reduced, and it was hoped that this would lead to more traffic using the line.

The next surprise, of which no mention had been made in the reports of meetings, was a dispute between Mathieson (the contractor) and the Bridport Railway Company, a report in the *Bridport News* on 4th September, 1858 stating, 'The case Mathieson v. The Bridport Railway Company which was due to be heard at the last Bristol Assizes, has been settled without the intervention of the court'.

The first public airing of the affair was at the seventh half-yearly meeting held on 28th September, when the true financial situation was partially revealed. A Director questioning the matter found only that their outstanding liabilities were £6,803 7s. 3d., but the report was silent as to the particulars. Mr Smith wanted to know why the Directors could not give the shareholders the particular amounts in the instance of the contractor's account! However, as these matters were in dispute it was considered best they were not discussed.

The Secretary said it would be imprudent that some of the items making up that account should be read to the meeting. The first was the amount of the judgement obtained by the contractor under the award of Mr Fowler. The next item would be the amount of costs which was not yet taxed and could only be estimated.

The Chairman added there was also a disputed claim for a very large sum from the contractor who had built the line, but as the materials and workmanship were very defective the Directors considered they ought not to submit to such a gross case of extortion. There was an outstanding amount of £25 to pay for the rails and this was not disputed. Nor was £14 15s. 6d. owing to a Mr Pearson and an outstanding amount due to Mr Wylie.

The state of the line, in particular at Witherstone cutting, gave the company much concern, and cash was required to put the line in order before the GWR would entertain any further agreements with the Bridport company.

The Chairman said that passenger receipts on the line had increased, and read out the statement of revenue accounts.

	Passenger			Parcels			Goods			Total		
	£	s	d	£	s	d	£	s	d	£	s	d
1857												
November	146	12	10	Included in the Dec figures						146	12	10
December	222	6	2	18	15	3	225	19	3	467	0	8
1858												
January	199	4	7	7	6	7	142	19	6	349	10	8
February	158	7	3	4	12	4	140	0	9	303	0	4
March	187	2	2	6	3	3	177	8	4	370	13	9
April	195	9	6	8	9	4	185	1	4	389	0	2
May	193	17	10	13	3	3	136	15	7	343	16	8
June	255	8	9	18	17	5	149	8	8	423	14	10
July	322	6	4	11	14	5	218	4	3	552	5	0
Totals	1,880	15	5	89	1	10	1,375	17	8	3,345	14	11

The safe working of the railway was also raised at the meeting, Mr Templer was concerned about the mixed train working as passengers were worried about coal wagons being placed at the rear of the train. Mr Flight replied that it had been put before the Great Western authorities who had said that the only way to avoid it was to lengthen the platform or delay the trains for a short time for the purpose of shunting. One passenger refused to travel on the line again until this dangerous practice was altered.

Although Bridport now had an established railway the stage coach was not yet dead. Every weekday morning the Bridport & Crewkerne Royal Mail departed at 7 am, calling at Martock station (on the Durston-Yeovil branch), to give connections with trains to Taunton, Exeter, Bristol and London, and the 'Coronet' coach left Bridport for Exeter daily at 3 pm after the arrival of the train.

The *Bridport News* for 16th October published a letter from Mathieson who was unable to attend the previous meeting, and parts of its contents reveal a different story!

Signed photograph taken in later years, of Daniel George Bingham, Bridport's first station
master.   *Gloucestershire Library Service*

I think it is right to explain that my only claims against the company as contractor are; for the amount of award by Mr Fowler, £3,151 11s. 8d. Half the costs of award etc. £1249 3s. Total £3,300 14s. 8d. To this there falls to be added the cost of obtaining judgement, probably amounting to £200. As a shareholder in the undertaking, I think that the shareholders are entitled to have a more explicit statement of the estimated liabilities of the company, given in the report as £6,803 7s. 3d.

Despite all the doom and gloom of 1858, it was a year that Bridport station master Daniel Bingham would never forget. He left the station in the hands of his successor, Henry Knowles who came from the goods department at Devizes, and took up the position of chief goods manager of the Dutch Rhenish Railway. This rapid rise from rural Dorset to such an exulted position was unusual but very interesting.

Bingham was born in 1830 at Cirencester, and came from a working family. He became a great friend of James Staats Forbes who, whilst district manager for the GWR, took lodgings with the Bingham family. About 1844 young Daniel become a junior clerk at the town station whilst Forbes went on to become the divisional superintendent at Cheltenham, and later chief goods manager at Paddington, Bingham then gaining promotion to Forbes' office in London during April 1855 at a salary of £64 pa.

Promotion was rapid for young Bingham. January 1856 gave him promotion within the department, and in July he transferred to Bristol with a salary increase to £80 pa. With the opening of the Wilts, Somerset & Weymouth line in January 1857 he moved to Dorchester, his salary increasing to £100 pa, and that November saw him in charge of Bridport.

Forbes' reputation as a good railway manager and his Dutch connections resulted in his appointment in 1857 as head of the Dutch Rhenish Railways, which at the time were on the verge of bankruptcy. Assembling chief officers of outstanding ability, Bingham joined his former boss in September 1858 as General Agent at Rotterdam, and in 1860 he took over the same post in Utrecht. He had developed the freight traffic to such an extent that when Forbes returned to England in 1861 to manage the London Chatham & Dover Railway, Bingham at 31 years of age was appointed as his successor.

Realising that whilst the top officials received very high salaries the remainder of the staff were underpaid, he increased their pay to give them an incentive to work. He also paid station masters a bonus when they secured a coal order, this being one of the principal traffics between Westphalia and Rotterdam. When the Dutch railways were nationalised in 1890 the Government paid 25 per cent over and above the value of each share, such was his success.

In retirement he and his wife stayed in Utrecht, where he had interests and held many shares in the coal industry, but he never forgot his native Cirencester. In 1904 he financed a collection of books and the construction of a public library, and later endowed the town with a public hall which in reality was a fully equipped theatre with a shooting range attached! Daniel Bingham died in 1913, and today the former public library (now the Council offices) is a memorial to a very outstanding man.

One other member of staff was not so outstanding, but was also on the move. William James was found unsuitable as station master at Maiden Newton and was moved back to Evershot in the June of 1858. By September his place was taken by Frederick Beauchamp.

On the 6th November, 1858 an advertisement appeared in the *Bridport News*, in which the local company were seeking power to raise yet more capital. They were going to apply in the next session of Parliament to raise further sums of money by the creation of new shares in the undertaking, or by mortgage, and to guarantee such amount of interest of dividend on all or any of the existing shares of the company. The advertisement was signed by Flight and Loggin, solicitors to the Bridport Railway.

In order to alleviate the difficulties at Witherstone, extra land was to be purchased as the banks had to be cut back. This land was owned by a Revd William Jenkins, who would only sell on the condition that a siding was put in at that point for his use. History does not record if this siding was ever laid. However, there is a section of the embankment cut back at this point where a siding could have been accommodated. The ordnance survey map of 1887 shows a brick works on the down side at this point.

The *Bridport News* in December 1858 reported the following:

> Although Witherstone has up to the present time been the bug-bear of the Bridport Railway Company and the thief of the shareholders, it is possible that the soil may be turned into some utility, as it is discovered to be a valuable clay and beautiful yellow bricks may be made from it in any quantity at almost nominal expense.

At the March 1859 meeting of the Bridport company, Mr Flight alluded to the prospects of raising income from the carriage of bricks from the site. He said that one of the best judges in the kingdom had pronounced the clay unsurpassed for the manufacture of bricks, drains and tiles, and there was no question that such a valuable material would find some party to work it. He went on that the bricks could be manufactured for between 25s. and 27s. per thousand, and he had one customer who was ready to take half a million! From this source he thought they might be able to raise £500 to £600 per year in traffic!

Although a kiln was constructed in Witherstone Woods near to the railway, there is little evidence of yellow bricks being used anywhere on or near the railway, although it is confirmed that large lumps of baked clay were used in places as retainers in cuttings and embankments. Likewise there is no evidence of bricks being transported from the site by rail. Today the remains of the brick kilns are preserved, a reminder of Witherstone's infamous past!

In February 1859 the slip at Witherstone was causing so much concern that its movement had to be checked every morning before the commencement of the day's train service. However, the contractor on the site, Mr W. Shaw, was gradually coming to grips with the situation.

The junction with the main line at Maiden Newton was very basic, there being no separate facilities for the branch train which had to use the down loop of the main line. This resulted in the branch train having to wait on the branch if the loop was occupied, or retreat to the branch approach if the loop was required to pass trains on the main line.

Plans by the GWR Civil Engineer for increasing the accommodation at Maiden Newton were postponed at the GWR Board meeting in January 1859. However there was a change of heart by the March meeting, when the Engineer recommended that a portion of the extended arrangement at Maiden Newton, which had been provisionally agreed, should be carried out at a cost of about £350, by which a separate siding for the Bridport trains would be provided. As there was much delay and difficulty in working the junction the Engineer was instructed to proceed with the work.

There had been little mention of trouble with the navvies during the construction of the line, until a report in the *Bridport News* on 5th March, 1859 blamed railway navvies for spreading smallpox in the Toller area. One navvy had the disease and passed it to another, and as a result both died. Consequently a widow and her family caught the deadly disease, as did a servant in another house, and three other cases were reported in other parts of the village, where it was now spreading among children.

At the eighth half-yearly meeting on 28th February, 1859 there was a move forward, with the agreement between the GWR and the Bridport company having been settled on 1st February. The main contents of the agreement were thus:

The GWR agree to take on the lease for 21 years from 1st July, 1858. The Bridport company are, within a reasonable time, to completely repair the permanent way, and all matters and things connected therewith especially repairs and works to the slip at Witherstone under the superintendence of a GWR Engineer. After all repairs have been carried out upon the line the works will be maintained in good working order at the expense of the GWR, who will also provide the staff.

The GWR will have the sole management of the entire traffic, the mode of working, and the number of trains and their times of running. The receipts of traffic on the Bridport Railway being divided between the two companies in the following proportion; the GWR shall be entitled to 52½ per cent of the gross receipts, and the Bridport company the remaining 47½ per cent of receipts. The Bridport company to pay all land tax, tithe rent or other burden.

Despite the life-saving nature of the GWR agreement, the question of the Bridport Railway accounts would not go away. Indeed, when the report of the above meeting appeared in the *Bridport News* Mr Templer had published two sets of accounts - his version, and the company version. The Mathieson affair was still hanging over their heads, with the fear that he might oppose the Bill going to Parliament to raise extra finances. Some shareholders just wanted to get out, one of them stating in a letter to the *Bridport News* the following week, 'I for one say if the GWR, or any other Company, will offer us anything above the cost price, let us sell, for it is certain with our present large annual expenditure, and interest (which must be paid) that we can never obtain the smallest dividend'.

The Mathieson affair again came to the fore, he having previously brought an action against the Bridport company in the County Court and obtained a judgement against them in respect of an outstanding account of £3,302 14s. 8d. for work done, and upon which the company had still not paid up. No settlement having been reached by the Spring of 1859, Mathieson returned to the Court seeking a distress order against the Bridport company to seize property to the value of that owed to him.

On Wednesday 30th March, 1859, at the Sheriff's Court in Dorchester, before Mr Under Sheriff Coombs and a special jury, the case of Mathieson v. The Bridport Railway Company was heard. Mr Brady of Brady and Scott appeared for Mathieson, Mr Flight for the Bridport company, and Mr Pearce of Maples, Pearce and Maples representing the interests of the GWR.

Mr Brady, addressing the jury, told them he intended to lay before them evidence of the property possessed by the railway company, and it would save a lot of time if Mr Flight would admit the company owned the line from Maiden Newton to Bridport. To this request Mr Flight had no objections, admitting they were the mortgagees of the line, but the mortgage consisted of debentures as allowed by law, and this barred Mathieson's claim on the company property. Mr Brady withdrew that part of the claim, but went on to make a claim against the sleepers and rails, stating that the rule applied to all things that were not permanently fixed, and which could be moved and seized under execution of a judgement.

Brady then referred to the presence of Mr Pearce of the GWR, and enquired what business he might have at the hearing, to which Pearce curtly replied that anyone could attend an inquiry of this nature and give evidence if it was pertinent. The Under-Sheriff agreed that he had a right to be there, but questioned his right to take part. Mr Brady made it clear that the dispute was only between his client and the Bridport company, and as the GWR had no lease to produce and were possessed only of a working agreement, they had no right to interfere with Mathieson's claim.

The first witness, Mr Flight, stated that the only goods and chattels owned by the company were two clocks, but Mr Mathieson (when called) said the rails came under the category of 'movables' as they could be removed independently of the sleepers, or vice versa, and the whole framework - not being secured to the soil of the railway - could be lifted up and carried away.

Mr Brady said his client was a large shareholder in the company, and of course, as such, did not want to lift the rails and stop the traffic literally, but he would like to be in a position to do so if necessary. 'I say to the Great Western company go on working as you are now, but instead of paying the Bridport Railway Company the specified proportion of the receipts, pay it to me until the debt is satisfied'.

In summing up Under Sheriff Coombs said that the only chattels the defendant appeared to possess were two clocks, except for the rails and sleepers, but he directed the jury to find that the case for the plaintiff had been proved, and that Mr Mathieson could seize the company's land from Maiden Newton to Bridport.

The jury's verdict was that the railway company was in fact owner of the rails valued at £2,000 and the land on which the railway ran. The effect of this judgement enabled Mathieson to obtain complete possession of the Bridport Railway!

The Bridport Railway Company now found itself in a situation where, by law, Mathieson could dismantle the railway in an attempt to recover some of his loss. However, as a major shareholder he was in a strange situation. The Bridport company appealed to the Vice-Chancellor's court on April 15th, asking for a restraining order on Mathieson's claim, and this order was granted. On Wednesday 4th May in the Vice-Chancellor's Court, Mr Legg - a substantial shareholder in the company - applied for an injunction to restrain the Sheriff of Dorset from delivering legal possession of the land on which the railway was constructed, or the rails, and from any interruption to the traffic of the railway. Mathieson did not appear at the proceedings. The Vice-Chancellor made an order for an injunction, and granted leave to serve the defendant Mathieson with the order in Scotland.

Although Mr Legg was the current Chairman of the Bridport company, he had loaned the company, as a private person, the sum of £600 (as had several others) as a mortgage loan. The injunction was granted to Legg against Mathieson, preventing him from taking possession of the land, rails and sleepers until such time as the mortgagees (Legg and others) were paid up in full. This had been allowed for by a clause in the original Act of Parliament in 1855. Mathieson was also ordered to pay the costs of all parties in the suit.

A special general meeting was held on 13th July to consider the provisions of a Bill to go through Parliament granting facilities for raising funds to complete the Bridport Railway. Mr Gundry observed that he had received a letter from Mathieson containing his views on the Bill, and also instructions on which way he wished to vote. The letter concluded with a request that he should vote against the Bill on his behalf (Mathieson's). Mr Gundry then added that 'I hope the shareholders will not consider the foregoing are my sentiments respecting the Bill. I merely had to fulfil a duty for Mr Mathieson; and I will vote for myself whatever way I think best'. Mr Templer remarked that Mathieson had sent a letter to him, which conveyed a somewhat different impression!

Whatever his differences with the Bridport company, Mathieson was well respected in Dunfermline where he had taken up residence as a young man. In 1853 he entered the Town Council, and 18 years later he was Chief Magistrate and served as Provost. His engineering knowledge was widely sought with the many improvement schemes that were carried out in the area during his years in office. When he retired to Edinburgh in 1891 he was presented with 400 sovereigns and a piece of silver plate. He passed away aged 81 on 21st November, 1897.

The Act for leasing the Bridport Railway to the GWR and for raising a further amount of capital received the Royal Assent on 13th August, 1859. The estimated liabilities for which such further capital was required was put at £19,600. The terms of the Act allowed the raising of a sum not exceeding £20,000.

Mr Kenneth Mathieson, the Contractor who built the Bridport Railway.

The Engineer's report on the line made interesting reading:

The slip on the South side of Witherstone cutting has at last been secured and no movement traced in the past two months. 50,000 cubic yards of clay have been excavated and deep drainage carried through several portions of the slip. The permanent way is now in as good a condition as it is possible the Macdonnell system can be, and the fencing along the entire line is rapidly decaying and needs replacing.

Mr Mathieson, who attended the meeting took exception to the last remark, stating that he had walked the line that morning for a mile and a half and saw no symptoms of decay, and if the fences along the line were as good as those he saw they would require no new fencing for many years to come. Mr Reader remarked that the posts should not have been Scotch fir or larch. However, the contract deed with specification of construction clearly stated, 'the fencing is to consist of oak, larch, or scotch fir. For the latter it is to be creosoted'! Mr Dunham said he would like to see a station erected at Great Toller, to which Mr Flight replied that the matter would now be in the hands of the GWR.

In the meanwhile works had been progressing well on the railway. In October the Bridport company paid Mr Shaw £921 3s. 2d. for his work on the line, and the GWR forwarded its account up to the 30th June for work carried out at Maiden Newton.

Materials and labour at junction	£156 4s. 8d.
Engineering and permanent way	£852 1s. 3d.
Rails	£3 8s. 0d.

The work at Maiden Newton had been quite substantial, involving a bay platform on the up side for the branch train, and a gravity siding to allow the engine to run round the stock. To accommodate the extra track an arch carrying a lane under the railway at the north end of the station had had to be extended, and other small works were carried out including extension of the station buildings. All the works were completed by the end of December.

In March 1860 Mr M. Lane, the GWR Engineer, in his report to the Bridport company stated, 'The line during the progress of the works has been greatly improved, and is now in very good condition. The GWR have from the 1st of January last taken, with the exception of the fencing, the charge of the line and works'. He was highly critical of the state of the fencing and estimated its replacement would cost £220 per mile.

The problems with the Macdonnell way were causing considerable concern. An examination of the line by Mr F. Fox, Civil Engineer of the Bristol & Exeter Railway, was published in the minutes of the Institution of Civil Engineers Vol. 20 1860-61, and gave a very pertinent description of the state of the track.

> The bearers are only 60 lb. per yard, the middle web projects but slightly above the bearer, and the rails are only 53 lb. per yard; the way is, therefore, very light and weak. There are no plates of any kind at the bearer joints, which are, in many cases, between 1 inch and 2 inches wide. The weakness at these points is most apparent, and considering that the line is traversed by heavy broad gauge engines, the omission of joint plates is most objectionable. The pine packing is only ¼ inch thick, laid longitudinally, and there is no hard wood at the rail joints. The packing being compressed out, it is of little service either as a cushion for the rail, or as a means of keeping the bolts tight. The latter are continually working loose, and owing to the threads not being cut sufficiently long, it is very difficult to tighten them; and this difficulty is increased by their being round instead of square at the shoulder, requiring the ballast having to be opened out and the bolt head held by a spanner. The transoms were exceedingly light, being of angle iron 2½ inches by 1½ inches, and they were only of sufficient length to admit of being secured by one bolt at each end. It was found essential to the safe working of the line to take out every alternate transom and to replace it by a strong transom of the kind used for the Barlow way. There is nothing to keep the way in its place in the ballast, beyond the slight curvature of the bearer, and it is found necessary to effect this, by driving stakes in the ballast on the curves, and even on the straight line. When it is added that the gradients are heavy, being 1 in 50 for some length, that the bottom is a yielding clay, and the chief part of the ballast is of a soft stone, broken originally into very large lumps, it is by no means surprising that, laid as it was, it should prove a partial failure; but it would be manifestly incorrect to condemn [sic] this system of iron way, from its having failed through an almost entire disregard of the appliances which the character of the gradients, the curves, the ballast, and the subsoil rendered more than ordinarily necessary.

Within a short time the Macdonnell way was replaced by the GWR standard baulk road with longitudinal timbers which remained in use for many years. The Macdonnell way passed into history - a brave attempt to overcome the problems of the period. Ironically some of the bearer plates remained on the branch until closure, used to cover storm water catch pits, and for any other job where an iron plate could be put to use.

Changes of station masters to give them promotion were again taking place, Henry Knowles moving from station master Bridport to goods canvasser at Yeovil for a salary of £120 pa. In January 1860 John Webber from the Yeovil goods department became the replacement Bridport station master. Knowles was destined for higher office, for in February 1862 he became the goods agent at Wolverhampton, only to resign for reasons unknown four years later!

Frederick Beauchamp moved from Maiden Newton in January 1860, his place being taken by William Mathews Mitcham. Aged only twenty, he had commenced his service as a clerk at Warminster in 1856, moving to Dorchester with the opening of the line in January 1857.

During 1859 there were proposals for a 'West Dorset Railway' - a local project to extend the Bridport branch to Charmouth via Bradpole and Symondsbury - but this was yet another scheme that failed to progress.

The question of a station at Great Toller was still being raised, the first official recognition of any progress being the signing of a Private Siding Agreement on 16th December, 1861 between the GWR and Mr Edward Pope, a Gentleman of the village. The siding was at 2 miles 46 chains and was to be used for the 'conveyance of goods and passengers from the same'.

As it would have been extremely difficult to operate passenger services from a siding, it is clear that a station of some description was envisaged, and one was finally opened on 31st March, 1862. Although the village was immediately alongside the railway, the long wait for a station had been caused by the awaited decision of the Authorities concerning the route of a new road!

The opening was celebrated by a little festive gathering at Great Toller, at the invitation of Mr Edward Pope. The Directors of the company arrived on the first train, and were later hospitably entertained with an excellent luncheon in the village. Among those present were Mr E.G. Flight (Sec.), a Mr J. Pope of Symondsbury, the Revd G.K. Weston, Mr E. Whittle and a number of Mr Pope's personal friends.

The new station was put under the charge of booking porter Arthur Henry Woodrow, who had previously served at Mells, but just a year after his appointment to Toller he moved to Limpley Stoke on promotion. Toller was the lowest grade of station for booking porters who were paid 21s. a week, so staff changes were very frequent as many moved upward on promotion and that few shillings extra!

It was more than a few shillings when William Mitcham moved from station master Maiden Newton to Bruton in April 1862, his annual salary being increased from £90 to £110. Three years later upon further promotion to Frome he received £130. The Maiden Newton vacancy was filled by John Girling.

The year 1863 saw the start of yet another set of proposals for railways in the Bridport area. As built, the Bridport Railway only just reached the town, the harbour being situated nearly two miles away. During this year the Bridport Harbour Railway and Pier Company was formed with the intention of constructing a deep water pier at the harbour, and a mixed gauge railway line to join up with the Bridport Railway. They also wanted to build a line to join the LSWR's main line at Wayford and continue with an extension to Martock (both places in Somerset), and there joining the Bristol and Exeter Railway's Yeovil branch. Both the GWR and the LSWR as well as the Bridport company opposed this scheme, and the Bill was withdrawn from the 1864 session of Parliament. In the same year a plan for the Bridport, Lyme Regis and Axminster Railway was deposited, this being a revival of the coastal route from Dorchester via Bridport and Lyme Regis to Exeter. In the same session of Parliament the 'Chard Road and Lyme Regis Harbour Railway' applied for powers to construct a line from Chard Road to Lyme Regis, with a tramway extension to the harbour. A branch from Birdmoregate to Bridport was also planned. This scheme also failed in the face of opposition.

The harbour line also made an abortive attempt to reappear as the 'Beaminster Railway'. This truncated version would have run from a junction with the LSWR main line at Crewkerne and terminated at Beaminster.

The Bridport, Lyme Regis and Axminster Railway scheme exposed some unsavoury business practices of the day. The cost of the line was to have been approximately £480,000 or approximately £30,000 per mile. It had been hoped that both the GWR and LSWR would provide the majority of capital for the project, but both companies declined to become involved so the Bill was about to be withdrawn.

BRANCH.
Up.　　　Bridport to Maiden Newton.　　　Up.

Dist.	STATIONS.	WEEK DAYS								SUNDAYS.		
		1	2	3	4	5	6	7	8	1	2	3
		Pass.	GOODS	Pass.	Pass.	Pass.	Pass.			Pass.	Pass.	Pass.
		a.m.	a.m.	p.m.	p.m.	p.m.	p.m.			a.m.	p.m.	
	Bridport ..dep.	9 0	11 *o	12 55	3 50	5 45	8 45	...	...	9 30	5 45	...
3½	Powerstock	9 10	11 10	1 5	4 0	—	8 55	...	...	9 40	5 55	...
6¾	Toller	9 20	—	S	4 10	—	9 5	...	...	9 50	6 5	...
9¼	Maidn.New.arr.	9 30	11 30	1 25	4·20	6 10	9 15	...	...	10 0	6 15	...

* No. 2.　This train will only run from Bridport when required.
S　To stop at Toller on Saturdays.

Working timetable for the Bridport Railway, January 1863.

Down.　　Maiden Newton to Bridport.　　BRIDPORT Down.

Dist.	STATIONS.	WEEK DAYS.								SUNDAYS.		
		1	2	3	4	5	6	7	8	1	2	3
		Pass.	Pass.	Pass.	Pass.	Pass.	Pass.			Pass.	Pass.	
		a.m.	noon.	p.m.	p.m.	p.m.	p.m.			a.m.	p.m.	
	MaidnNew dep.	10 15	12 *o	1 55	4 50	6 25	9 35	...	...	11 10	6 25	...
2⅓	Toller	10 20	—	2 0	—	6 30	—	...	...	11 15	6 30	...
5¾	Powerstock	10 35	12 20	2 15	5 10	6 45	—	...	...	11 30	6 45	...
9¼	Bridport ..arr.	10 45	12 30	2 25	5 20	6 55	10 0	...	...	11 40	6 55	...

* No. 2.　This Train will only run to Bridport when required.

However a letter was intercepted by a correspondent in the *Bridport News*, and was published on 18th February. The letter was written by the solicitors for the scheme, Baxter, Rose, Norton & Company, and addressed to John Hawksworth FRS, the Consulting Engineer, and contained reasons both why the Bill was to be withdrawn and why the clients had decided not to go ahead and make the obligatory Parliamentary deposit. Here the letter became controversial and soon sparked off a disagreement, for it said,

> To carry the Bill in any altered shape we felt we could not be positive, acting as we do for the Great Western Railway Company in other matters, and more-over those of the Directors associated with the same who are connected with the Bridport Railway Company, would have good reason to complain of our adopting such a course.

The letter continued at some length and was signed by the solicitors.

The *Bridport News* commented, 'The idea of Bridport being able to raise £480,000 is somewhat startling, but where there's a will there's a way, but not always a railway'. This angered Mr Flight, the Bridport company Secretary, and the following week his reply was published.

> Sir,
> In your last week's paper is a supposed copy of a letter from a firm of London Solicitors, from which it might be inferred that they acted for the Bridport Railway Company in promoting the railway scheme from hence to Lyme Regis and Axminster.
> Who were the clients of these gentlemen in that important scheme, I do not know, but certainly not the Bridport Railway Company who did not promote it, and who never in any way, directly or indirectly, employ them.
>
> Yours Respectfully
> E.G. Flight

The 1865 'Bridport, Lyme Regis and South Coast' appeared again to join the LSWR main line near Wayford. This went through Parliament as far as the House of Lords and was then withdrawn.

On 14th August, 1871 the Lyme Regis Railway Bill received Royal Assent to build a line from Axminster to Lyme Regis, and at the end of 1874 the company sought powers to construct an extension to Bridport to join the existing railway and form a branch to the harbour. Again after passing through the House of Commons, the Bill was withdrawn in the House of Lords. As for the original planned line to Lyme Regis, three years after the passing of the Act the first sod was cut ceremoniously at Lyme Regis - this was in September of 1874 - but little else was done and the powers lapsed in 1876. Consequently Lyme Regis had to wait until 1903 for its railway.

Turning back to the domestic affairs of the Bridport company. By 1863 their offices had, for some reason not recorded, moved to premises in Barrack Street, and on 12th April, 1865 they moved into Mr Flight's residence in Bradpole Road - only to move again on the 10th October, 1866 into what was reported to be Mr Flight's new residence in East Street.

In December 1865 John Webber resigned as station master Bridport. This gave promotion to Henry Alfred Bond, an experienced clerk who had previously worked in the goods departments at Frome, Bristol and Warminster, and as station master at Wilton.

January 1866 saw John Girling move from station master Maiden Newton to Devizes, William Edward Bock taking his place. Previously employed in the goods department at Bruton he was no stranger to the district, having commenced his employment with the GWR at the age of 19 in 1859 as junior goods clerk at Bridport.

Charles Gardner, the original booking porter at Powerstock, resigned in November 1867, his pay having been £59 per year plus accommodation. However this meant promotion for F.W. Green who had been booking porter at Toller since July 1866, his new position earning him 23s. a week. H.C. Fisher took over Toller, moving on in November 1868 to Lawrence Hill, Bristol. Again his replacement, J. Liddiard, soon moved to Limpley Stoke in January 1870.

W.E. Bock moved from Maiden Newton in November 1869 to a clerical position at Swindon, then upwards again to the senior clerk at Swindon and the divisional manager's office in Gloucester two years later. He became chief clerk at Oxford in June 1876, but was dismissed at the end of September!

Henry Yeo, formerly booking porter at Grimstone & Frampton, moved to Maiden Newton as station master at £80 per year. In 1872 this was raised to £90, and £100 in 1874. Yeo was one of the few booking porters to break through as station master at a larger station, such positions usually being awarded to clerical grades, although his starting salary at Maiden Newton does tend to indicate that the GWR were trying to cut staff costs at the time!

At 5 pm on Monday 6th February, 1871, at the age of 68 years, Edward Gill Flight died after four days' illness with congestion of the lungs. He had married late in life and left a widow and six children, the youngest being only 15 months old. The son of a London merchant, he had been born locally and had been responsible for bringing the railway to Bridport, having been Secretary to the company from the start, and through its most difficult times. Indeed, he was a man to whom the town owed much.

The tragedy was that, although he brought the railway to Bridport, he died penniless and his widow and children were left destitute. At a meeting of the Board on 8th February his death was discussed and it was decided an appeal should be sent to the GWR asking the Directors of that company to provide financial aid to help the distressed family as Mr Flight, through starting the Bridport Railway Company, had in fact brought quite an amount of useful business to the GWR. Nicholas Loggin, a partner in the firm of solicitors Flight and Loggin, was appointed Company Secretary in his stead.

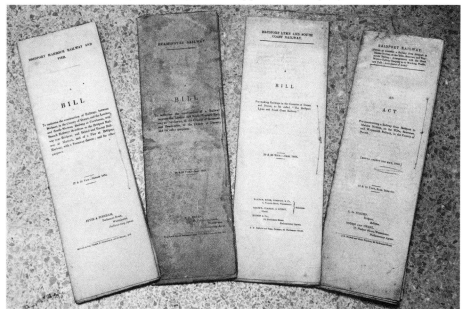

Various Bills for railways in the Bridport area. *Left to Right*: Bridport Railway and Pier 1864. Beaminster Railway 1865. Bridport Lyme and South Coast Railway 1866. Bridport Railway 1855.

Chapter Four

The Final Years of Independence

The end of the year (1871) also saw the death of Flight's contemporary, Wylie, the Engineer. Following his work on the Bridport Railway, other schemes in Scotland, including the Kirkcubright Railway and the Berwickshire Railway were completed before he took up an appointment with the Home Department of the Indian State Railways in 1868; but following a controversy arising over the best gauge to be adopted, he accepted an appointment as consulting engineer to the Tasmanian Railways. The exertion of this visit aggravated a pulmonary complaint, his death taking place at his sister's home in Melbourne, Australia, on 3rd November at the young age of fifty.

The 1870s were to see a new era in the fortunes and misfortunes of the Bridport Railway, which commenced with the conversion of the entire Wilts, Somerset & Weymouth line including branches to standard gauge in the period between 18th-22nd June, 1874. This involved alteration to 131 miles of railway excluding sidings. Unfortunately shortly before the demise of the broad gauge a derailment had taken place at Maiden Newton. On Thursday 28th May the 2.10 pm train departed from Maiden Newton in charge of driver Taylor and fireman Frost, the train consisting of the usual carriages and four goods wagons. Whilst rounding the curve heading away towards Bridport the trailing wheels of the engine left the rails, but with only a handbrake on the engine and another in the guard's van it took 200 yards to stop the train, the track being damaged over that length. A telegram was promptly sent to Weymouth for an engine and men to clear the track, and by good fortune a spare engine was at Bridport. This brought coaches to the scene of the derailment and then conveyed the passengers to Bridport where they arrived at 5.50 pm.

A service was maintained by the Bridport engine operating a shuttle service to the scene of the derailment and the Weymouth engine using the stock of the derailed locomotive to operate the same to Maiden Newton station, passengers alighting and walking past the derailment. The offending engine was re-railed at 8.15 pm and removed. The *Bridport News* reporting that upon the 'engine being examined it was found that the tyres of those wheels that had run off the line were too thick'. The paper also remarked 'it is strange that this accident should have taken place just as the arrangements for converting the broad into the narrow gauge had commenced'. This statement raised the question of whether maintenance of the track had slipped owing to the pending change, or if preparatory work for the conversion had involved a little too much slackening of fittings!

A great deal has been written concerning the gauge change in general so only the local events require explanation. On the Bridport branch, as elsewhere on the system, a considerable amount of preparatory work had been carried out. For some weeks previously men had been engaged in clearing out ballast to facilitate the movement of sleepers and rails, and also partly sawing through the transoms. Where the rails were laid on conventional chairs and sleepers, additional chairs were placed on the sleepers set at the new gauge, and all bolts and fittings freed ready for a swift change over.

The majority of broad gauge stock had already been removed from the branch by Thursday 18th June, the remainder departing that evening, many local people going to the station to witness the departure of the last broad gauge train. With this went the certificate from station master Bond of Bridport and station master Yeo of Maiden Newton to the effect that all broad gauge stock was clear of their stations and district.

Down.
Witham to Wells.
On Week Days Only.

Single Line.		1	2	3	4	5	6	7	8	9	10	11
Dist.	STATIONS.	Goods	Pass. and GOODS A	Pass.	Pass.	Pass.	Pass. and GOODS	Pass.				
		a.m.	a.m.	a.m.	p.m.	p.m.	p.m.	p.m.				
	Witham J. dep.	8 15	8 45	11 5	12 50	3 40	6 40	9 0	...	...	...	...
2¼	Wanstrow	—	—	11 12	—	3 48	—	—	...	...	...	...
5¾	Cranmore	—	9 0	11 25	—	4 0	6 55	9 15	This	Line	is	Worked
7	Doulting	—	—	—	—	—	—	—	by	Train	Staff.	
9	Shepton Mallet ..	8 55	9 15	11 35	1 10	4 10	7 10	9 25	...	...	...	...
14	Wells......arr.	9 10	9 30	11 50	1 25	4 25	7 30	9 40	...	...	...	...

A This Train will run on Sunday mornings, but not on Monday mornings.

BRIDPORT

Down.
Maiden Newton to Bridport.

Single Line, worked by Train Staff		WEEK DAYS.								SUNDAYS.		
Dist.		1	2	3	4	5	6	7	8	1	2	3
	STATIONS.	Pass.		Pass.		Pass.		Pass.		Pass.	Pass.	
		a.m.		p.m.		p.m.		p.m.		a.m.	p.m.	
2¼	Maidn New dep.	10 15	.	2 10	.	5 20	.	10 5	.	11 20	9 5	...
5¼	Toller	10 20	..	2 15	..	5 27	..	C R	..	11 25	9 10	...
9¼	Powerstock	10 35	...	2 30	...	5 35	...	C R	...	11 40	9 25	...
	Bridport ..arr.	10 45	.	2 40	.	5 50	..	10 30	..	11 50	9 35	...

R Calls when required.

BRISTOL AND SOUTH

Down.
Bristol to New Passage.

Single Line, worked by Train Staff and Auxiliary Disc Teleg'ph.		WEEK DAYS.									SUNDAYS.			
Distances		1	2	3	4	5	6	7	8	9	1	2	3	4
	STATIONS.	Pass.	Pass.	Pass.	Goods.	Pass.	Pass.	Pass.			Pass.		Pass.	
		a.m.	a.m.	p.m.	p.m.	p.m.	p.m.	p.m.			a.m.		p.m.	
1	Bristol (G.W.Stn.) dp	7 30	10 30	12 35	12 45	2 50	5 10	7 15	...	.	8 10	...	3 0	...
1¼	Lawrence Hill	7 35	10 35	12 40	12 55	2 55	5 15	7 20	...	.	8 15	...	3 5	...
2¼	Stapleton Road	7 40	10 40	12 43	C R	3 0	5 20	7 25	...	...	8 18	...	3 10	...
4¼	Ashley Hill	7 45	10 45	—	—	—	5 25	—	...	...	8 22	...	3 15	...
6¼	Filton	7 51	—	—	C R	—	5 31	—	...	...	8 28	...	3 23	...
	Patchway	7 57	10 55	12 55	1 20	3 20	5 38	7 40	...	...	8 34	...	3 30	...
9¼	Over Siding.	—	—	—	C R	—	—	—	...	...	—	...	—	...
11¾	Pilning	8 5	—	—	C R	—	5 46	—	...	...	8 42	...	3 40	...
12	New Passage	8 12	11 7	1 5	1 45	3 30	5 54	7 50	...	...	8 48	...	3 47	...
	Pier............ arr.	8 15	11 10	1 10	...	3 35	5 55	7 55	...	.	8 50	...	3 50	...

C R To call when required.

(Single Line.)

PORTLAND

Down.
Weymouth to Portland.

STATIONS.		WEEK DAYS.											SUNDAYS.				
Distance. 4½ miles.		1	2	3 S. W. Goods	4 G. W. Goods	5	6	7	8	9	10	11	1	2	3	4	5
		Pass.	Pass.	Pass.	Pass.	Pass.	Pass.	Pass.	Pass.	Pass.	Pass.		Pass.	Pass.	Pass.	Pass.	
		a.m.	a.m.	a.m.	a.m.	a.m.	p.m.	p.m.	p.m.	p.m.	p.m.		a.m.	p.m.	p.m.	p.m.	
Weymouth		7 25	9 30	10 40	11 10	11 20	1 43	2 50	4 55	6 5	8 40	...	9 30	12 30	3 0	8 35	...
Rodwell		7 35	9 40	10 50	11 20	11 30	1 53	3 0	5 6	6 15	8 50	...	9 40	12 40	3 10	8 45	...
Portland		7 45	9 50	11 0	11 30	11 40	2 3	3 10	5 15	6 25	9 0	...	9 50	12 50	3 20	8 55	...

This Line is worked by Train Staff.

Extract from the working timetable 1873, down trains.

Wells to Witham.
On Week Days Only.
Up.

	Single Line.	1	2	3	4	5	6	7	8	9	10	11
Dist.	STATIONS.	Pass. and GOODS	Pass.	Pass.	Pass.	Pass. and GOODS	Pass. and Goods	Goods				
		a.m.	a.m.	p.m.	p.m.	p.m.	p m.	p.m.				
	Wells .... dep.	6 30	10 10	12 5	1 40	5 30	7 40	9 40	...	...	...	...
5	Shepton Mal. dep.	6 42	10 25	12 20	1 55	5 50	7 55	10 0	...	...	...	...
7	Doulting............	—	—	—	—	—	—	—	...	...	...	...
8¼	Cranmore	6 52	10 35	—	2 5	6 0	8 5	10 15	...	...	...	...
11¾	Wanstrow	—	10 45	—	—	C R	—	—	...	...	...	...
14	**Witham J.** arr.	7 5	10 50	12 40	2 20	6 20	8 20	10 40	...	...	...	...

BRANCH.

C R   To call when required.

Bridport to Maiden Newton.
Up.

	Single Line, worked by Train Staff.	WEEK DAYS								SUNDAYS.		
		1	2	3	4	5	6	7	8	1	2	3
Dist.	STATIONS.	Pass.		Pass.		Pass.		Pass.		Pass.	Pass.	
		a.m.		p.m.		p.m.		p.m.		a.m.	p.m.	
	Bridport ..dep.	9 0	..	12 40	.	4 30	.	8 15	.	10 30	5 0	.
3½	Powerstock	9 10	..	12 50	..	4 40	..	8 25	..	10 40	5 10	..
6¼	Toller	9 20	..	Sat.	...	4 50	...	8 35	...	10 50	5 20	...
9¼	**Maidn. New.** ar	9 30	..	1 5	.	5 0	.	8 45	.	11 0	5 30	.

WALES UNION LINE.
New Passage to Bristol.
Up.

Distances.	Single Line, worked by Train Staff & Auxiliary Disc Telegraph.	WEEK DAYS.									SUNDAYS.			
		1	2	3	4	5	6	7	8	9	1	2	3	4
	STATIONS.	Pass.	Pass.	Pass.		Goods.	Pass.	Pass.	Pass.		Pass.		Pass.	
		a.m.	a.m.	p.m.		p.m.	p.m.	p.m.	p.m.		a.m.		p.m.	
	New Passage dep	9 15	11 35	3 5	...	3 55	6 0	8 0	8 20	...	10 5	...	5 30	...
2¼	Pilning	9 21	—	—	...	C R	—	—	8 26	...	10 11	...	—	...
	Over Siding.........	—	—	—	...		—	—	—	...	—	...	—	...
5¼	Patchway	9 31	11 47	3 20	...	4 25	6 15	8 15	8 35	...	10 21	...	5 42	...
7	Filton	9 37	—	3 26	...	C R	—	—	8 40	...	10 27	...	5 48	...
9	Ashley Hill	9 43	—	3 32	...		6 25	—	8 46	...	10 33	...	5 55	...
10	Stapleton Road	9 47	12 0	3 36	...	C R	6 30	8 27	8 50	...	10 36	...	6 0	...
10¾	Lawrence Hill	9 50	12 3	3 41	...	4 45	6 35	8 30	8 55	...	10 39	...	6 3	...
11¾	**Bristol** .... arr.	10 0	12 10	3 51	...	4 55	6 45	8 40	9 5	...	10 45	...	6 10	...

Train Staffs work as under:—Bristol and Patchway, Staff and Ticket Red and Square ; Patchway and New passage, White and Round.

BRANCH.
(Single Line.)
Portland to Weymouth.
Up.

STATIONS.	WEEK DAYS.											SUNDAYS.				
	1	2	3	4	5	6	7	8	9	10	11	1	2	3	4	5
				S.W.	G.W.											
	Pass.	Pass.	Pass.	Goods	Goods	Pass.	Pass.	Pass.	Pas.	Pass.		Pass.	Pass.	Pass.	Pass.	
	a.m.	a.m.	a.m.	noon.	p.m.	p.m.	p.m.	p.m.	p.m.	p.m.		a.m.	p.m.	p.m.	p.m.	
Portland ...	8 10	9 55	11 55	12 0	12 25	2 10	4 10	5 20	6 30	9 5	...	10 0	1 0	4 0	9 0	...
Rodwell	8 20	10 5	12 5	12 12	12 37	2 20	4 20	5 30	6 40	9 15	...	10 10	1 10	4 10	9 10	...
Weymouth...	8 30	10 15	12 15	12 25	12 50	2 30	4 30	5 40	6 50	9 25	...	10 20	1 20	4 20	9 20	...

Extract from the working timetable 1873, up trains.

GREAT WESTERN RAILWAY.

The Alteration of the Gauge

BETWEEN

CHIPPENHAM, WEYMOUTH, SALISBURY, BATH, *and on the* EAST SOMERSET AND BRIDPORT BRANCHES, *will be completed on the*

NIGHT of the 24th INSTANT.

The Ordinary Service of Passenger Trains will be resumed on

THURSDAY, the 25th of JUNE.

Paddington, June, 1874.

J. GRIERSON,
Genl. Manager

Public notice advising of change of gauge on the Bridport Railway.

The *Bridport News* estimated that about 180 men were engaged in the conversion of the branch, many of them being brought in from other parts of the Great Western system and arriving on the Thursday evening. Work commenced at 2 am on the Friday morning, and continued to dusk, the men sleeping in makeshift accommodation where they worked. Those at Bridport had the luxury of sleeping on straw in the goods shed, as did those at Maiden Newton. The men were allowed 1s. 3d. a day for rations and the company provided a drink consisting mainly of oatmeal mixed with sugar called 'skilley'. It was the duty of one of the men on each gang to brew this mixture and distribute it in large buckets into which indivual workers dipped a tin cup.

Local people showed a great interest in the work and went to view the progress. At 11.40 am on Sunday 21st the first standard gauge engine arrived at Bridport with a party of GWR officials testing the line at a speed of 15 mph. Upon arrival it was discovered that the clearance in the platforms was not sufficient for the new coaches so both sets of rails had to be moved over. At 5 pm a locomotive and the new coaching stock for the branch arrived, the *Bridport News* observing:

> The carriages are first, second and third class; besides there are two guard's vans. They are altogether of a more modern make than the old ones, being much loftier, with more room between the seats, some of the third class being merely padded, while the second and first were also padded only in a better degree. Each of the third seats was not entirely enclosed in some instances, a partition reaching only half way up the carriage separating them.

Although the running lines had all been successfully converted during that historic weekend, there was still a considerable amount of work to be carried out. Many sidings were no doubt converted during the following week, extra gangers being employed at Bridport until Thursday 25th June. The conduct of the platelayers during the conversion was excellent, assisted by the fact that the men were not allowed to bring alcohol to the work. At Maiden Newton the Revd Hankey held a service in the goods shed on Sunday afternoon, during which he preached the parable of the Prodigal Son, doubtless a reference to the errant 'Broad Gauge' coming home to join the universal family of the standard gauge. Passenger services had returned to normal on Monday 22nd, although they were subject to some speed restrictions until works were completed. Goods traffic was however delayed for a considerable time. To enable wagons to be cleared from the area no goods had arrived for several days before the conversion, and afterwards the need to reinstate sidings caused further delay. There were also several other major factors involved with the change, five narrow gauge wagons being required to carry the contents of two broad gauge wagons. The same applied to coaching stock, and consequently the length of trains was increased simply to carry the previous loadings, which in turn resulted in extra siding accommodation being required and the lengthening of station platforms. These tasks were carried out over a long period in the following years. It was however a new beginning, opening up the Bridport branch and the Wilts, Somerset & Weymouth to the remainder of the country without the problems of transhipment at various places.

One might have thought that the Board of Directors of the Bridport company would have been very pleased at having all the track of their railway replaced by the GWR, which made the changeover its entire responsibility, but at a Board Meeting on the 5th August they complained that the GWR had altered the gauge of their railway and at no time had consulted them about it!

At the Bridport company half-yearly General Meeting on 30th September it was announced that no dividend would be paid to the shareholders. When Captain Groves asked the Chairman for an explanation, he received the simple one that there were insufficient funds!

An omen of future locomotive failures, of which at one stage the branch suffered a surprising number, took place on New Year's Day 1876, when the horse power of the station bus failed. The *Bridport News* reported:

A horse named Turpin, the property of Mr Knight of the Bull Hotel, died suddenly at Allington under the following circumstances. The horse was one of two which was taking up passengers at Allington for the 12.5 pm train, and where it suddenly fell down and died. The cause of death was the bursting of a blood vessel. The horse was one which Mr Knight purchased a few weeks since in London. Other vehicles had to be sent out to collect the passengers by reason of the mishap, and we understand it was a case of 'sharp work' to catch the train.

January 1876 saw the departure of station master Yeo from Maiden Newton, moving to Dorchester in the same position from which he later took retirement. His place at Maiden Newton was filled by George Hyrons, although his was a short stay, moving on to become station master at Devizes that November. Walter Thompson Gray from Devizes goods department then took over at Maiden Newton. Again he had local connections, having entered railway service at Bridport in April 1872, aged 20, as a clerk in the booking office.

Also departing in January was Miss Devenish who for the past 16 years had been manageress of the refreshment room on Maiden Newton station, the station staff and a few friends presented her with a suitably inscribed silver watch.

On Tuesday 10th October, 1876 Witherstone cutting was again a source of trouble, when the 4.30 pm mixed train from Bridport became derailed as it was rounding a sharp curve at that point.

The cause was a truck near the centre of the train which left the rails and drew with it three others, together with two carriages and a brake van. No-one was injured and the passengers were taken on to Maiden Newton in the stock which had formed the forward part of the train.

During 1877 the agreement which had been made in 1858 between the Bridport Railway Company and the GWR still had two years to run, and with this in mind the GWR was asked if it would like to purchase the line. The GWR replied that it was not interested and did not intend to modify the terms of the agreement if the contract was renewed.

At this stage the relationship between the two companies was a little strained to say the least, which resulted in a plan for a railway to link Bridport with the LSWR at Chard and Crewkerne being put forward in November 1877. An engineer had asked the council for co-operation in a project to construct a railway line to Chard Road (Chard Junction), leaving the present railway just outside Bridport station and crossing the countryside via Bradpole, Netherbury and going near Beaminster, Stoke Abbot and Broadwindsor with a branch to Crewkerne station. The *Dorset County Chronicle* in reporting this scheme said 'It is evident Bridport people no longer desire the monopoly of the Great Western Railway, and would hail any feasible scheme which would open up a communication either with the South Western or Midland Company lines'.

The same newspaper for 21st November, 1878 gave the following account of the proposed railway,

There are a variety of opinions respecting the proposed railway to Chard Road. Of course the object is to have a ready communication between Dorchester and Exeter, and the scheme now advocated seems to be the most feasible, but it is contended that in going through The Vale of Marshwood it passes no town and scarcely a well populated village. It is argued a line to Beaminster, Broadwindsor and Winsham could be made at a little more expense, and the country would be opened up abounding with factories, for instance Pymore, Slape, Broadwindsor and

Greenham. Of course the Directors of the Bridport Company have considered the best scheme and have very good reasons for adopting the choice they have made. We have not yet heard a word as to the estimated cost, nor of the method of raising the money.

It was quite clear that the Bridport company now wanted to extend its spheres of operation. It wanted to construct a line to Bridport harbour, and another to join the LSWR, and also sought powers to sell or lease the new lines to either the GWR or the LSWR, and running powers over the GWR main line between Maiden Newton and Dorchester were also to be requested.

In February 1879, an extraordinary meeting of the shareholders to consider the Parliamentary Bill for the extension to the railway and other powers that were sought was held at the Bull Hotel, Bridport. Mr Swatridge, the Chairman, was unable to attend so the chair was taken by Mr J.P.F. Gundry. It would appear that cash was not as forthcoming as expected, and it was decided that only the harbour extension was to be proceeded with, although certain shareholders were still interested in the Chard line. Major Groves asked the Chairman 'I understand the Bill is now simply to extend the line to the harbour and obtain running powers between Maiden Newton and Dorchester', to which the Chairman replied 'Yes, and obtain powers to enter into a contract with the London South Western Company'. Major Groves then expressed his firm opinion that the extension to Chard would pay. The Chairman announced that votes representing a capital of £33,200 were recorded in favour of the harbour extension.

In May of that year the harbour extension Bill was heard by a Parliamentary Select Committee of the House of Commons. Among those present at the hearing were Mr Shopland, an engineer of Windsor, Mr Loggin, the Bridport company Secretary, Mr Grierson, the General Manager of the GWR, and Mr Graham, a GWR superintendent.

Mr Shopland told the committee that there were no difficulties in the proposed construction, which would cost about £21,600. As the majority of the shareholders were local people, so long as they were provided with proper train accommodation they did not care about getting a dividend.

Mr Loggin agreed and said,

Five-sixths of the shareholders were interested in Bridport and they desired a better service rather than a dividend. Complaints have repeatedly been made of the inadequacy of the present working, passengers going to Dorchester in the middle of the day were being kept waiting at Maiden Newton about 1½ hours and similar delays occur to people travelling in the other direction.

Mr Loggin estimated that traffic to the value of £35,000 was sent on to the GWR from the Bridport line each year.

The Bridport company wanted the GWR to work the line for 50 per cent with a rebate on traffic passing on to the GWR system, or it should be guaranteed 4 per cent on its ordinary capital; failing this the GWR should purchase the line for 75 per cent.

To all these proposals the GWR refused to agree, but offered three alternatives:

1. If the Bridport Company wished to work their own line the Great Western would provide stock, station accommodation and service at Maiden Newton at a cost to be agreed by an arbitrator.

or

2. The Great Western would provide rolling stock and staff, work and maintain the line and provide accommodation at Maiden Newton at such a percentage of the gross receipts as a competent person might decide.

or

3. The Great Western would renew the present agreement on the old terms.

Mr Grierson replied, 'Whilst negotiating with the Bridport Company last year they never asked for a better service, but better terms. If a better train service was really wanted, it could be had, it was only a question of terms'.

Mr Loggin on behalf of the Bridport company pressed for running powers over the line between Maiden Newton and Dorchester, but Mr Graham pointed out that it would obstruct traffic.

The committee retired to deliberate in private, later returning to say that they would not give running powers over the single line from Maiden Newton to Dorchester, but if the Bridport company would like to take steps to make this section a double line, the committee would give them running powers over it. As a result a new clause was added to the Bill, which required the Great Western to provide and lay an extra line between Maiden Newton and Dorchester. This must be laid within a reasonable time and permit running powers to the Bridport company, the GWR paying a large amount of the cost.

The Bridport Railway Act 1879 was passed on the 21st July of that year with a capital of £42,000 and borrowing powers of £14,000. This no doubt altered the positions of both the GWR and the Bridport company. The Chard line had been dropped from the Bill, and powers to enter into a contract with the LSWR were no longer mentioned.

The GWR extended the old working agreement until 30th June, 1881 and as from the 1st July that year the line was leased to them. The matter of the running powers into Dorchester appear to have died a natural death, the entire main line as far as the county town not being doubled until May 1885, and then at the expense of the GWR.

Whilst all these company matters had been taking place, the guard of the branch train, Shepherd, had gained promotion. The *Bridport News* for 11th July 1880 reported, 'Mr Shepherd who has been guard on this line for 16 years has left Bridport for another sphere. He will now be travelling with the express train between London and Milford'. However the following week it was reported, 'We regret to learn that on his first journey between London and Milford he met with a rather serious accident, which necessitated his returning to his home in Bridport. It appears that Shepherd was holding the handle of the brake which jumped out of his hand and struck him a heavy blow to the body !'; Shepherd returned to his previous job as branch guard.

The blizzard that swept the West of England on Tuesday 18th January, 1881 caused disruption to both the branch and main line trains, the last train from Maiden Newton on the Tuesday evening, due to arrive at 10 45 pm eventually arrived at 7 am the following morning! On the Wednesday trains ran subject to slight delay until the 2.25 pm which departed an hour late. However, after travelling about 2½ miles it was stopped by a snowdrift between eight and ten feet deep, the train having to be dug out before returning to Bridport with its one passenger.

On Thursday 20th at 9 am Mr Bond the station master and other members of the station staff travelled on a light engine in an attempt to get through, their efforts failing before Bradpole Crossing owing to the accumulation of snow. At noon a train containing 16 men for the purpose of clearing the line succeeded in getting within a mile of Powerstock station where it came to a standstill, a number of men being left to clear the line. The train returned to Bridport before making another unsuccessful attempt at 2.30 pm. Eventually at 5 pm a train departed from Bridport and with much delay and difficulty reached Maiden Newton. After waiting there a while it returned to Bridport, having collected 15 mail bags from the one train that succeeded in travelling from Yeovil to Weymouth.

The following morning several passengers joined the 8 am departure which reached only the first cutting at Browns Farm (near Powerstock) where a fresh fall of snow had blocked the line. The passengers walked back to town, and after a while the train returned to Bridport before setting off again at 10 30 am with the station master and 14 men in an attempt to clear the snow. After leaving men at various points to clear the line the train returned to Bridport. At 5 pm another train departed, and succeeded in reaching Maiden Newton where it waited for three hours for any passengers off the main line before returning at 9 pm with a number of passengers and 13 mail bags.

In May 1881 station master Gray departed from Maiden Newton to West Drayton, and his later moves show a man with determination to succeed: Southall 1885, Barnstaple 1888, New Milford 1890. His final appointment in July 1906 was as station & quay superintendent Fishguard, but unfortunately he died in March 1909 aged 57. His place at Maiden Newton was taken by Arthur Dagg.

During this time William Collins, booking porter at Toller, had been replaced by Samuel Chalk, who in the 1881 census had been honest enough to put his occupation as 'booking porter', not 'station master' as many of his rank did. Chalk moved on shortly after to work at Holt Junction, Hannington, Marston and Limpley Stoke where he served from 1906. Staying on owing to the Great War, he was eventually forced to retire owing to ill health in late 1917. At the time of his death, aged 71, in December 1920, four of his sons were in the service of the GWR, two being station masters at Wrington and Nailsea. Chalk's position at Toller was taken by Edmund Dale.

The antiquated methods of working at Bridport station were clearly demonstrated in a fatal accident on 21st January, 1882, in which a passenger died, Richard Thorner, aged 32, of Burton Bradstock. Thorner, who had been to Dorchester to sell a horse, returned by train arriving just after 6.30 pm. There being no run-round facilities at the platform, it was the custom for inward trains to stop opposite the goods shed whilst the tickets were collected. As this took place the engine moved to another line and horses pulled the coaches into the platform, or sometimes the engine moved to the rear of the train and propelled it into the platform. On the fateful night a soldier decided to leave the train whilst it stood outside the station. He was followed by Thorner, at which moment the engine propelling a truck it had removed from the front of the train, came up the line alongside. Despite warnings shouted by station staff and others, he was cut in two by the passing engine, his remains being removed to the Railway Terminus Hotel where two doctors pronounced life extinct. Ironically, on Monday 23rd, work commenced on the extension of the platform which put an end to the previous practice.

It was, however, rather more than a mere platform extension, as the impending extension to Bridport Harbour made it necessary to generally alter the arrangement of the station. The terminal end of the covered train shed had to be removed and the track curved to join the alignment of the extension, which resulted in the main platform face being reconstructed on a curve to match. To allow for this the other platform track was removed, and a run-round loop was provided running from the beginning of the extension and around the back of the train shed to join the engine shed siding. The importance of this work brought the GWR General Manager, Mr Grierson, to Bridport early in February to see the situation for himself.

At a Bridport company meeting held on 17th March it was reported that houses and gardens near the station had also been purchased, and that the improvement works by the GWR were nearly completed.

The last statement would not appear entirely true, as the *Bridport News* for 14th July more than four months later reported;

The alterations to the present station are being proceeded with, and are so far advanced as to allow the engine to run through the station and passengers can alight on the extended platform. Among other improvements are the erection of a signal box and the building of a new office for the use of the station master and the goods clerk. The office which was formerly occupied by them, in company with the booking clerk, is now being used as a booking and parcel office. The old parcels office will come down.

Serious business in connection with the proposed extension of the line to Bridport Harbour had been discussed at an extraordinary meeting of the Bridport Railway Company on 31st May, 1882, and a circular was sent to the shareholders which contained the following.

The Directors have been in communication with the Great Western Railway Company with a view to the construction of the extension line to Bridport Harbour, and if £10,000 or more be subscribed towards the cost by the shareholders of the company or the public in preference shares at the same rate, provided the present working agreement be extended 21 years from the 1st day of July 1882 and that the work is carried out under the superintendence of an engineer to be appointed by themselves. It is estimated that the cost will not exceed £23,000, the Directors unanimously approve of this proposal and recommend it for the approval of the shareholders.

There was much discussion, Sir Charles Whetham demanding a poll, the result of which was 1,014 votes in favour of the extension (representing £43,020 capital) and 111 against (representing £2,430 capital). The motion was therefore carried.

By early July it was reported that the route was being surveyed and marked out. At the half-yearly meeting held on 27th September it was revealed that applications for the £23,000 new preference shares at 4 per cent, issued for the purpose of carrying out the extension, had been fully taken up, that notices to treat had been served on all owners of land required and advertisements inviting tenders for the construction would shortly be issued. It was also reported that work on the extension of the platform at Bridport station had been completed, together with the extension of the goods shed and other work in the goods yard.

In March 1882 station master Bond was transferred from Bridport to the goods department at Frome, his annual salary - which had been in excess of £110 - being reduced to £100. Later appointed station master at High Wycombe he eventually gained a salary of £120 before retirement in February 1897. He passed away during July 1898.

His successor at Bridport was the former Bruton station master Walter Titball. In August 1882 station master Dagg moved from Maiden Newton to Bruton, his place being taken by Alfred Reeve who came from the booking office at Chippenham.

Torrential rain on Monday 23rd October, 1882 caused severe flooding in the West Dorset area the following day. The early train ran as usual to Maiden Newton, but experienced difficulty in returning as the line near Toller was under water. The second train commenced its journey but at Bradpole Crossing the safety of the bridge beyond was in question so the train returned to Bridport.

Later in the day an engine conveyed Mr Titball the station master on an inspection of the line, but this had to be curtailed short of Maiden Newton as the collapse of a culvert prevented the engine reaching the station.

Tragedy had also occurred on the main line, where the 8.10 am from Yeovil, running late through flood water and past a landslip at Evershot, ran off the track following a bridge failure near Cattistock Mill. The engine was thrown across the track and the first two coaches fell back onto the damaged bridge. Unfortunately the driver later died of injuries caused by escaping steam. Owing to the main line being blocked by this accident no further attempts were made to run branch trains that day.

The year 1883 started literally with a bang - at least according to a report in the *Bridport News*! This gave details of a locomotive boiler which had exploded in Bridport station, but in reality it had been a tube failure which caused large amounts of steam and hot water to escape. To the untrained eye it doubtless looked more dangerous than it was, and the event certainly lost nothing in the telling!

Work actually commenced on the West Bay extension in mid-February 1883, when the appointed contractors Messrs Mousley & Lovett arrived at Bridport with a large amount of equipment for use in the construction of the line. A stable, blacksmith's shop and other buildings were erected in a field near the Crown Inn, and an old cottage on the brow of the hill above Wanderwell was put to use as an office.

Excavations soon commenced near the main road at Wanderwell, earth moved from the hill being taken back to the valley extending towards Flood House. Temporary rails were laid to enable tip wagons to continue the work.

On Tuesday 22nd a small contractor's locomotive weighing 12 tons arrived at Bridport station. The following night (at midnight, and with steam up!) the engine was driven from the station through the streets of Bridport to West Bay, assisted by a team of six powerful horses. The reason for the late departure was the reaching of an agreement with Bridport Town Council to allow the engine to be moved by that method. A large crowd followed its progress. It was later reported that no serious obstacles were encountered on the way, and the turning of corners did not present any special difficulties. At 6 am on the Thursday morning the engine was driven up a ramp onto rails at Bridport Harbour. Although the whole episode seems as comical as that well known Ealing Comedy *The Titfield Thunderbolt* it was not unusual to move small locomotives in such a way at the time, and there were no reports of the local steam roller being hard pressed to repair the roads afterwards!

At an extraordinary meeting of the Bridport Railway Company held at the Bull Hotel on Wednesday 13th June, those present were informed that a Bill being raised in Parliament would authorise the GWR to make and maintain certain railways and works, and vest in the GWR the undertakings of the Stratford-upon-Avon Railway Company, and the Watlington and Princes Risborough Railway, and for other purposes. Mr Swatridge, the Chairman of the Bridport company, explained that the object of the meeting as far as they were concerned was to allow the GWR to subscribe £13,000 in Bridport Railway preference shares towards the extension to Bridport harbour, and adding these powers to the existing Bill would save both time and money for all concerned.

The *Dorset County Chronicle* for 13th September, 1883 reported the formation of a limited liability company, which had been incorporated under the Companies Act, named the West Bay, Bridport, Land and Building Company Limited. It had a capital of £50,000 in £20 shares and had Mr J.P.F. Gundry as Chairman. The Directors were S. Whetham, W.H. Chick, A.W.H. Dammers, W. Hounsell, Job Legg and R.F. Roberts. Messrs Loggin and Nantes were the company Secretary and Solicitors respectively.

Arrangements had been made to acquire building sites near the seaside, and the scheme envisaged the construction of an Esplanade and sea wall with walks, drives and gardens etc. on the west side of the harbour, and the erection of modern residences. It was intended to commence the scheme at once by the building of a row of about a dozen houses, and several thousand pounds had already been subscribed by gentlemen of the town and neighbourhood.

It was quite clear that most of the Directors of the building company were also involved with the Bridport Railway, probably in the hope that a profit would be made from the land and property market. Certainly none had made a fortune from the dividends paid out on their railway shares, so to them this venture must have appeared the best way of making Peter pay for Paul.

At the 57th half-yearly meeting held on 27th September a statement of expenditure on the extension to date was given.

	£	s.	d.
Construction of ways and stations etc.	2,970	0	0
Purchase of land and compensation	5,616	12	3
Law, engineering, survey and Parliamentary fees	1,309	8	6

Mr Clarke, the Engineer, in reporting the progress of the new works to the Board said,

There has been a little delay in completing the earthworks as there was a difficulty in obtaining a sufficient and a continuous supply of labour. The masonry and minor works at the Harbour Station and the alterations at the old terminus at Bridport are well advanced, the rails and many of the sleepers have been delivered.

He thought the line could be ready by the first of November.

The meeting was told of the financial affairs for the working part of the line between Maiden Newton and Bridport, and the fact that the Great Western were now taking only 47½ per cent of the gross receipts for working the line instead of the previous 52½ per cent gave many shareholders fresh hopes. The following dividends were declared: 6 per cent on preference shares on the 1879 Act, 5 per cent on the first issue of preference stock under the same Act, and 4 per cent on the second issue, 1¼ per cent was paid out on ordinary shares. Although during the first half-year 3,384 more passengers had been carried, passenger receipts were down by £129. This was due to the introduction of third class carriages on to the line.

Later the same evening the Board of Directors were shocked to hear of the sudden death of one of their number, Mr Richard Francis Roberts. At the age of 52 he suddenly collapsed and died whilst entertaining guests at his country residence 'Cogden', near Burton Bradstock. Mr Roberts was Solicitor to the London & North Western Railway Company (LNWR) and had not long been a member of the local company's Board of Directors .

The funeral took place the following week at Burton Bradstock. A special train left Paddington at 8.55 am conveying the many people who came to pay their last respects. They included Mr Grierson, General Manager of the GWR, and other senior officers of the company, Mr W. Crankwell, Deputy Chairman of the LNWR, Mr G. Findlay, the General Manager and the heads of various departments; also representatives of the Midland Railway (MR), other railway companies and Parliament. They arrived at Bridport at 1 o'clock and partook of luncheon at the Bull Hotel. Afterwards they were conveyed in carriages supplied by Mr Knight, proprietor of the Bull Hotel, to Burton Bradstock for the burial, which took place at 3 pm. Upon the return of the mourners to Bridport, the saloon carriages of the special were attached to the rear of the 5 pm up train. At Maiden Newton an engine was waiting to take the special back to Paddington. It is doubtful whether so much top brass had ever visited Bridport station before, or for that matter since. It certainly gave Mr Grierson and his officers a view of the improvements being carried out; he travelled by special saloon and not in the usual passenger stock used on the line, which was shortly to be the cause of complaint.

Meanwhile work was progressing on the construction of the extension, although it was disrupted by a dispute on 4th June when the navvies engaged in the work went on strike over their wages which were between 2s. 6d. and 3s. a day. They returned to work the next morning following a promise by the contractor to look into the matter. Work on the extension was progressing well, the contractor's locomotive being in daily use moving spoil wagons, and by the end of the month the embankment from Wanderwell to the harbour and from Wanderwell to Flood Lane was almost complete. The iron girders over the road at Flood Lane and the bridge over the Asker at East Road were also complete, leaving only the bridge over the Burton Bradstock road to be constructed. During August the vessel *Ivyholme* brought materials for the extension into Bridport Harbour,and it was reported that although operations were still taking place in Wanderwell Cutting the locomotive had been moving material towards East Road where the thatched cottage formerly occupied by Mr Bowden was being converted into a station master's house, booking office and waiting room to save the expense of constructing a new station, as the cottage lay only a few feet away from the platform.

Work was delayed by a flood in mid-October, but on Tuesday 30th an engine crossed East Road and the river bridge for the first time, and by the beginning of November rails were being laid towards Bridport station, although fears were expressed in the *Bridport News* over the dispersal of water at East Road when the Asker ran high! At the same time it was reported that permanent rails, sleepers and ballasting had been completed from the harbour up to Mr Hounsell's fields. At the beginning of February 1884 the contractor's locomotive was taken away and a majority of the workmen discharged.

Newspapers reported that the line was almost completed and could be ready for traffic in a few days, but the formal opening would now be delayed until the spring.

The new line was inspected by Col Rich of the Board of Trade on Monday 3rd March, 1884. A powerful engine and two carriages were sent by the GWR for the test. The Inspector was met at Bridport station by the Directors of the Bridport company, together with Mr Clarke, the Engineer, and Mr Mousley, the contractor, who also represented his partner Mr Lovatt. Also present were officers of the GWR. So the inspection took place. On the journey towards the harbour the train stopped at bridges and other points that the Inspector wished to view, including signalling and interlocking at both East Street and West Bay stations. The train returned to East Street where the party was conveyed by carriage to the Bull Hotel for luncheon. Col Rich expressed himself perfectly satisfied with the construction and stability of the line and stated that he would be able to report favourably upon it to the authorities so that it could be opened to the public in due course.

Over the years the importance of the harbour as a commercial port had dwindled as goods that once came by sea were transported to and from the town by the railway. As a result the future prospects for the harbour now lay in its redevelopment as a seaside resort, and the new station was named 'West Bay'. The West Bay/Bridport Building Company had high hopes for a rapid expansion of the small hamlet that had grown up around the harbour.

The opening of the new line on Monday 31st March, 1884 caused much excitement in the area. A special committee was formed to make sure the day was celebrated in style - indeed a carnival atmosphere prevailed. In the town most of the shops closed for the occasion, flags and bunting flew from buildings in South Street and East Street and an arch was erected near the East Street station. It was decorated with flags and greenery and on one side was a scroll which said, 'Success to the railway' and on the other 'Prosperity to West Bay'. A great number of people travelled on the first train down at 7.32 am and returned on the next train leaving West Bay at 7.45 am.

On that very morning the 58th half-yearly meeting of the Bridport Railway Company took place at the Bull Hotel. Mr W. Swatridge, the Chairman, was indisposed so the chair was taken by Mr J.P.F. Gundry. He remarked that it was customary for the Chairman to say a few words on such an occasion, and as this was rather more than an ordinary occasion he would like to take the opportunity of addressing the shareholders. He thought they might be congratulated upon the state of things presented before them. They had been, especially during the last two years, passing through a severe crisis in their existence as a railway. He thought - and he hoped - that everyone would agree with

BRIDPORT AND WEST BAY RAILWAY TIME TABLE.

DOWN.

	A.M.	A.M.	P.M.	P.M.	P.M.
Bridport depart ..	7.32	9.25	3.35	6.38	8.39
East Street ,, ..	7.35	9.28	3.38	6.41	8.33
West Bay arrive ..	7.40	9.33	3.43	6.46	8.33

UP.

	A.M.	A.M.	P.M.	P.M.	P.M.
West Bay depart..	7.45	10.10	3.50	6.55	9.0
East Street ,, ..	7.50	10.15	3.55	7.0	9.5
Bridport arrive ..	7.53	10.18	3.58	7.3	9.8

There will be no trains on Sundays.

Opening timetable for the West Bay Extension.

him, that they had come fairly out of that struggle and time of trial with fair and tolerable success. There had been considerable expense incurred as they knew, and a considerable extension made to the line was now concluded, and they proposed to open it that day.

The present state of the revenue of the railway was also satisfactory. The Directors now proposed to declare a dividend of 1s. per share on the ordinary shares of the company, carrying forward an even larger balance than was carried forward during the last half year. This had been done in the face of having to pay interest upon the £19,000 of additional capital which had absolutely not been earning a single penny. If they took this as a fair example as to what the future might be, certainly the bulk of the 52½ per cent on the gross earnings of the new line could be applied as dividend to the ordinary shareholders.

The Chairman wished to put the matter in the right light and not deceive them in any way, and he should therefore say that the interest on the £19,000 had not been paid for the whole year because it was not due, and as the amount required in all for the extension of the line was £23,000, there would be something more in the shape of interest which would have to be brought to bear in a future account. The earning of the extension line, however, it was hoped would meet all that, and he trusted in the course of a few years to see their little watering place extended, and the result would be satisfactory and bring an increasing dividend for the shareholders of the company.

After reflecting upon other matters concerning the line he said, 'I'm glad to say that a different feeling has sprung up between the Board of the Company and the Great Western and of quite a different kind to that which existed in former years'.

At 2 pm a procession left the Bull Hotel for the station at East Street. It was headed by the band of 'A' Company of the Dorset Rifle Volunteers under the direction of Bugle Major Foster. The band was followed by the Directors, shareholders, guests and friends. A special train of 14 coaches hauled by two engines was waiting at the decorated station to take the party down to West Bay, where they alighted and proceeded to a building normally used as a store, this having been decorated for the holding of a public luncheon, tickets for which had been sold at 2s. 6d. each.

About 110 people sat down to dine at this excellent meal provided by Mr W. Trump of the Cross Keys Inn, Bridport. During the after dinner speeches the late Mr Roberts was mentioned. Mr Loggin, the Secretary, said that Mr Grierson had told him that the actual success of the line just built was mainly due to Mr Roberts, inasmuch as he exerted himself to an enormous extent to get money to bring the railway to West Bay. Nothing could be done without money. Mr Roberts not only got an immense number of people to give money, but he persuaded the GWR to supply any balance that was necessary, and had also got a number of his friends to put money into the scheme.

The subject of the building company was raised, and it was hoped that within a short time they would see scaffold poles rising from West Bay. Mr Loggin said he hoped they would all meet there again in less than 10 years to celebrate the fact that West Bay had become a place of larger population than the present town of Bridport. Mr W. Colfox said the place was little known, but it was the nucleus of a watering place which might rival those established on the coast. 'Why should West Bay not rival Bournemouth in the future?' asked Mr Colfox.

Whilst the luncheon was being proceeded with, about 1,100 Sunday School children from the town were each given a bun and an orange and taken to West Bay by train, but owing to the inclement weather they were not allowed out of the train at the terminus but were taken straight back to Bridport.

Later in the day the band positioned themselves in a field near West Bay station and played a selection of tunes to entertain the many people who turned out to see the event. Games were organised in a field nearby. Obstacle races, bucket-of-water races, and climbing the greasy pole were all well contested, prizes being given to the winners. Confectionery vendors pitched their tents nearby. The ships in the harbour were bedecked with flags and during the evening bonfires were lit on the cliffs.

At last the complete railway line, with a total track length of 11 miles 18 chains, was running. People travelling over the extension on the first day numbered 5,100, of which 2,100 paid their fares. The total amount of cash taken in fares was £72 14s., against the cost of running the trains that day which amounted to £66 11s. 3d. The remaining £6 2s. 9d. was donated to a fund for a regatta and sports to be held at West Bay later in the year.

Whilst the extension had been under construction, the main line and the junction at Maiden Newton were not neglected. By the 10th June, 1881 the men employed in doubling the line between Evershot and Maiden Newton had been paid off, and the double line was being worked. During 1882 a footbridge was added and other alterations carried out at the station. The section southwards to Grimstone was opened as double line on 18th May, 1884, and the final section to Dorchester on 19th July, 1885, at last freeing the main line of the restrictions of single line working.

By this time Alfred Reeve had been appointed station master at Maiden Newton and was to remain there until promoted to Bradford-on-Avon in late 1897.

The weakness of a branch line operated by only one engine was demonstrated on Monday 19th May, when the engine of the 7.40 am arrival at West Bay became derailed whilst running round its train, it later being found that the shingle ballast had interfered with the proper working of the points at the end of the platform. The delay in obtaining an engine from Weymouth resulted in the first train not reaching Bridport until lunch time.

The extension soon proved an attraction for children from the town. In June seven lads from the South Street area were fined 4s. 5d. each for damaging gradient posts, a warning being given that future cases would not be let off so lightly. On 26th December, 1884 Nicholas Loggin, the Bridport company Secretary for the the past 13 years, passed away, his place being taken by his nephew Charles George Nantes who had been in partnership with his uncle since 1876.

Early in 1885 the roof of East Street station had to be rethatched, and in view of its close proximity to the railway, one wonders why a different material was not chosen. It is surprising that over the years a passing train had never reduced the station to a smouldering ruin in one puff!

Indeed 1885 was not a good year for the Bridport Railway. During the small hours of Tuesday 26/27th October a burglary took place at Bridport station, the station master's

West Bay station soon after the opening. A '1016' class saddle tank stands at the platform with its train, consisting of four very rudimentary four-wheel coaches. Note the ballast covering the sleepers - a practice prevalent at the time.   *K. Bakes Collection*

An unidentified saddle tank stands at West Bay station awaiting departure with a mixed train for Maiden Newton. The starting signal on the right, which at the time was fitted with only a single spectacle lens, was supplied (with the remainder of the signalling equipment for the extension) by the Gloucester Carriage & Wagon Company.   *M.J. Tattershall Collection*

office being broken into, his desk forced open, and £1 5s. in money removed as well as a packet addressed to Lady Nepean of Loders Court containing an unknown quantity of jewellery. Nearly every parcel in the parcel office was ransacked, and a quantity of tobacco was taken together with a parcel of clothing. Despite enquiries by the local police the theft remained a mystery. A story soon spread that one of the porters was in custody on suspicion, but this of course was a complete fabrication as the man in question would have been one of the last to be accused of such an act.

Sadly, this event took place whilst the Bridport station master Walter Titball, was lying at his home in Bradpole Road dangerously ill. He passed away two days later having suffered from Brights disease (kidney failure). Tragically he was only 34 years of age.

The *Bridport News* remarked, 'No one who visited Bridport station since Mr Titball has been the station master can fail to have been impressed with his courteous and agreeable manner and his earnest desire to study the comfort and convenience of passengers and those who have business there'. He left a widow, four children, and an aged mother who were all dependent on his earnings, and an appeal was set up by local traders on their behalf. The following month George Peach from the clerical staff at Weymouth was appointed as Mr Titball's successor.

Of the many excursions organised over the years only a few were reported in the local press following the event. However, the excursion to London organised by the local Oddfellows in September 1886 caused dissension. Departing from West Bay at 4.20 am, the loud whistling of the engine on its way to Bridport woke many inhabitants who saw fit to complain! Some 200 passengers joined the train at Bridport, others at Powerstock, Toller, Maiden Newton, Evershot and Yetminster, arriving in the capital at 10.10am.

BRIDPORT BRANCH. Narrow Gauge.

Single Line, worked by Train Staff—Shape, Square ; Colour, Red.

Distances.	DOWN TRAINS.		WEEK DAYS.								SUNDAYS.			
			1	2	3	4	5	6	7	8	1	2	3	4
			Pass.	Pass. and Goods	Pass.	Pass. and Goods	Pass. and Goods	Pass. and Goods	Pass.	Pass.	Pass. and Goods	Pass. and Goods	Pass. and Goods	
			A.M.	A.M.	A.M.	P.M.	P.M.	P.M.	P.M.	P.M.	A.M.	P.M.	P.M.	
	Mdn. Newton	dep.	....	9 30	11 10	1 30	3 10	5 50	7 50	10 20	11 15	....	10 5	....
2¼	Toller	,,	....	9 37	11 20	1 40	3 19	6 0	8 0	CR	11 25	....	10 15	....
5¾	Powerstock	,,	....	9 46	11 30	1 50	3 28	6 10	8 10	CR	11 35	....	10 25	....
9¼	Bridport	{ arr.	..	9 54	11 40	2 0	3 37	6 20	8 20	10 45	11 45	....	10 35	....
		{ dep.	7 0	10 4		2 2		6 29	8 30			2 30		....
9¾	East Street	,,	7 3	—	..	2 5	..	6 32	8 33	..	..	2 33	..	..
11¼	West Bay	arr.	7 8	10 9	..	2 9	..	6 37	8 38	....	....	2 38	....	..

Distances.	UP TRAINS.		WEEK DAYS.								SUNDAYS.			
			1	2	3	4	5	6	7	8	1	2	3	4
			Pass.	Pass.	Pass.	Pass.& Goods A		Pass.& Goods B	Pass. and Goods	Pass.	Pass. and Goods	Pass. and Goods		
			A.M.	A.M.	A.M.	P.M.		P.M.	P.M.	P.M.	A.M.	P.M.		
	West Bay	dep	7 45	10 14	....	2 13	....	....	6 47	9 0	....	4 50	....	....
1½	East Street	,,	7 50	10 18	..	—	..	..	6 52	9 5	..	4 55	..	....
2	Bridport	{ arr.	7 53	10 20	....	2 19	....	....	6 55	9 8	....	4 58	....	....
		{ dep.	8 0	10 23	11 55	2 21	....	4 45	7 5	9 40	10 30	5 0	....	....
5¼	Powerstock	,,	8 10	10 33	12 5	2 30	....	4 55	7 15	9 50	10 40	5 10	....	....
8¾	Toller	,,	8 20	10 42	12 15	2 39	....	5 5	7 25	10 0	10 50	5 20	....	..
11¼	Maiden New	arr.	8 30	10 50	12 25	2 47	....	5 15	7 35	10 10	11 0	5 30	....	....

No Block Telegraph.   **A ST** No. 120.   **B ST** No. 121.

Only one Engine in Steam allowed on this Branch, or two coupled together.

Special instructions are in force for working the Inclines on the Bridport Branch, dated April 1885, and Guards and others must make themselves acquainted with them.

Working timetable July–December 1885.

Severe weather caused chaos in the Bridport area at the end of the year, heavy rain during October causing a small amount of flooding, but the severe gale, rain, and a snowstorm that struck the county on Boxing Day, Sunday 26th December was to leave Bridport as what would today be described as a 'disaster area'. As the rivers Brit and Asker burst their banks the low lying areas to the East, West and South of the town were flooded, causing widespread damage and loss of livestock both in the town and the surrounding countryside. The brewery was flooded, and the gas works put out of action. The entire area was cut off, there being no postal, telegraph, road or rail communication for several days. The railway line was severely damaged in several places, with trackwork washed out and bridges weakened.

The last train to leave Bridport had been at 5 pm on the Sunday evening. After leaving Toller the train was running through water, and the guard requested the line be examined before the next down train travelled over the line. In the deteriorating weather the train which ran direct from Weymouth to Bridport on Sunday evening was struck by a falling tree near Grimstone, and after arrival at Maiden Newton it returned on the down line to clear five fallen trees before returning to the junction, where Bridport passengers had been waiting 3½ hours! It then set off for Bridport at just after 1 o'clock in the morning, but had to return to Maiden Newton owing to a bridge being washed out near Toller. The unfortunate passengers, of whom there were a good number, had to seek the limited hospitality available in the village, and some were reported to have spent the night in the station waiting room, the signal boxes, the goods shed, and any other covered accommodation available.

Daylight on Monday revealed the full extent of the damage to the line. A bridge at Loders was damaged, and the stone buttresses of the bridge over the river at Bradpole had been moved from their foundations. The area around East Street station was totally flooded, water reaching half way up the stairs of the station house. The track being washed out and under water, it was eight days before the West Bay extension was restored to traffic.

Repair gangs were quickly brought in, the *Bridport News* reporting that 130 men were employed on the Monday under Inspector Ivens, and an engine was brought onto the line to test the metals. By Tuesday sufficient temporary work had been carried out to allow the passage of trains during daylight. The stranded Maiden Newton passengers who had spent their second night of forced encampment were first away - but only as far as Boarsbarrow Crossing near Bradpole, from where they either had to walk or travel by horse-drawn conveyance. On Wednesday and Thursday four trains each way shuttled during daylight between Maiden Newton and the same crossing, where station master Peach sold and collected tickets alongside the track. On Friday an attempt was made to bring the 2 pm train over the repaired bridge at Bradpole and into Bridport station, but when the engine arrived at the spot Inspector Ivens decided it not advisable to cross, and the passengers again had to leave the train at Boarsbarrow Crossing.

Normal service was restored the following day, as was the telegraphic communication with Maiden Newton station although much of the National system was still unusable.

On the following Monday, 3rd January, another storm struck the area, and it was decided not to run the last two trains that night on account of the temporary bridge at Bradpole becoming unsafe, but sufficient repairs had been carried out to enable the 10.20 am train to cross on Tuesday morning.

Two weeks later the following appeared in the *Southern Times*,

On Friday morning some gangers and packers were taking a trolley of clay from Whitherstone Cutting to fill a slip above Powerstock station, the speed of the truck increased so greatly that the men were unable to restrain it. They were obliged to let go their hold and the trolley rushed off down the line at great speed increasing in its velocity till it came to the gates at the East Street crossing, which were shut.

The gates were much damaged the trolley forcing its way through them and coming to a standstill on the up incline just below. The gates at the level crossing at Bradpole were also damaged.

The line had been fully repaired by the 26th March when at the half-yearly meeting of the Bridport company the Deputy Chairman, Mr R.D. Thornton, was able to report that the damage had been repaired by the GWR authorities, who had a contract to keep the line in repair. Care had been taken by the Directors to see that substantial bridges had been built.

At the same meeting, driven on by either blind optimism or delusions of grandeur, the Secretary was asked to write to W.H. Smith and Sons enquiring about the provision of a bookstall at West Bay station, although at that time West Bay had still not developed into any of the things suggested at the opening of the line.

The year 1887 also saw the renaming of Bridport station to 'Bridport Bradpole Road'. This lasted until 1902 when the name 'Bridport' was restored.

The company, always looking for ways of raising cash, was told at a Board Meeting in November 1888 that five trees at Loders Bridge had been sold for £2, the best price obtainable.

At the same meeting it was agreed that the Secretary write to the GWR asking its advice on the construction of a tramway to the quay at West Bay. The GWR did not reply until early in 1889, and then wrote saying there were several difficulties in the construction of a tramway. However, an extra siding was being considered for West Bay, the cost of which was estimated to be £320. The Board, on receiving this reply, decided to postpone the matter of the tramway.

At East Street station passengers who wanted shelter from the weather had to wait in the station building which was a little distance from the platform, so in July 1889 it was decided to erect a waiting hut on the platform itself at a cost of £15.

The state of the carriages used on the line at the time left a great deal to be desired, and the GWR was approached and asked to supply newer ones. Although new coaches were not forthcoming, by December the old ones had been returned to Swindon for repairs. They were eventually returned with the interiors untouched, which caused a number of complaints and resulted in their return to the works for internal renovations to be carried out.

The railway had been extended to West Bay, and alterations carried out at Bridport (Bradpole Road) station, but there were no crossing facilities for trains on the branch. As things stood only one train could work on the line between Maiden Newton and West Bay at a time as no passing loops were provided. With a loop, together with the necessary signalling, two or more trains could occupy the branch. Realising the situation, the Directors discussed the subject of a crossing place, but came to no decision. It was again brought up in January 1890 with the same result. On Monday 9th March, 1891 a severe blizzard struck the South and West of England paralysing railways from Kent to Devon, the famous 'Flying Dutchman' being snowbound at Tiverton Junction. The situation was made worse by fresh falls of snow during the night.

The Yeovil-Weymouth line was also closed, with the last down train becoming trapped in snow north of Dorchester. This resulted in the following boat train being stopped at Maiden Newton, where the passengers had to take what shelter they could for the night. The train eventually arrived at Weymouth at 6 pm the following day. On Tuesday morning the 6.40 am train from Bridport departed from the station, but only succeeded in reaching a point between Bradpole and Loders. It then returned to Bridport, and an attempt was made with the 8.3 am departure. This was slightly more successful, but it ran into a snowdrift a mile short of Powerstock station. Several attempts were made at forcing the train through before it returned again to Bridport. On Wednesday morning at 8 am an attempt was made to send an engine to West Bay, this

The oldest known photograph of Bridport station, taken between 1884 and 1891. The original signal box is to the right, and behind it at right angles is the Somerset Trading Co. warehouse. At that stage the station retained its overall roof, but a section had been removed from the end wall - as can be seen behind the coaches - to allow the extension to West Bay which goes off to the left. *By permission of the Bridport Museum Service*

Locomotive No. 1308 is photographed alongside the station staff at Bridport. It would appear that this photograph was taken shortly after the opening of the new down platform in 1894. The engine is in its original form; in 1898 it was reconstructed and was fitted with a full length saddle tank. *By permission of the Bridport Museum Service*

also being unsuccessful. A gang of workmen dug away the snow at Powerstock and on Thursday morning the service was resumed. However, during the night high winds filled the cutting again and Mr Peach, the Bridport station master, and a gang of men spent the morning clearing the cutting before the trains could get through.

The subject of crossing places on the branch again came to the fore in April when plans were sent by the GWR. Two alternative sites were selected, one at Powerstock costing £2,511, and one at Bridport (Bradpole Road) costing £3,868, or both could be made for the cost of £4,900. The Board considered Powerstock to be the best scheme, for after all it was the cheapest!

About this time, the Board was considering the idea of making East Street the main station and not Bradpole Road as was then the case. At a meeting in September 1891 the matter was discussed, and had the suggestion come about it would have certainly altered subsequent events. However, it was decided in June 1892 to make Bradpole Road the main station and crossing place at a cost of £3,860, and on 22nd June an extraordinary meeting was held at the Bull Hotel to raise the £4,000 required for this work to be carried out.

The Chairman, Mr R.D. Thornton, said that as the railway stood not all trains could travel through to West Bay. The timetable would not allow it, but this could be overcome if two trains could work the line. The GWR was prepared to place an extra engine on the line for a period of two years to see how things would work out. The required money was raised by mortgage, and in October the Great Western sent a letter requesting a cheque for £3,860, the estimated cost of the crossing place. The Bridport company asked to see, and received, detailed plans of the work before sending a cheque for £2,000 and informing the GWR that the remainder would be paid when it was required. The plans for the alterations were submitted by the GWR to the Board of Trade on 26th April, 1893 for approval.

An unfortunate incident took place on Saturday 9th July, 1892. The 9.33 pm train to Maiden Newton had left Bridport as usual. Two or three miles up the track the fireman saw the driver move his lunch basket; he did not see the driver again and assumed that he had climbed outside the cab to oil the engine.

As the train approached Powerstock, driver Snook had still not returned to the cab. The train was stopped at the station and, as the driver could not be found, the fact was reported to the guard.

On receipt of this information, the guard started to walk back along the line towards Bridport whilst the train was slowly reversed behind him.

At Loders Bridge the driver's hat was found, and nearby driver Snook lay unconscious on the embankment. He was put on the train and immediately returned to Bridport.

The injured man was removed to the cottage hospital, where despite prompt medical attention, William Snook died on the following Tuesday morning at the age of 32 years.

The question of an additional siding for West Bay was raised again in June 1893, the cost of which had now risen to £383. The Board turned the idea down at this time, but had a quick change of mind in October when they told the GWR that they wanted the extra West Bay siding after all. One of the Bridport Directors asked 'Could one of the sidings at Powerstock be removed and used at West Bay'? This suggestion was never acted upon.

The eventual cost of the siding was £465. In five years the price had risen by £120. The Bridport Board could never be accused by their shareholders of parting with cash easily, for in February 1894 the Great Western sent them a letter asking for the £465. As the work was not completed the Bridport company paid 50 per cent of the bill and the rest when the work was finished.

A pre-1894 view of Bridport station viewed from the north-east. In the centre (partly obscured by a tree) can be seen the original signal box. To the left between trees is the engine shed and the original overall roof of the station.

M.J. Tattershall Collection

In November 1893, the Bridport company sanctioned the provision of a waiting shelter at Toller station. This was the result of complaints received over the years from passengers about waiting accommodation at that station. At a Board Meeting in March of the previous year, the estimated cost of alterations to Toller station to provide the waiting accommodation had been given as £230. The Directors decided that a simple shed was all that was needed, and they were not prepared to spend more than £40. However, by 1893 £45 was allowed for the provision of a hut.

The Directors were certainly splashing out in 1893, for in March they ordered a cast-iron 'double whelk' gents' toilet from Messrs Thomas and Company to be erected on East Street station platform.

In June of the same year it came to the notice of the Directors that the GWR had been quarrying stone from the goods yard at Powerstock and had taken it off the line. The Bridport company asked for 3d. per ton for the stone they had already taken, but they had to be satisfied with the GWR offer of 1d. per ton.

During 1893 there was a threat - if ever it was one - of a second railway route being built to Bridport by the Abbotsbury company who had succeeded in opening a branch from Upwey Junction, near Weymouth, to the village of Abbotsbury in 1885. Despite many initial problems and a grave financial situation, this company refused to admit defeat, and was talking in terms of a grandiose scheme of extending its line to Axminster. It was yet another version of the famous 'Coast Scheme' that had been pushed around for nearly 50 years. However, owing to its financial circumstances, nothing ever materialised.

The original plan to construct a crossing place at Powerstock having been rejected in favour of Bridport, work actually commenced early in January 1893. By the 20th of that month the overall roof had been removed, being soon followed by the supporting wall on the east side.

A considerable amount of work had to be carried out to improve the layout for two-train operation. An additional platform, complete with canopy, was constructed on the down side for arrivals from Maiden Newton and departures for West Bay, whilst up trains would depart from the main platform. No footbridge was provided, passengers having to cross the line by means of board walks which were provided at both ends of the platforms. A new signal box was built at the Maiden Newton end of the up platform, and additional siding accommodation provided.

Although the dangers of the pre-1882 shunting arrangements had been reduced, accidents could still occur to railway staff engaged in shunting work. During April porter White, who was engaged in shunting the train to form the 5.5 pm to Maiden Newton, either slipped or fell off the running board, the wheels of the coach passing over his left foot and resulting in his leg being amputated just above the ankle.

In general affairs were not going too well for the Bridport Railway Company, for it appears that work had stopped on the reconstruction. A letter in the *Bridport News* on 2nd February, 1894, signed 'H.G. Slape House Bridport' complains as follows:

Will you permit me to draw attention to the timetable inefficiency and sloth of the Bridport Railway. Twelve months ago the roof of the station at Bradpole Road was removed for the purpose of making certain alterations, and in this condition the station has remained ever since. The work is apparently at a complete standstill. Passengers on the platform are unprotected from both sun and rain. The only part of the station that remains covered is the miserable hovel which forms the ticket and waiting room etc.

After moaning about the timetable the letter continues. 'It not infrequently happens that passengers, who are desirous of travelling by the Bridport Railway, find that the one asthmatic old engine is indisposed, and that their journey, in consequence, must be postponed'.

BRIDPORT BRANCH.

Single Line, worked by Electric Train Staff. Crossing Place, Bridport.

DOWN TRAINS.

Distances M C	DOWN TRAINS.	1 D Goods ST 42 arr	dep	2 A Passenger arr	dep	3 A Passenger arr	dep	4 A Passenger arr	dep	5 D Goods arr	dep	6 A Passenger arr	dep	7 A Passenger arr	dep	8 D Goods arr	dep	9 A Passenger arr	dep	10 A Passenger arr	dep
		A.M.	A.M.	A.M.	A.M.	A.M.	A.M.	P.M.	P.M.	P.M.	P.M.	P.M.	P.M.	P.M.	P.M.	P.M.	P.M.	P.M.	P.M.	P.M.	P.M.
	Maiden Newton	—	8 45	—	9 30	—	11 0	—	1 10			—	3 27	—	6 5			—	8 10		
.44	Toller	8 51	8 55	9 35	9 36	11 5	11 6	1 15	1 16	1 46	1 50	3 32	3 33	6 10	6 11			8 15	8 16		
3.62	Powerstock	9 5	9 10	9 43	9 44	11 13	11 14	1 23	1 24	2 0	2 5	3 40	3 41	6 18	6 19			8 23	8 24		
5.21	Bridport	9 20	—	9 51	9 56	11 21	11 24	1 31	1 34	2 15	2 45	3 48	3 51	6 26	6 29	—	6 30	8 31	8 34	—	10 26
9.54	East Street						11 26		1 36				3 52		6 31				8 36		
11.19	West Bay				10 0		11 30		1 40		2 55		3 57		6 35	6 55		8 40		10 45	

SUNDAYS.

DOWN TRAINS.	1 A Passenger arr	dep	2 A Weymouth Passenger arr	dep
	A.M.	A.M.	P.M.	P.M.
Maiden Newton	—	11 35	—	9 54
Toller	11 40	11 41	9 59	10 0
Powerstock	11 48	11 49	10 7	10 8
Bridport	11 58		10 15	
East Street				
West Bay				

UP TRAINS.

Distances M C	UP TRNS.	1 D Goods arr	dep	2 A Passenger arr	dep	3 A Passenger arr	dep	4 A Passenger arr	dep	5 D Goods arr	dep	6 A Passenger arr	dep	7 D Goods arr	dep	8 A Passenger arr	dep
		A.M.	A.M.	A.M.	A.M.	A.M.	A.M.	A.M.	A.M.	P.M.	P.M.	P.M.	P.M.	P.M.	P.M.	P.M.	P.M.
	West Bay					10 10		11 42				2 30				4 35	
1.45	East Street					10 14		11 46				2 35				4 40	
1.73	Bridport	—	7 30	—	8 20	10 15	10 17	11 47	11 54	12 15	12 25	2 37	2 41	—	3 15	4 41	4 45
6.37	Powerstock	7 40	7 45	8 27	8 28	10 27	10 28	12 2	12 9	12 30	12 39	2 48	2 49	3 20		4 52	4 53
8.65	Toller	7 54	7 58	8 35	8 36	10 35	10 36	12 9	12 10	12 43	12 50	2 57				5 0	5 1
11.19	M. Newton	8 5	—	8 41		10 41		12 15				3 2				5 6	

SUNDAYS.

UP TRNS.	9 D Goods arr	dep	10 A Passenger arr	dep	11 A Passenger arr	dep	2 A Weymouth Passenger arr	dep
	P.M.	P.M.	P.M.	P.M.	P.M.	P.M.	P.M.	P.M.
West Bay				7 5		9 15		5 10
East Street			7 9			9 20		5 1...
Bridport	ST 171, 176, 175		7 12	7 15	9 19	9 22	5 17	5 1...
Powerstock	5 24		7 22	7 23		Q	5 25	5 2...
Toller	5 35		7 30	7 31		Q		5 2...
M. Newton	5 45		7 36		9 58		5 31	5 34

Q On Saturdays calls at Powerstock 9.48 and Toller 9.56, and arrives Maiden Newton 10.1 p.m.

Special instructions are in force for working the inclines on the Bridport Branch dated March, 1884, and Guards and others must make themselves acquainted with them.

In accordance with an understanding that has been given to the Board of Trade, all Trains on the Bridport Branch must be worked by Tank Engines.

Engineers' Occupation.

The Engineers will have occupation of the Bridport Branch every night (Sundays excepted) after last Passenger Train till 6.45 a.m., for the purpose of working a Ballast Train.

Working timetable September–December 1894.

The *Bridport News* the following week contained a reply from the Bridport Railway Company Secretary, Mr Nantes, who dealt with some of the complaints concerning the timetable and then continued: 'I may state that the engine on the line is not old or inferior, and is constantly changed by the GWR from Weymouth Depot'. Although the engine failures were in themselves of a minor nature, and it would seem mostly caused by tube problems, they do appear to have been rather too frequent, with instances recorded in January, May, August, September and October 1893, and another on 8th March, 1894 followed by a derailment that June. Unfortunately, with no spare engine at Bridport when these incidents did happen, a replacement engine had to be obtained from Weymouth, and the single line staff being at the Bridport end caused further delays!

On 7th March, 1894 £800 was sent to the GWR for work that had been completed to date.

The content of the letter from 'H.G.' was raised at the 1894 half-yearly meeting of the Bridport company on 28th March. Mr F.W. Gundry wanted to know about the delay to the station alterations, and commented: 'The station roof was taken off 14 or 15 months ago and the bulkhead that protects the platforms from the prevailing winds blowing from the sea has been removed. The place is reduced to a state of semi ruin'. He continued: 'I hear that the GWR are at fault. Bridport station is so disgraceful it has become a byword for miles around. It might be said, Oh, you must not say anything against the Great Western, but why not? Why should we care about the Great Western if they should show a want for the comfort of the people of Bridport?'

It would appear however that the payment of £800 to the GWR speeded things up, the *Bridport News* on June 15th reporting:

The alterations and improvements at Bridport station are now practically complete. The roof over the two platforms is finished and will prove a welcome protection to passengers after a long spell of bare walls and roofless platforms since the alterations were commenced. The two roadways are complete and the new arrangements for working passenger and goods traffic separately will commence on the 1st July, when we shall see two engines instead of one on the line.

The *Bridport News* was able to announce in its edition for 6th July that:

An additional engine was put on the Bridport Railway on Monday, and the two engines have been working satisfactorily. The trains have been running punctually, and the improvement thus effected in the service is a great boon to the public. We may mention that now the goods traffic is worked separately from the passenger traffic, the passenger trains are running much quicker than formerly. All through trains from Maiden Newton reach Bridport in 20 minutes and West Bay in 26 minutes.

The improvements to the service were reflected by the traffic carried on the August Bank Holiday Monday, it being reported that about 300 excursionists came off main line trains and about 400 local people departed from East Street and Bridport bound for destinations beyond Maiden Newton. Twenty-four trains were run in and out of West Bay.

Although the main improvements had been completed in July 1894 the Board of Trade inspection of the works was not carried out until that October. The only fault the inspecting officer could find was that a separate waiting room was required for ladies with an entrance from the platform which he considered could be easily provided. With the main part of the original station buildings being incorporated in the reconstruction, it was to remain without much change - except for minor details - for the next 58 years.

In January 1895 the Bridport company received an unexpected bill from the GWR. The original estimate for the work had been £4,000, but there had been an overspend, and it was decided that the difference should be divided between the GWR and the Bridport company, the latter having to pay £217 5s. The GWR also refused to provide a

Long-serving branch guard Shepperd, whose service dated back to broad gauge days stands by his train at West Bay station. The locomotive is believed to be No. 1307. Note the old type of communication cord fitted to the coach and just visible in the top right corner.

By permission of the Bridport Museum Service

waiting shed at Toller, and in view of the expenses incurred on the branch recently the Board would not consider further expenditure for the moment. This shelter had been discussed between the companies since November 1893 and was estimated to cost £45.

The fact that the GPO were still relying on horse-drawn carts was brought to light on Saturday 12th January, 1895, when due to severe weather with gales and snowstorms and winds at almost hurricane force at times, it was found impossible to send the mails by cart from Dorchester to Bridport on Sunday morning. Instead they were dispatched by train, reaching Bridport by the 12 noon train. Again on Monday the mail carts were unable to get through due to heavy snow drifts, so the mails had once more to be sent by train from Dorchester to Bridport reaching Bridport at about 10 am.

In the same month some staff changes along the line took place. Edmund Dale, who had had charge of Toller station for the past 12 years, transferred to Powerstock in the place of Mr F.W. Green who retired after 40 years service, of which 24 had been spent at Powerstock.

In April George Peach, who had been station master at Bridport for the past 10 years, departed to take up the appointment of station master, Frome. It was a richly-deserved reward with an increase of annual salary from £140 to £155. During his time at Bridport he had dealt with many problems - including the upheaval of the reconstruction work.

Unfortunately for his successor it was a demotion. William Mathews Mitcham had been station master at Frome for almost 30 years and was reduced to Bridport as a disciplinary measure. It did however show that the Directors and management of the GWR had both loyalty towards, and compassion for, a good servant. Early in 1895 he issued (on two separate occasions), privilege tickets in favour of his son, who was not in the service of the GWR, and also to his son's wife who visited him on the occasion of the illness and subsequent death of his daughter. However having regard to all the circumstances, and particularly to the length of Mitcham's service (nearly 40 years) it was considered that instead of dismissal, he be removed to a station of lesser importance and reduced in salary.

At the end of September 1896 a presentation was made to guard John Edwin Shepperd upon his retirement after 44 years service with the GWR, for 32 of which he had worked the Bridport train. Owing to age and with infirmity creeping upon him he was obliged to relinquish his duties, and a presentation of £27 10s. 6d. in a purse was presented to him together with a framed illuminated address which read as follows.

BRIDPORT RAILWAY COMPANY

The Directors of the Bridport Railway Company, upon the retirement from the service of the Great Western Railway of Guard John Edwin Shepperd, after 44 years service, desire to testify to the high character and unsurmounting attention to his duties which Guard John Edwin Shepperd maintained during the 32 years which he latterly spent in charge of the Bridport train. The Directors are pleased to present Guard John Edwin Shepperd the sum of £27 10s. 6d. which has been numerously subscribed as a gift to him on his retirement and the acknowledgement of his civility to passengers at all times.
Dated Bridport Railway Company. Bridport 30th September 1896.

R.D. Thornton Chairman

Although nothing more had been heard about the request for a bookstall at West Bay station, one was now being provided at Bradpole Road. In September 1897 letters were received by the Bridport company containing complaints that the boy was absent from the stall and passengers could not buy papers.

Every branch line had its characters. On the Bridport branch it was 'Big Bill' - a man of massive proportions who stood 6 ft 6 in. tall. A platelayer on the railway, he lived at

Toller and to many was known as 'Cant' or 'Canterbury', although his real name was William Legg. There are many stories and much folklore about this well known gentle giant who (it was reputed) could carry railway sleepers on his back, and had to have his boots specially made. Unfortunately, as the years progressed he suffered from deafness, and was eventually sent for a medical at the end of July 1898. Faced with dismissal from the railway, he went missing on the Saturday evening only to be discovered the following morning hanging from the bridge over the railway at Little Toller. Weighing well over 20 stone, he had used fencing wire instead of rope to bring about his end. He was unable to face a bleak future with only 4s. a week railway pension which could have resulted in both his wife and himself ending their days in the Workhouse. Such was the fate of many of the working classes who had no other means of support.

Maiden Newton's longest serving station master, Alfred Reeve, departed after 15 years in February 1897 to become station master at Dorchester, and in March 1901 he moved on to Warminster. His successor did not stay at Maiden Newton long - just 10 months. Frederick William Cooper had previously been a booking clerk at Bath, and went on to Melksham that December. E.C. Beard a Yeovil booking clerk, was appointed to Maiden Newton in his place.

During 1898 there were plans for the Axminster and Bridport Junction Railway. It was intended to join the two towns with a railway to run via Lyme Regis. At this stage Lyme Regis was still without a railway and was served by horse buses from Bridport and Axminster. The Bridport and Lyme Regis horse bus service was started in September 1858 with a coach named 'Defiance' operating one round trip each day meeting the trains at Bridport station. This service lasted until August 1922 when the motor bus superseded it, unlike the Axminster to Lyme Regis coach, which had started in the 1870s and ceased to operate when the Lyme Regis Railway opened in 1903.

The projected 16¾ mile Axminster and Bridport Junction Railway of 1898 was described as 'one of the most feasible and important projects to connect Bridport with Lyme Regis', or so Mr Nantes was told when Messrs Smith & Cotterell, the Civil Engineers for the project, called on him at his Bridport office in the September. The plan was to form a connection with the Bridport branch on the West Bay extension and then cross South Street and proceed to Lyme Regis and Axminster, there joining the LSWR main line.

The scheme was described as nothing less than 'of National importance', as it would form the much vaunted connecting link in the coast line from Sussex, Southampton, Bournemouth and Weymouth, as a line already ran from Axminster to Exeter and Plymouth. It is clear the promoters were still thinking along the lines of schemes from the 1840s, when a continous line of railway along the coast was desired because of the French invasion threat, which made the movement of troops a matter of importance. Despite the change in the international situation, the promoters hoped the scheme would receive the moral support of the Government, and hopefully, the active support of the Bridport Railway Company.

On 1st November Mr Cotterell chaired a public meeting at the Town Hall, at which he explained the proposal to a packed assembly. He estimated the line would cost less than £7,000 per mile. The Bridport branch would be doubled and become part of the main line. The difficulties at Charmouth could be overcome by utilising the substantial foundation of rocks along the foreshore on which they would build a stone viaduct, well clear of the cliffs which had a tendency to fall occasionally, but there would be no danger of this interfering with the railway.

It is clear that the promoters had not kept up with the international situation, and nearer to home they must have failed to note the difficulties then experienced (and still encountered) on the South Devon sea wall section of the GWR! However, talk is cheap, and everyone at the meeting voted in favour of the scheme and approved the suggested railway.

On 5th November the scheme was discussed by the Bridport Board, when the estimated cost was put at £200,000. The annual gross earnings were expected to be around £19,000. The Board would not form an opinion on the scheme before consulting the GWR and the LSWR companies. Although taken very seriously, the scheme was abandoned, as in June 1899 the Axminster and Lyme Regis Light Railway Order was passed, authorising the construction of a light railway between these two towns, this being opened on Monday 24th August, 1903.

The last attempt to have a second railway line to Bridport had ended, as had the coastal route, except for short section between Budleigh Salterton and Exmouth opened by the LSWR in 1903.

A report of June 1898 clearly demonstrated the cost-conscious management. The authorised clerical staff at Bridport consisted of the station master, an audit clerk, and two lad clerks, but officers visiting the station found this insufficient to carry out the work. It was therefore decided that another audit clerk be appointed at £70 per annum, but a saving would be effected by the replacement of a 28s. a week member of wages staff with one at 21s. a week!

Mr E.C. Beard moved from Maiden Newton in May 1899, his place being taken by Arthur John Campfield, formerly station master at Keynsham. However his stay was extremely short. In January 1901 he was appointed to Bristol parcels department, becoming station master at Wootton Bassett during 1910. His successor at Maiden Newton, Frank George Dunsford, also moved from being station master at Keynsham. A local man born at Maiden Newton, he commenced his service in 1885 at Chippenham goods, later moving to Swindon, Portland, and Yeovil, then being appointed station master at Witham in September 1899 before moving to Keynsham the following year.

At that period a vast amount of valuable traffic was carried on the railways under conditions that today would be considered most insecure, but owing to the honesty of both public and staff there were few problems. But what was described as 'systematic pilfering' took place at Bridport in July 1900, when four young engine cleaners employed during the night made a habit of going to the goods shed, forcing the doors open, and stealing a quantity of butter cloths, sweets, cigars, and ale, the total value of which came to around 10s. Caught in a trap set by the railway police, two of the four received three weeks hard labour, the third one week's hard labour, and the fourth who had just received the goods was fined 10s., such were the deterrents handed out by the magistrates court!

At Bridport an era was coming to an end with the retirement of station master William Mitcham on 12th August, 1900. His entire railway career had been spent on the former Wilts Somerset & Weymouth lines and the Bridport Railway Company. He had seen the beginning of the local company in his early days at Maiden Newton, and a year after him it was also to retire from the scene.

To see in the new century William Francis Vaughan was appointed as Bridport station master. Commencing his career in Cardiff booking office during 1875, following a spell at Newport he became station master at Cardiff Clarence Road in 1894, moving to Presteign in 1897 and Grange Court in March 1899.

As the century drew to a close, the Bridport company had extracted itself from the financial débacle of the early days, mainly by transferring money from the revenue account each half-year until the deficiency of £5,866 was extinguished. The capital account to 30th June, 1897 showed that £143,683 had been received and expended, the amounts received on shares being as follows.

Ex-Monmouthshire Railway tank No. 1305 stands at Powerstock station with a Bridport-bound train about the turn of the century. In the foreground is a 'Hybar' wagon an idea going back many more years than one imagines. In the background Egardon Hill overshadows the scene in this rural part of Dorset.   *M.J. Tattershall Collection*

West Bay station in June 1900; ex-Monmouthshire Railway & Canal Co. 4-4-0 tank, No. 1305, stands at the station with a train of four-wheelers. In the foreground is a selection of wagons including an 'Iron Mink' van, to the right of which is a PO wagon of the Somerset Trading Company.   *By permission of the Bridport Museum Service*

£10 ordinary shares	£64,431
£10 preference shares at 6 per cent	£20,000
£10 preference shares at 5 per cent	£4,000
£10 preference shares at 4 per cent	£23,000
	£111,431

The amount received on loans at 3½ per cent was £25,600 and on sundries £6,652.

For the half-year ending 30th June, 1897 the net earnings sufficed for the payment of dividends at the rate of 6 per cent, 5 per cent and 4 per cent per annum on the preference shares (less tax), and 1 per cent per annum free of tax on the ordinary shares. However, for the previous half year the dividend on the ordinary shares had been 1½ per cent.

It was clear the company, although out of debt, was not out of danger, and many were questioning whether it was worth all the trouble as the shareholders and Directors grew older.

At the half-yearly meeting of the Bridport Railway Company held at the Bull Hotel, Bridport in March 1900, a dividend of 2¼ per cent was sanctioned, but the Chairman, Mr R.D. Thornton, said,

> Questions have recently arisen between the Directors and the Great Western Railway Company, and in the course of them, negotiations have taken place as to whether some arrangement can be made for the sale of the railway to the Great Western, with terms materially advantageous to both companies.

Experience had shown that the large railway companies were willing to give more than the real value to acquire the control and possession of subsidiary lines. Mr Thornton spoke of the question being discussed with the GWR and said after some lengthy and very careful considerations that the Directors had come to such a point that they were hoping shortly to place before the shareholders a proposal for the purchase of the line by the GWR, and such a proposal they would recommend them to accept. They were certain it would be beneficial to them all.

As regards the ordinary shares, they hoped that the GWR, or somebody acting on its behalf, would be willing to buy them outright at £6 per share, whilst in dealing with the preference shares, they hoped the holders of preference stock in the Bridport company would receive GWR preference stock for an amount sufficient to yield them the same income as they were now receiving, as soon as the necessary Parliamentary authority was obtained.

With regard to the debentures, they would be paid forthwith. They had arranged for the Great Western to pay the sum of £1,300 in order to provide for all expenses and pay compensation to their officers.

It was pointed out that the scheme would not only be of great advantage to the shareholders, but it would be of considerable advantage to the town. He wished to place on record his expression of thanks for the way the GWR had always helped them. The GWR had done its best to forward any proposals made, and if the line became its property he was of the opinion that it would add to the prosperity of the town.

The Bridport company and the GWR agreed the terms of the sale in April 1900; the GWR to pay the ordinary shareholders £6 for every £10 share and to exchange its own preference shares for those of the Bridport company.

At a special meeting of the shareholders held on 1st May, 1901, a resolution was passed allowing the Bill to go before Parliament for the amalgamation of the two companies. This received Royal Assent on 26th July, 1901, the amalgamation taking place from the first day of the month in which the GWR lease of the line expired, the purchase price being £111,145 5s. 0d. The final meeting of the Bridport company to wind up its affairs was held at the Bull Hotel, Bridport, at noon on Wednesday 25th September, 1901.

A '2021' class saddle tank, still fitted with a domeless boiler, stands at the main platform of Bridport station shortly after the turn of the century. The staff pose while the photographer captures the scene for posterity. Note the flat bottomed rail with baulk road sleeper arrangements.   *Lens of Sutton*

A view of Bridport station taken in 1906, looking towards Maiden Newton, and clearly showing the reconstruction of 1894 with the platform curving away at an angle to the main station building. Longitudinal baulk road is still in place, and the rolling stock is typical of a branch train of the period.   *By permission of the Bridport Museum Service*

Chapter Five

The Great Western Era

At last the GWR had complete control over the Bridport branch. No longer was there a local Board of Directors to contend with, and all decisions could be made solely by the GWR either at Paddington or at Divisional Headquarters. One of the first decisions was to let Bradpole Road station revert to its original name of 'Bridport', this happening in 1902, and between the take-over in 1901 and 1907 four bridges were renewed at a cost of nearly £5,000.

One item that they had not planned to renew was the station building at Toller, which burnt down on Sunday 12th October, 1902. It appears that at about 11 pm Mr Brayley (the station master) was in his office and had an accident with a paraffin lamp. An explosion occurred, and the wooden building burst into flames. Earlier, from the vicarage which overlooked the station, the Revd D. Clarke had noticed a light in the office and thought it unusual at that late hour, as the last down train had departed at 9.56 pm. Retiring to bed he soon smelt burning wood, and looking out of the window, saw a cloud of smoke coming from the station office. Quickly dressing, he ran to the scene, meeting the station master who was coming from the Sexton's house where he had gone for help. He noticed the station master had severe burns on his hands and arm and his fingers were badly cut.

Upon reaching the station the Vicar threw water over the table in the office, upon which were piles of documents in flames, and then turned his attention to moving hampers and other things from the platform out of harm's way. By this time other villagers had arrived on the scene, cut down a fir tree close to the station to prevent the fire spreading, and extinguished a fire which had began to burn the ground frame hut. At one stage both the vicarage and the Swan Inn (both with thatched roofs!) together with other buildings in the village were threatened as the wind carried showers of sparks over them. When the fire died out at 1 am there was little left. The books, papers, and everything in the station office was destroyed - even those in the safe being burned! Only the fire grate and a few iron fittings remained.

During the following week no tickets were issued at Toller, passengers paying at either end of their journey, and the *Bridport News* reported: 'Mr Brayley, the station master, carries an injured arm in a sling and still suffers from the shock caused by the disaster, and is attended by Mr Hay of Bridport, the local GWR medical officer'.

Within a short while a temporary shed was erected to serve as a booking office and waiting room, but it was not until 31st May, 1903 that the management approved plans for a new station building, an extended platform, and a connection at the West end of the siding at a total cost of £798, the plans being forwarded to the Board of Trade for approval on 3rd July.

Sadly John Cowell Brayley was not to see the new station. He died of apoplexy (a stroke) on 14th June, 1903 at the age of 56, having complained of feeling unwell the previous evening. Apparently he had suffered agonising head pains for a fortnight, but had not consulted a doctor. Unfortunately life had not run smoothly for Brayley. Originally a porter at Sandford & Banwell, he was promoted to second class inspector at Winscombe in March 1895, where he soon found himself in trouble by causing the derailment of an engine through 'careless working of the points'. In December 1897 he was moved to Toller, his pay being reduced from 25s. to 23s. a week. He was, however, a well respected man at Toller - both as station master, and through his formation of a swimming club, his enthusiasm for the latter extending to taking a dip at noon each Christmas day!

Maiden Newton station, looking towards Yeovil. In this view taken around 1905 the station was in its prime. The signal box of 1885 is shown on the down platform, the portly figure of station master Frank Dunsford in the foreground. Timetables and period adverts adorn the walls of the up platform, and the entrance to the refreshment room can be seen behind the group of staff standing on the left.   *K. Bakes Collection*

East Street station photographed shortly after its rebuilding. The new station master's house is on the left, and the new station building on the platform. The hut housing the ground frame controlling the crossing is on the right, GWR Whitsuntide excursions to Scotland and Ireland are advertised on the bill board. The train approaching from West Bay is hauled by a '2021' class 0-6-0ST, thought to be No. 2115.   *I.D. Beale*

Whether as a direct result of the Toller fire or not, the thatched station building at East Street was replaced during 1904, a new brick building of GWR standard design being erected on the platform and a fine new station master's house constructed nearby. This work was carried out by Messrs J. & H. Childs of Bridport. The new station at Toller was a little longer in arriving, this not being completed until the last week of June 1905, and whereas East Street had been executed in brick, Toller was of timber on a brick base - although again a standard GWR design of the period was used. At the same time the timber bridge over the line near the station was replaced by a steel girder structure. The *Bridport News*, in reporting the re-opening, remarked:

It is hoped another improvement will soon be put in hand, viz., the provision of pens for loading cattle. At present cattle have to wait outside the railway gate until the arrival of the combined passenger and goods train, and then be driven onto the passenger platform to be entrained. The practice is both unpleasant and dangerous.

Following the death of John Brayley, H.S. Hill, formerly a porter at Evershot - was appointed station master at Toller, although his stay was short. Destined for higher office, he moved on during 1905, when John Churchill moved back to the branch from his previous position of station master at Stratton (Wilts).

One other improvement on the branch during this period was the construction of a new stable for the accommodation of the railway dray horses at Bridport station during 1909, again the work being undertaken by a local firm of builders, Jesty & Baker.

Whilst the railway was being brought up to a higher standard, other affairs were taking place. The opening of the Axminster-Lyme Regis branch of the LSWR on 24th August, 1903 was to have an effect on the Bridport-Lyme Regis coach service operated by Mr Warren who was also a GWR agent. Since April 1902 Warren had received a payment of £40 per annum as a subsidy. The service having been carried on in a satisfactory manner, Mr Warren considered that in order to improve it a new omnibus was required at a cost of £100. The Directors of the GWR decided to assist Warren in his efforts and reduce the capital outlay on his part by increasing the subsidy to £50 per annum.

However, the age of the horse-drawn omnibus was rapidly ending, for early in 1904 the *Bridport News* reported that

. . . it is understood that the Great Western Company look with favour upon a motor service between Lyme Regis and Bridport and a representative of the company has inspected the route with a view to reporting upon the feasibility of the project.

The only drawback is said to be the steep hills, but there is reason to hope a service will be established before very long, and it is reported a motor car will run twice a day between the two towns.

However, this turned out to be wishful thinking as no such GWR motor bus service ever operated in the district, the nearest being a local service in Weymouth which started the following year! The horse bus connection survived until 1st August, 1922, by which time the motor bus had greatly improved.

The *Bridport News* for 8th May, 1903 reported that employees of the LSWR were taking levels and marking out a light railway route between Crewkerne and Bridport.

The paper was obviously enthusiastic about the scheme and wrote in exuberant terms of its prospects, but the following week a letter from a local inhabitant was far nearer the truth in saying,

When one considers the character of the country between Crewkerne and Beaminster, there can be no doubt as to the answer. In order to gauge the need for a railway in any neighbourhood we

Bridport station, viewed from the east. The new roof of the goods shed extension can be clearly defined. A clerestory bogie coach stands on the siding, while undeveloped farm land and Waddon Hill dominate the scene.   *B.L. Jackson Collection*

A branch train arriving at West Bay. In this pre-World War I view the driver can be seen handing over the single line staff to the signalman. The engine is thought to be '2021' class 0-6-0 No. 2115.
By permission of the Bridport Museum Services

must look at the present amount of traffic between two places. Multiply the present amount of traffic between Bridport and Crewkerne tenfold, and would it not better be served by a well appointed system of omnibuses, possibly motor buses meeting the principal trains at Crewkerne?

Wise talking indeed, and a sentiment so often expressed in later years. As to the actual project, a certain amount of mystery surrounded it for several weeks. Later the *Bridport News* printed a retraction, stating that the LSWR was in no way connected with it. It has never been recorded as a 'proposed' railway, but has to be regarded as the final verse in a chapter of unsuccessful schemes.

The year 1905 saw the departure from Bridport of one of the sons of the late W. Titball - Mr Cecil Hubert Titball, a clerk in the goods department - being presented with a dressing case by the staff on his promotion to chief passenger clerk at Yeovil Pen Mill. In 1911 he became chief clerk at Devizes, and in 1920 station master at Wells Tucker Street. Unfortunately following many months illness, he died in January 1937 aged 58. His son, R.C. Titball, became a goods clerk at Devizes during the 1930s, moving to the divisional superintendent's office at Bristol in late 1941.

In April 1907 Bridport station master W.F. Vaughan moved to Yeovil Pen Mill station, his fine singing voice having made him welcome in many social circles within the town. Mr Vaughan was succeeded by Frederick Weeks, formerly station master at Shepton Mallet GWR.

The sleepy station at Powerstock came alive on Saturday 6th February, 1909 for the funeral of local man Peter Meech. Born at Beaminster in 1826 he had gone to London to make his fortune - a latter day 'Dick Whittington'. A butcher by trade, he had an extensive business at Smithfield and was most successful, and like Daniel Bingham, he never forgot his roots, donating a substantial sum towards the building of Beaminster village hall.

His body and 30 of his friends who travelled down from London arrived in a saloon coach attached to the 1.48 pm train. On leaving the station the hearse was followed by 15 coaches taking the mourners to Powerstock church where he was laid to rest. He bequeathed £500 for the maintenance of his grave and the provision of coal for the poor of the parish at Christmas.

On Thursday 7th April, 1910 large crowds gathered at Bridport station to witness the arrival of a coffin containing the body of Mr William A. Hart MVO, - one of the town's most successful sons, who had passed away at his London home aged 64. Born at Bradpole on 31st July, 1846, he was educated at Bridport General School and later a local grammar school. His education complete, he commenced work at Bridport station as a parcel clerk, being appointed to Swansea in September 1866. The following year he moved to the divisional superintendent's office at Newport, then to the goods department at Cardiff. In 1872 he was appointed head clerk in the parcel department at Bath.

The following year he was selected for special duty in connection with traffic generated by Army manoeuvres on Salisbury Plain, during which his superiors noticed him as future management material, and shortly after he was appointed head of the parcels department at Bristol. From there he soon moved on to become station master at Slough, which brought him into contact with Royal Train working. On one occasion the Royal train conveying the Empress of Austria was trapped at Slough following a severe snowstorm, and Mr Hart promptly took Her Majesty to his own house for comfort until the train could proceed.

In 1877 Hart became station master at Bristol Temple Meads, and two years later he was appointed station master at Paddington. On 28th February, 1884, fearing terrorist

BRIDPORT BRANCH.

Single Line, worked by Electric Train Staff.   Crossing Place, Bridport.

DOWN TRAINS.

WEEK DAYS.

Distances M C	DOWN TRAINS.		1 B Pass. MFO A.M.	2 K Goods A.M.	3 B Pass. A.M.	4 B Pass. A.M.	5 B Pass. A.M.	6 B Pass. W P.M.	7 B Pass. P.M.	8 B Pass. W P.M.	9	10 B Pass. W P.M.	11 B Pass. P.M.	12 B Pass. P.M.	13 K Goods P.M.	14 B Pass. P.M.	15 B Pass. P.M.	16 B Pass. P.M.	17 B Pass. P.M.	18 Pass. THO P.M.	19
	Maiden Newton	dep.	Bank Holiday	9 X 0	....	9 38	11 6	...	1 34	...	...	3 X 0	4 0	5 0	6X50	...	7 28	8 45	July and August only	10 55	...
	Toller	arr.		9 6		9 44	11 12		1 40			3 16	4 6	5 15			7 34	8 51			
2 44	"	dep.		9 11											6P58						
3 00	Stop Board	dep.		9P15																	
	Powerstock	arr.		CR		9 52	11 20		1 48			3 24	4 13	5 23			7 42	8 53			
5 62	"	dep.		0P23																	
6 0	Stop Board	dep.		10X25											TP6						
	Bridport	arr.	8 5	9 33		9 59	11 27		1 55			3 31	9X22	5X30	7 16		7 49	9 6		11 15	
9 21	"	dep.	8 8	10X25		10 3	11 31		1 59			3 35	4 27	5 33		7 30	7X54		9 13		
9 64	East Street	dep.	8 8	10 30		10 6	11 34		2 2			3 38	4 30	5 36		7 33	8 1		9 16		
11 21	West Bay	arr.	8 12	ST41		10 10	11 38		2 6			3 42	4 34	5 40		7 37			9 20		

SUNDAYS.

DOWN TRAINS.		20	21	22 B Pass. P.M.	23 B Weymouth Pass. P.M.
Maiden Newton	dep.	...	...	5 52	9 52
Toller	arr.			...	9 57
Powerstock	arr.			5 59	9 50
Bridport	arr.			6 8	10 8
"	dep.				10 8
West Bay	arr.			6 15	10 15

UP TRAINS.

WEEK DAYS.

UP TRAINS.		1 B Mxd. A.M.	2 K Pass. MFO A.M. R	3 B Pass. A.M.	4	5 B Pass. A.M.	6 K Gds. A.M.	7 B Pass. A.M.	8 B Pass. W P.M.	9 B Pass. W P.M.	10 B Pass. V P.M.	11 B Pass. W P.M.	12 B Pass. P.M.	13 B Pass. P.M.	14 K G'ds P.M.	15 B Pass. P.M.	16 B Pass. P.M.	17 B Pass. P.M.	18 B Pass. P.M.	19 Pass. THO P.M.	20
West Bay	dep.	...	8 20	8 23		10 15	10 20	11 50	1 55	2 50	2 33	4 10	...	4 45	5 35	6 15	7 45	8 30	...	10 20	
East Street	"		8 23	8 25		10 20		11 55	2 0	2 55	2 38	4 15		4 50		6 20	7 50	8 33			
Bridport	arr.		8 27			10X22	10 55	11 57	2X2	2 57	2 40	4 17		4 52	N	6 22	7X52	8 37		10 27	
"	dep.	7 30	R	8 35		10 28	10 55	12 1	2 15	3 1			4X30		5 35	6 25	8 2			10 27	
Powerstock	arr.	7 40													5 46		8 11				
Toller	arr.	7 45				10 37		12 10	2 24	3 10			4 39		6 1	6 34	8 11				
"	dep.	7 54				10 46		12 19	2 33	3 19		4 46	4 46		6 8	6 43	8 20				
Maiden Newton	arr.	8 5	BX58	8 53		10 51	11 2	12 24	2 38	3X8	3 1	4 53			6 15	6X48	8 25				

SUNDAYS.

UP TRAINS.		21	22	23 B Pass. P.M.	24 B Weymouth Pass. P.M.
West Bay	dep.	...	...	2 5	7 5
East Street	"			...	...
Bridport	arr.			4 14	7 14
Toller	arr.			4 23	7 23
Maiden Newton	arr.			4 29	7 28

Down trains notes:

R Wagons attached to this Train at Powerstock and Toller must be picked up next Coaches and run in proper order at Maiden Newton.

V July 1st to 15th only.
W Commencing July 10th.
Y Will not run after third Thursday in September.

Up trains notes:

N ST 219 220, 221 222.

Bank Holiday, Will not run.

Engineers' Occupation.

The Engineers will have occupation of the Bridport Branch every night (Sundays excepted) after last booked Train till first booked Train for the purpose of working a Ballast Train.

Working timetable 1910.

Mr William Albert Hart MVO who went from parcels clerk to
divisional superintendent, London Division, Great Western Railway.

activity following the discovery of explosives at other stations, he had all items in the
parcel office and cloakroom examined, and a portmanteau was opened containing 20 lb.
of dynamite and a clock detonator. The Directors of the GWR later presented him with
an inscribed marble clock in recognition of his actions.

In 1893 he became superintendent of the London Division, in which office he was
responsible for Royal Train journeys to and from Paddington and Windsor. King
Edward VII decorated him for his efforts, Hart becoming the first railwayman to be a
member of 'The Royal Victorian Order'. There were also awards from distinguished
foreign visitors, including a diamond and turquoise pin from Archduke Francis
Ferdinand of Austria in 1894, and having the order of the Red Star Eagle Class conferred
on him in 1907 by the Emperor of Germany.

Over 1,000 people attended his memorial service at St James, Sussex Gardens, after
which his coffin was taken to Paddington station for conveyance to Bridport where he
had commenced his successful career. He had been a frequent visitor to the town, and
despite his exulted position never forgot the friends of his boyhood, often being seen
talking to some companion of his school days. He also helped many to find
employment on the railway. He was a true friend of Bridport, and proof that anybody
with determination could rise to the top of his profession. He was buried in the east end
of the church yard of Holy Trinity Church, Bradpole, within sight of Bradpole Crossing
and the GWR to which he gave a lifetime of service.

The dangers of crossing the line were demonstrated by a sad occurrence on the night of
25th September, 1910, when Mr Richard Gill of Uploders, aged 77, was killed by the last
train of the day into Bridport. Having attended a late dance at the Foresters Hall Institute,
he had crossed the line by a footpath a short distance from Bradpole Crossing gates. Later
at 12.15 am a local lady who had locked the hall followed by the same route and discovered
the body. At the inquest it was revealed that on Thursdays an extra late train arrived in
Bridport at 11.18 pm, which for some reason Richard Gill had failed to take into account.

During June 1910 authorisation was given by the Directors to lengthen the platform at
Powerstock, the estimated cost being £95. The following year track renewal took place at
Bridport, where much of track and pointwork was still laid with baulk road. This was
replaced by the then standard cross-sleepered road. At the same time a short loading dock
was added behind the platform at the south end of the station. During this period the three
permanent way gangs employed on the branch were reduced to two. The down platform
at Bridport and the up platform at Maiden Newton were both widened during October 1913.

Bridport station, viewed from the north-east before World War I. A saddle tank stands at the platform, whilst the siding in the foreground contains coaches and some wagons loaded with artillery equipment. At that time many Territorial Army manoeuvres took place in the West Dorset area, and the local Territorials also travelled to carry out their annual training elsewhere.

K. Bakes Collection

In the same year staff were again on the move, commencing with William Pound, a Bridport parcel porter, being promoted to station master at Portesham (on the Abbotsbury branch), and Mr F. Dunsford, the Maiden Newton station master, being transferred to Radstock.

A popular local man, Frank Dunsford was presented upon his departure with a pair of silver candlesticks by the station staff, and a gold hunter watch and chain together with a suitably-inscribed book containing the names of 64 subscribers in Maiden Newton and surrounding district. Upon his marriage in April 1907 to Miss Frances Brown, the station staff had presented him with a handsome silver biscuit box.

His replacement was Mr W.G. Stickland, formerly station master at Clutton, and previously (to 1906) a clerk at Dorchester. At the same time Richmond Roberts, formerly a parcel porter at Wootton Bassett, was appointed station master at Powerstock.

In 1913 there were additional comforts for clerical staff at Bridport, with the provision of a new office for the goods department. Great interest was created at Maiden Newton in July 1914 when an exhibition train of the National Poultry Organisation Society, visited various stations in the West Country. The display was housed aboard the LSWR train consisting of two 48 ft former brake/kitchen cars and one 56 ft former dining saloon.

The war was declared on Germany on 4th August, 1914 and was to change the British way of life for ever. Immediately all lines of communication were protected. Volunteers kept watch on the telegraph lines, and a guard was put on Bridport railway station and the local reservoirs in case of sabotage.

A Voluntary Aid Detachment of the Red Cross Society was formed in Bridport with the intention of turning St Andrews Road School, which was convenient to the station, into a hospital for wounded servicemen. After a lengthy delay a reply was received from the War Office declining this offer as Bridport was at the end of a branch line, and Bridport station was not large enough to receive a complete hospital train.

In the early days many horses in the area were commandeered by the War Office, the railway being left with only two dray horses to perform all the delivery work. The German invasion of Belgium caused many to flee the atrocities. On 26th November, 1914 the first batch of nearly 40 refugees arrived at Bridport station, one carrying all his worldly goods in a galvanised bucket! These and others were housed in empty property in the town. The girls were taught the art of net making at Edwards & Son and were quickly absorbed into the labour force.

During the first week of January 1915 around 1,000 men of the 'Howe' Battalion of the Naval Brigade arrived at Bridport station, quickly marching off into town where they were billeted. They camped under canvas whilst training took place on Eype Down.

As the war progressed the railways became hard pressed as staff joined the forces, and extra traffic added to the problems of the shortage of materials and coal supplies which resulted in non-essential services being withdrawn. To release staff for other work the Bridport-West Bay section closed to passenger traffic from the 31st December, 1915, and there was also a reduction in the passenger service between Bridport and Maiden Newton. From 1st January, 1916 only four trains each way were run daily, the first down train being 'mixed', as was the 6.5 pm, the last up train from Bridport. On Wednesdays and Saturdays an extra train to and from Weymouth ran, mainly for the benefit of passengers wishing to visit Dorchester market, the down train leaving Maiden Newton at 8.25 am, running non-stop to Bridport, and returning at 10.32 am. On Sundays the service was reduced to one train in each direction during the afternoon, provided by the through working of a Weymouth auto-train.

By 1st May, 1917 the Sunday service had been withdrawn, although the daily passenger service had been increased to five trains each way, of which two each way were mixed. The local rope and net industry played a vital part in the war effort, the vast amounts of material all having to be conveyed by goods train. Supplies of hemp lanyards for the Army and

BRIDPORT BRANCH.

Single Line, worked by Electric Train Staff. Crossing Place, Bridport.

DOWN TRAINS.

Distances	Station No.	DOWN TRAINS.	2 K Goods A.M.	3 D W80 'C'hes A.M.	4 B Mixed A.M.	6 K Goods A.M.	7 B Pass. P.M.	12 B Pass. P.M.	15 B Pass. P.M.	18 K Goods; P.M.	SUNDAYS 20 B Wey-mouth Motor P.M.
M 0	621	Maiden Newton … dep.	7 45	8¼25	9 38	…	1 45	5 12	7 35	9 26	3 23
2 44	667	Toller { arr.	7 51	…	9 44	…	…	…	…	…	…
		{ dep.	7 56	…	9 49	…	1 52	5 18	7 41	9P36	3 30
3 60	—	Stop Board	…	…	…	…	…	…	…	…	…
5 62	668	Powerstock { arr.	CR	…	9 58	…	…	…	…	…	…
		{ dep.	8P0	…	10 2	…	2 1	5 26	7 49	…	3 39
5 65½	—	Stop Board	…	…	…	…	…	…	…	…	…
9 21	670	Bridport { arr.	8P8	8¼18	10X10	10 45	2 8	5 33	7 56	9P50	…
		{ dep.	8·18	…	…	…	…	…	…	10 0	…
9 54	672	East Street … arr.	…	ST41	…	…	…	…	…	…	…
11 18	673	West Bay … arr.	…	…	…	10 50	…	…	…	…	3 48

UP TRAINS.

UP TRAINS.	1 K G'ds A.M.	3 B Pass. A.M.	4 B Wey-m'th Pass. A.M.	6 K Gds A.M.	7 B Pass. P.M.	12 B Pass. P.M.	15 B Mixed R N P.M.	18 K Goods Z P.M.	SUNDAYS 23 B Wey-mouth Motor P.M.
West Bay … dep.	6 30	…	…	11 15	…	…	6 5	…	…
East Street …	…	…	…	…	…	…	…	8 20	…
Bridport { arr.	—	…	WS0	—	12 5	…	…	8 30	…
{ dep.	6 40	8·52	10X52	11 20	12 5	4 30	6 15	8 35	3 55
Powerstock { arr.	6 45	9	10 41	…	12 14	…	6 20	8 44	…
{ dep.	6 54	9 10 41	…	…	…	4 39	6 29	…	4 4
Toller { arr.	6 58	9 10 50	10 50	…	12 23	4 48	6 33	8 48	4 13
{ dep.	…	…	…	…	…	…	…	…	…
Maiden Newton … arr.	7 5	9 15 10 55	10 55	…	12 28	4 53	6 40	8 55	4 19

N ST 219, 220. Z, S T 221, 222.

R To convey goods traffic only for 6.25 p.m. Weymouth.

Engineers' Occupation.

The Engineers will have occupation of the Bridport Branch every night (Sundays excepted) after last booked Train till first booked Train for the purpose of working a Ballast Train.

Working timetable January–July 1916.

Drastic situations require drastic remedies! Owing to a shortage of timber during the World War I vast quantities were felled in Powerstock Forest. To avoid extra haulage it was loaded direct into wagons standing on the branch line from adjacent fields.

By permission of the Bridport Museum Service

A '645' class 0-6-0 ST heads away down Witherstone cutting with a train load of timber during World War I. The timber had been loaded directly into the wagons from the side of the cutting.

M.J. Tattershall Collection

WEEK DAYS.   SUNS

	A.M.	A.M.	P.M.	P M	P.M.	P.M.	P.M.	A P.M.	M P.M.			
MAIDEN NEWTON ....dep.	9 40	11 15	12 26	1 30	4 15	5 25	8 5	9 0	2 46			
Toller .... ,,	9 46	11 21	12 32	1 36	4 21	5 31	8 11	9 7	2 53			
Powerstock .... ,,	9 54	11 28	12 40	1 44	4 29	5 39	8 19	9 18	3 2			
Bridport .... arr.	10 1	11 36	12 47	1 51	4 36	5 46	8 26	9 27	3 9			
Bridport .... dep.	10 8	11 42	....	1 56	—	5 55	—	—	—			
BRIDPORT East Street... ,,	10 11	11 45	....	1 59		5 58						
West Bay ... arr.	10 15	11 49	....	2 3		6 2						

	A.M.	A.M.	A.M.	P.M.	P.M.	P.M.	P.M.	P.M.	SUN P.M.			
BRIDPORT West Bay dep.	......	10 20	......	12 15	2 15	......	......	6 55				
East Street ,,	......	10 25	......	12 20	2 20	......	......	7 0				
BRIDPORT arr.		10 27		12 22	2 22			7 2	M			
dep.	8 50	10 30	11 48	12 52	—	3 10	3 50	7 10	3 20			
Powerstock ,,	8 59	10 39	11 57	1 1		3 19	4 59	7 19	3 29			
Toller ,,	9 10	10 48	12 6	1 10		3 28	4 8	7 28	3 38			
MAIDEN NEWTON ...... arr.	9 15	10 53	12 11	1 15		3 33	4 13	7 33	3 43			

A—Third Class only.   M—Rail Motor Car, Third Class only.

BRIDPORT TO DORCHESTER AND WEYMOUTH.   Suns

	a.m.	a.m.		p.m.	p.m.	p.m.	p.m
BRIDPORT .... dept.	8 50	10 30	12 52 p.m.	3 10	3 50	7 10	3 20
DORCHESTER .... arr.	9 46	11 18	1 38 ,,	4 8	5 0	8 0	4 14
WEYMOUTH .... arr.	10 5	11 30	1 50 ,,	4 20	5 20	8 15	4 30

WEYMOUTH TO DORCHESTER AND BRIDPORT.   Suns

	a.m.			p.m.	p.m.	p.m.	p.m.
WEYMOUTH .... dept	8 55	10 30 a.m.	11 50 a.m.	3 25	4 15	7 25	2 0
DORCHESTER .... dept.	9 11	10 47 ,,	12 7 p.m.	3 45	4 32	7 41	2 23
BRIDPORT .... arr.	10 3	11 38 ,,	12 49 ,,	4 36	5 46	8 26	3 9

BRIDPORT TO PADDINGTON.

BRIDPORT	...	...	... dep. 8 50 a.m.	PADDINGTON	...	...	... arr. 12 55 p.m.
,,	...	...	,, 10 30 ,,	,,	...	...	,, 3 20 ,,
,,	...	...	,, 11 48 ,,	,,	...	...	,, 3 52 ,,
,,	...	...	,, 3 10 p.m.	,,	...	...	,, 6 50 ,,
,,	...	...	,, 3 50 ,,	,,	...	...	,, 8 10 ,,
,,	...	...	,, 7 10 ,,	,,	...	...	,, 2 45 a.m.

Sunda Service—Depart from Bridport 8 20 p.m.   Arrive Paddington 7 45 p.m.

PADDINGTON TO BRIDPORT.

PADDINGTON	...	...	... dep. 5 30 a.m.	BRIDPORT	...	...	... arr. 11 38 a.m.
...	...	...	,, 10 30 ,,	,,	...	...	,, 1 51 p.m
...	...	...	,, 12 30 p.m.	,,	...	...	,, 4 36 ,,

Timetable published in the *Bridport News* in 1919.

Navy were required in their millions and sometimes as much as 300 tons were dispatched, and as many were required as 'pull-throughs' for rifles. At one period 50,000 hay nets for feeding Army horses were dispatched every week, as were tent ropes and seaming twine for sewing canvas, and those were just a few of the many items in constant demand.

One manufacturer alone was, at one stage, sending 6 tons a week of balloon and aeroplane cordage, and there were also nets for covering spherical balloons and airships - some of these weighing half-a-ton each.

In January 1915 the Admiralty asked if the Bridport factories could produce anti-submarine indicator nets, which had to be made of steel cord, and it was duly done, the largest nets made in Bridport being 300 ft by 180 ft. When these arrived at the station they must have been very heavy and difficult to handle. The idea of camouflage netting was introduced during 1917, and vast quantities were soon arriving at the goods depot.

At the other end of the scale was the transport of eggs. Being in very short supply, an appeal went out from Military Hospitals and a receiving station for local contributions was set up at the Town Hall, where Mr J.E. Smith the 'Egg Controller for Bridport' received, packed, and sent off consignments. Between March 1915 and March 1919 no less than 64,428 eggs were contributed by the people of Bridport, 1,636 to the Exeter Military Hospital and 62,792 to HQ for base hospitals in France and others at home.

Towards the end of the war an Admiralty Airship Mooring was established in the wooded hills north-west of Grays Farm, Powerstock, 1½ miles west of Toller. Although later referred to as 'Powerstock Air Ship Station', its official name was 'Toller Airship Mooring', the only accommodation being provided by tents. It was a satellite station for patrols against U-Boats between Start Point and Portland Bill, flying SSZ ('Sea Scout Zero') airships. Opened in the spring of 1918, it closed that November. Apart from a few personnel using the branch as transport it was of little significance to the railway except on one occasion in July 1918, when SSZ 45 flying in from the coast over Bridport damaged its control gear in some tall trees. After jettisoning a 100 lb. unfused bomb the ship crashed into a hill alongside the railway near Loders, where villagers were soon on the scene salvaging the balloon fabric in preference to assisting the injured crew, one of whom had great difficulty in persuading the postmistress to let him use the phone without paying!

Vast amounts of timber were also required for the war effort and much of this was felled in the surrounding area and transported by rail. Oak trees felled in Powerstock Forest were brought to the lineside and loaded directly into wagons standing on the single running line.

The difficulty of transporting goods other than war supplies was demonstrated in the Summer of 1917, when the number of visitors to the area played havoc with the supply of meat. Local slaughterhouses and butchers were unable to supply demand and difficulties in rail transport precluded bringing in supplies from outside. The shortage of coal also had an effect in both 1918 and 1919, the Council purchasing lots of 100 and 200 tons as an emergency supply which was stacked in the station yard.

In April 1918, to ease congestion on the railways, Government legislation was passed which allowed railway companies to restrict the issue of return tickets, and also freed them of the 'Common Carrier' clause so goods could be refused if another means of transport existed.

As there was no public broadcasting system at the time, the first news of the armistice was received by wireless at Powerstock Air Station at 6.30 am on 11th November, 1918. The most bloody conflict ever fought by man was over, and there were high hopes of a new beginning. It was however a different world. The motor vehicle had been

A 'Buffalo' '1076' 0-6-0PT arriving at Bridport with a train from West Bay. Although by this time the engine had been rebuilt from its original condition as a saddle tank, the coaches are a collection of relics from a past age.   *B.L. Jackson Collection*

A '655' class 0-6-0PT No. 2703 stands at Bridport station with a Maiden Newton train. Originally built as saddle tanks, several members of this class survived on the branch until the end of World War II. No. 2703, built in February 1896, was converted to a pannier tank in June 1920 nad was finally withdrawn from service in November 1945.   *M.J. Tattershall Collection*

developed during the war years and was now a proven reliable machine. The railway had a new competitor - motor transport. The expectations of the people had also changed, bringing a different way of life and a demand for higher living standards, and industrial unrest was shortly to follow.

The West Bay section reopened to passenger traffic on 7th July, 1919, but on 26th September it had stopped again owing to a national railway strike.

During the war railwaymen had received a war bonus, but this was to be stopped from the 1st January, 1920 with the result of large reductions in pay ranging from 1s. to 16s. per week. A railway employee interviewed by the *Bridport News* said that he received £2 10s. a week, and if the bonus was taken away his wage would drop to £1 18s. a week.

The stoppage was complete, the first train to reach Bridport was on Wednesday 1st October when an auto-train ran from Weymouth manned by two old pensioners. It brought a number of people into the town and returned with others. There were allegations at the time that the railway dray horses stabled at Bridport were being neglected and that the striking railwaymen were being inhuman to them, but the truth of the matter was that before the men went on strike they had arranged for the feeding of the animals, and this was done without pay.

On Sunday 5th October, 1919 the strike was amicably settled at No. 10 Downing Street, and the railway returned to normal running. However, the tide had turned, and a quote from the 3rd October edition of the *Bridport News* demonstrates that the railway already had competition, 'The Daily papers have been brought in by motor, and taken altogether, the public inconvenience has not so far been so great as might have been expected'.

The motor bus had arrived, albeit in a crude form, and these together with the lorry, were destined to become the railways' greatest rival. In June 1919 the Beaminster Garage Company commenced a service to Bridport connecting with trains at the station. In January 1920 adverts for the Swanage & Bridport Motor Co. - operating a 12-seat motor wagonette to Dorchester and Weymouth - appeared, and the following month Butler Brothers, trading as 'Bridport & District', commenced an elaborate set of services joining the town to Axminster, Crewkerne, Martock and Dorchester and connecting with certain trains at railway stations. The *Bridport News*, in reporting the forthcoming service, said 'the fares are reasonable and 1st class vehicles alone are used'. In fact they were a Daimler CK and a Thornycroft 'J' type - both lorry chassis with Spartan bodies, the seating being reached by a ladder!

The *Bridport News* for 15th April, 1921 carried the following: 'In consequence of the miners' strike, there has been a slight curtailment of the local train service. In the event of a stoppage of trains, Messrs Butler Bros we are given to understand, are prepared to extend their motor bus service to Exeter and Bournemouth'. From 23rd May they extended their services to include Lyme Regis, Colyton, Colyford and Seaton. On the excursion side Messrs Bonfields offered char-a-banc trips to Weymouth, Salisbury, Bath, Bristol and Exmouth. The railway monopoly was over!

Meanwhile the business of running the railway continued. In January 1919 Mr Sidney Evans, formerly station master at Dulverton, was appointed to Maiden Newton, replacing W.G. Stickland who moved to Porthcawl. Bridport goods clerk G. Taylor also received promotion at this time, moving to become station master at Witham.

In August 1920 the gruesome discovery of a body near Bradpole Crossing was all the more sad because, despite extensive enquiries, the police were unable to identify the man who was well dressed in a grey suit and new boots. Ironically, the body was removed to the Boot & Shoe Inn for the inquest.

Bradpole Crossing was again in the news on 17th December when the 6.30 am from Bridport smashed through the gates. It would appear that at the time the usual practice was to leave the gates open for rail traffic during the day and open them to road vehicles as necessary. The local Council took exception to this practice, writing to the Ministry of Transport in protest. Giving themselves time to write a suitable reply a letter was received by the Council early in February 1922 stating:

> Respecting the Bradpole Level Crossing on the GWR, it would appear to be subject to the provisions of Section 47 of the Railway Clauses Consolidation Act 1845, which required that the gates should be kept constantly closed across the road on both sides of the railway, excepting during the time when horses, cattle, carts of carriages pass along the road and have to cross over the railway. The minister had no other power to issue an order requiring the gates to be kept closed during the day or at night.

At a subsequent Council meeting a local resident of 25 years standing told them he had never known the gates closed at night, but the Council were not satisfied with the reply from the Minister, and the Clerk was instructed to write forthwith to him on the subject.

During 1920 Mr Roberts, the Powerstock station master, transferred to West Bay, his position at Powerstock being taken by A.F. Wheeler, previously a member of the platform staff at Westbury. Wheeler's stay was brief, for the following year he moved to become station master at Grimstone & Frampton, A.G. Hacker from the station staff at Wishford taking his place at Powerstock. That year also saw the retirement of John Churchill from Toller. He had been there for 15 years, making him the longest serving station master there. In retirement he took up the position of assistant overseer and rate collector in the village, his position as station master being filled by Alfred James Pike.

In January 1921 Thomas Tuck retired from the position of station master at East Street, having been appointed in March 1884 when the extension opened. He commenced his railway service at Bristol in 1872, later becoming a ticket collector at Bath and then signalman at Wootton Bassett station signal box. In 1883 he was appointed station master at Stanton on the Highworth branch. He could claim that during his 36 years at East Street not a single person was injured on the crossing. He was succeeded by Frederick Gillingham, formerly station master at Monkton Coombe, previous to which he had been ticket collector and foreman at Bath.

At the end of December 1922 Frederick Weeks retired from the position of station master at Bridport. A local man educated at the Bridport General school, he commenced his career in 1877 at Bridport station, moving on promotion to Frome where he became the chief goods clerk. In 1898 he moved to Shepton Mallet, where he later became station master. It was at his own request that, when the vacancy arose, he moved to Bridport to take up the position of station master in his home town.

In appreciation of his services the Bridport Manufacturer Association presented him with a handsome silver rose bowl, and from the station staff a massive marble clock. A man well respected by all, he served the railway well throughout those difficult days of the Great War, during which the station managed to win the award for the best station garden in the Westbury area during 1915.

At a farewell dinner attended by 70 guests at the Greyhound Hotel the following verse was displayed for all to see.

For weeks and weeks and weeks and weeks
Weeks gave the 'Right Away'
And now we give him greeting
To cheer him on his way.

Amongst the railway officials present were H.R. Griffiths OBE (divisional supt Bristol), Mr R.G. Pole (assistant divisional supt Bristol), his brother C.W. Weeks, of Bristol, the station masters from stations on the Bridport branch and his son Frederick Weeks Jnr, station master at Camerton.

The replacement station master at Bridport was Charles Widdows formerly the Radstock station master. A native of Churchill, Oxfordshire, he joined the GWR at Chipping Norton, subsequent moves taking him to Watchet and then back to Chipping Norton as station master in 1906, thence to Kingham and Radstock.

During 1923 Mr Roberts, the West Bay station master, moved to Winscombe, his position being taken by Mr H. Toller who was nearing retirement.

The general unrest in industry during the previous years reached a head with the General Strike of 1926, railwaymen joining the strike at midnight on Monday 3rd May. On the Tuesday morning the only staff on duty at Bridport station were Mr Widdows the station master, the clerical staff, and one lone member of the platform staff. There was, however, activity in the station yard, where tradesmen and others were allowed to unload their goods which consisting mainly of coal, timber and oil cake. The local coal merchants stated that they had sufficient stocks of coal in hand to last for over a month and probably six weeks, and householders would be allowed one cwt. per week. Four trucks of general merchandise for the branch were at Maiden Newton, the contents being collected by the GWR motor lorry and taken to Bridport where they were distributed around the town by the driver of the usual horse-drawn vehicle. At Maiden Newton only the station master and a member of the clerical staff were on duty, assisted by Mr A.J. Pike the station master from Toller.

From Thursday 6th several trains commenced to run along the main line, and on Monday 10th May it was reported that one engine was available at Bridport and one at Weymouth which was working a railmotor service to Dorchester. By Wednesday 12th one of the three daily trains on the branch was extended to Dorchester.

There was not the total isolation caused by previous strikes, as the buses of the National Omnibus & Transport Company were running normally, and the other operators in the town soon took advantage of the situation. A notice outside Messrs Bonfields Garage in West Street advertised buses running to Dorchester daily at 10 am and 4 pm. Mr B. Samways, the driver of Messrs Kitcham & Dunham's 'Greybird' coach, had travelled to London to collect a party who could not return owing to the strike, and was stopped by strikers in Whitechapel and only allowed to proceed when they were satisfied with his explanations!

Although the strike ended at midnight on the 12th it was to be a slow process to get the railways back to full operation. At first there was a service of three trains daily, but from the 17th this was raised to four with three running through to West Bay, although the last arrival at Bridport from Maiden Newton was at 5.11 pm. The railway companies decided that they would take men back at places where they needed them, and would also pick *who* they wanted, a matter that caused much ill feeling. Several days after the end of the strike none of the 34 strikers had returned to work, declining to do so unless they could all resume together. Eventually services returned to normal, although the damage had been done both to staff relationships and the future of the railways.

The months following the strike saw many staff changes throughout the railway. Locally, A.J. Pike moved from Toller to become station master at Easton on the Portland branch, his successor being A.J. Mount-Stevens, a relief signalman from Trowbridge.

Towards the end of the year station master Widdows took his retirement at Bridport, his replacement being George Barnby, formerly station master at Castle Cary. He had joined the GWR as a junior clerk at Hayes in June 1894 and held other clerical appointments at

The station bus operated by Mr Trump of the Greyhound Hotel. Note the overall advertising for the GWR! This the first motor bus owned by Trump, was typical of many lightweight buses of the period, consisting of the famous Ford Model 'T' chassis, and a body that appears far superior to many of the period. It was indeed a sign of the times, while the train was travelling to Maiden Newton, a bus of this type could reach Dorchester!

By permission of the Bridport Museum Service

National Omnibus & Transport AEC 'YC' type, Y 8983, No. 2085 stands at West Bay, having travelled from Yeovil via Crewkerne, Beaminster and Bridport. This 1920 vehicle, with its 31-seat Dodson body, passed to the ownership of Eastern National in December 1929.

B.L. Jackson Collection

Kensington (Addison Road) and Henley-on-Thames. Appointed station master at Wooburn Green in January 1905, he moved to Savernake in March 1914, and then to Codford in April 1919, before going to Castle Cary. Early in 1927 A.G. Hacker, station master Powerstock, was promoted to Ogborne on the former MSWJR, his replacement being A.S. Chapman.

By this time the local bus services were well established, although an early casualty was the financial failure of Butler Bros in November 1922, their services being acquired by Kitcher & Dunham in March 1923 and operated under the fleetname of 'Greybird'. The Axminster service was diverted to include Lyme Regis, and more importantly they were agents for the LSWR, traffic being routed via Lyme Regis and Axminster stations! Greybird had also commenced a service to Powerstock and Nettlecombe by 1927.

The National Omnibus & Transport Company first appeared during the Summer of 1921 when they commenced a Yeovil-Crewkerne-Beaminster-Bridport-West Bay service. On 8th July, 1922 two major routes were commenced, West Bay-Bridport-Charmouth-Lyme Regis-Axminster-Seaton, and Bridport-Winterbourne Abbas-Dorchester-Weymouth. A garage was established in South Street and other local services soon commenced. In 1928 a Weymouth-Exeter-Torquay limited stop service was introduced.

Although only a small town, Bridport had a selection of small independent operators. Although National had bought out 'Greybird' for £4,750 in December 1927, there remained several other independents. The original horse and carriage service operated between the Greyhound Hotel and the railway station by Thomas Tucker had, by 1911, been taken over by Mr W. Trump, and later the horse and carriage was replaced by a motor bus and other services were developed - including a route to West Bay. Edwards & Hann, trading as 'Beaminster Bus', operated a service between Beaminster-Bridport and West Bay, and added to this, National purchased a Guy Toastrack (open-sided bus) to operate between Bridport and West Bay during the Summer months.

The bus had taken away the monopoly of the railway, and direct access to places both east and west of Bridport was now possible whereas before it involved a circuitous journey by train. Furthermore, the railway now had strong competition at West Bay, for at Bridport both the stations were virtually out of town on the east side, whereas the buses commenced from the centre and picked up and set down *en route*.

Economies started to be made on the railway. In April 1927 Mr Frederick Gillingham retired from the position of station master at East Street. Although he had been at East Street for only six years he was a popular figure, and received a 365-day clock, a silver cigarette case, and a box of cigars before retiring to Bath. His position at East Street was not filled.

In November 1928 Mr W.R. Williams the West Bay station master moved to Wookey (Somerset) to replace Mr F.B. Weeks, (son of former Bridport station master Frederick Weeks) who was moving to Chipping Sodbury. Williams was the last station master at West Bay, his place being taken by Ernest Burgoyne, who acted as leading porter and general factotum.

During August 1929 West Bay station was broken into, and a trunk belonging to a visitor which had been sent in advance was broken open. The burglar merely substituted his much worn pair of socks for a clean pair! Later apprehended by the police, a 24-year-old farm labourer was sentenced at Bristol Quarter Sessions to 15 months with hard labour for burglaries at railway stations including Chudleigh, Plymouth, Evershot, Tavistock, Cullompton, Upwey, Portesham, and Bridport.

West Bay had still not developed, and the promised 'new town' had not materialised 46 years after the opening of the railway. All there was to show for the grandiose plans was some spasmodic building of a few houses here and there, and many huts of various descriptions serving the holiday trade.

The early competition on the West Bay extension, and the branch in general. National Omnibus & Transport No. 2173 stands at West Bay after operating a Weymouth-Dorchester-Bridport-West Bay service. As well as providing a convenient service between Bridport and West Bay, it also linked Bridport directly with the towns of Dorchester and Weymouth. The vehicle is NO 9540, fleet No. 2173, an AEC 'Y' type of 1923, had a 30-seat body.   *B.L. Jackson Collection*

An early view outside Bridport bus garage, National Omnibus & Transport No. 2104 stands with staff for the photographer. The bus AD 8461, was an AEC 'YC' type, fitted with a Dodson 26-seat body. They were built in 1918 and supplied to London General, who ran them as 'Lorry Buses' to overcome a severe shortage of vehicles, in which form they carried open lorry bodies with primitive seating and steps at the rear. Originally registered as LU 8117, she was sold to NOTC, rebodied and re-registered the following year.   *B.L. Jackson Collection*

Rumours abounded about the future of the West Bay Extension, prompting the *Bridport News* for 31st May 1929 to say: 'The *Bridport News* is assured from a reliable source, that there is no foundation in the rumour circulated in the town, that a proposal is being considered for the discontinuance of the rail service from Bridport to the Harbour'. Despite this seemingly positive statement, the following poster appeared in the town in September 1930:

> On and from Monday 22nd September the passenger train service between Bridport and Bridport (West Bay) will be withdrawn and the following stations closed for passenger traffic: Bridport (East Street) and Bridport (West Bay). Merchandise and minerals will continue to be dealt with at Bridport (West Bay).

There is little doubt that the close association between the bus and railway companies had helped bring about the closure of the West Bay section. Whereas the railway had failed to pay its way, the railway company could now take its share of the profits from its new investment without the problems of operating it.

Indeed no objections were raised in 1931 when a local service between North Allington and West Bay was proposed, and more importantly a West Bay-Bridport-Lyme Regis-Seaton-Sidmouth service, the latter commencing the following June, later becoming joint with Devon General. At the same time a service between Bridport and Weymouth along the coast via West Bay and Abbotsbury commenced, but like the Sidmouth service, it was Summer only.

In April 1933 a Chard-Bridport-West Bay service commenced, and in the same month the services of Edwards & Hann were acquired by Southern National, thus eliminating one competitor from the area. West Bay was nurtured by Southern National, and in 1929 a Guy open-sided 'Toastrack' had been purchased for Summer use between Bridport and West Bay. In January 1935 a 1923 Leyland 'G7' fitted with a 1929 55-seat body was purchased from Southdown for £75, and CD 7713 (Fleet No. 3506) commenced to operate the service until sold during 1939.

Time takes its toll, unfortunately for some before they reach the retirement they deserved, and Frank Dunsford passed away on 3rd March, 1926, aged 57, having suffered indifferent health for some time. Following his move from Maiden Newton to Radstock, he had been appointed station master at Yeovil Pen Mill early in 1917. Born at Frome Vauchurch, Maiden Newton, he was laid to rest in the family grave at Maiden Newton at a service attended by many railway colleagues and friends who had come to pay their last respects to one of the most popular station masters in the area.

In December 1932 Frederick Weeks passed away, aged 70. Apart from his railway work he had served the people of Bridport well, being elected to the Town Council in 1912 and becoming Mayor in October 1924. The following year he was re-elected by a unanimous decision, and became an Alderman in 1928. He was also Chief Magistrate for the town, and had many interests within the Borough, and for a number of years represented Bridport on the Dorset County Council.

Perhaps unusually for a station master, Weeks was also well known in the brewing industry, becoming a Director of the Lamb Brewery, Frome, in 1916. In 1921 he occupied the position of Managing Director, and in April 1930 was elected Chairman of Directors. Although of small stature he was a very energetic man, held in high regard by all. Following a civic funeral, he was carried to his grave by six railwaymen from Bridport station.

Again tragically, having reached the high point of his career, Sidney Evans, aged 57, passed away on 12th November, 1933 after a long illness. Following his move from Maiden Newton to Devizes he was appointed station master at Westbury in August 1932.

Maiden Newton looking towards Dorchester. To the left is the new signal box of 1921. A goods train, headed by an 'Aberdare' 2-6-0 stands in the down refuge siding, whilst an up auto-train hauled by a '517' class 0-4-2 tank stands at the inner home signal.   *National Railway Museum*

Toller station, photographed in the early 1920s. Standing on the left is station master A.J. Pike.
M.J.Tattershall Collection

MAIDEN NEWTON AND BRIDPORT.

		Week Days.													Sundays.	
		a.m.	a.m.	a.m.		p.m.	p.m.	p.m.			p.m.	p.m.	p.m.		p.m.		
Maiden Newton	dep	8 10	9 40	11 15		12 20	1 35	3 42	...		4 50	8 0	9 45		10 32	...	1 50
Toller	,,	8 17	9 46	11 21		12 26	1 41	3 48	...		4 56	8 6	9 51		10 38		1 57	M
Powerstock	,,	8 26	9 54	11 29		12 34	1 49	3 56	...		5 4	8 14	9 59		10 46		2 6
Bridport { arr.		8 37	10 1	11 36		12 41	1 56	4 3	...		5 11	8 21	10 6		10 53		2 13
{ dep.		W	10 8	11 42		12 55	2 1	4 8			5 20						...
Bridport { East Street			10 11	11 45		12 58	2 4	4 11			5 23				T		...
{ West Bay	arr.		10 14	11 49		1 2	2 8	4 15			5 27						...

		Week Days.											Sundays.	
													M	
		a.m.		a.m.	a.m.	p.m		p.m.	p.m.	p.m.	p.m.	p.m.	p.m	
Bridport { West Bay	dep.	...		10 20		12 15	...	1 13	2 53	...	4 55	6 55		...
{ East Street	,,	...		10 25		12 20		1 18	2 58	...	5 0	7 0		...
Bridport { arr.		...		10 27		12 22		1 20	3 0	...	5 2	7 2	T	...
dep		8 50		10 30	11 40	12 52			3 5	4 10		7 10	9 0	2 50
Powerstock	,,	8 59		10 39	11 49	1 1			3 14	4 19		7 19	9 9	2 59
Toller	,,	9 10		10 48	11 58	1 10			3 23	4 28		7 28	9 18	3 8
Maiden Newton	,,	9 15		10 53	12 3	1 15			3 28	4 33		7 33	9 23	3 13

M—Rail Motor Car, one class only.   T—Thursdays only.

Timetable July–September 1927.

Timetable published in the *Bridport News* on 1st August, 1930.

LOCAL RAILWAY TIME TABLES.

July 7th to September 21st, 1930, inclusive.

MAIDEN NEWTON AND BRIDPORT.

		WEEK DAYS.													Sundays.	
		A.M.	A.M.	A.M.	A.M.	P.M	P.M.	P.M.	P.M.	P.M.	P.M.	P.M.	P.M.	P.M.	P.M.	P.M.
MAIDEN NEWTON	dep.	8 10	9 40	11 15	12 20	1 36	3 42	4 50	8 18	9 45	11 38	12 43	1 50	9 38		
Toller	,,	8 17	9 46	11 21	12 26	1 41	3 48	4 56	8 24	9 51	11 44		1 57	9 44		
Powerstock	,,	8 26	9 54	11 29	12 34	1 49	3 56	5 4	8 32	9 59	11 52		2 6	9 52		
Bridport { arr.		8 37	10 1	11 36	12 41	1 56	4 3	5 11	8 39	10 6	11 59	1 13	2 13	9 59		
{ dep.			10 8	11 42	12 55	2 1	4 8	5 20								
BRIDPORT { East Street	,,		10 11	11 45	12 55	2 4	4 11	5 23				T		M		
{ West Bay	arr		10 14	11 49	1 2	2 8	4 15	5 27								

M—Rail Motor Car, one class only.   T—Thursdays and Saturdays only.

BRIDPORT AND MAIDEN NEWTON.

		dep	A.M.	A.M.	A.M.	A.M.	P.M.	P.M	P.M.	P.M.	P.M.	P.M.	P.M.	P.M.	A.M.	P.M.	P.M.
BRIDPORT { West Bay	,,				10 20		12 15		1 13	2 53		4 55	6 0				
{ East St.	,,	B			10 25		12 20		1 18	2 58		5 0	6 5				
BRIDPORT { arr.					10 27		12 22		1 20	3 0		5 2	6 7				
{ dep.		6 30	8 50	10 30	11 40	—	12 52		3 5	4 10		7 10	9 10	10 15	2 50	8 0
Powerstock	,,	6 40	8 59	10 39	11 49		1 1		3 14	4 19		7 19	9 19	10 24	2 59	
Toller	,,	6 35	9 10	10 48	11 58		1 10		3 23	4 28		7 28	9 28	10 3	3 8	
MAIDEN NEWTON	arr.	7 5	9 15	10 53	12 3		1 15		3 28	4 33		7 32	9 33	10 38	3 13	8 20

B—Mondays only.   M—Rail Motor Car, one class only.   T—Thursdays and Saturdays only.

BRIDPORT TO DORCHESTER AND WEYMOUTH.

	N.S.									T		
		a. m.	a. m.	a.m.	p.m.	p.m.	p.m	p.m.	p.m.	A.M.	P.M.	P.M.
BRIDPORT	dept.	8 50	10 30	11 40	12 52	3 5	4 10	7 10	9 10	10 15	2 59	8 0
DORCHESTER	arr.	9 44	11 20	12 42	1 43	4 4	4 58	8 0	9 49	10 50	4 0	8 33
WEYMOUTH	arr.	10 0	11 32	1 2	1 55	4 15	5 10	8 15	10 0	11 3	4 20	8 45

N.S.—Saturdays excepted.   T—Thursdays and Saturdays only

WEYMOUTH TO DORCHESTER AND BRIDPORT.

		a.m.	a.m.	a.m.	a.m	p.m	p.m.	p.m.	p.m	p.m.	p.m	p.m	p.m	p.m
WEYMOUTH	dept	7 18	8 55	10 30	11 45	12 50	3 5	4 15	7 45	9 0	11 0	12 15	1 0	9 10
DORCHESTER	dept.	7 31	9 11	10 47	12 0	1 14	3 21	4 32	8 0	9 15	11 20	12 30	1 23	9 24
BRIDPORT	arr.	8 37	10 1	11 36	12 41	1 56	4 3	5 11	8 39	10 6	11 59	1 3	2 13	9 59

T—Thursdays and Saturdays only.

BRIDPORT TO PADDINGTON.

M.O.

		a.m.	a.m.	a.m.	a.m	p.m.	p.m.	p.m.	p.m.	p. m.
BRIDPORT	Depart	6 30	8 50	10 30	11 40	12 52	3 5	4 10	7 10	2 50
LONDON (Paddington)	Arrive	10 50	12 55	3 25	3 45	5 30	7 0	8 10	11 20	7 5

M.O.—Mondays only.

PADDINGTON TO BRIDPORT.

		a.m.	a.m.	p.m.	p.m	p.m.	
LONDON (Paddington)	Depart	5 30	10 30	1 30	3 30	5 0	...
BRIDPORT	Arrive	11 36	1 56	5 11	8 33	10 6	...

These tables are believed to be correct and care is taken to give accurate times, but we are not responsible for any error.

Bridport station viewed from the air during August 1928. The line to West Bay leads away towards the top left, and St Andrews Road which leads towards the town is in the centre. The main town is just out of the picture (to the top right) giving an idea of how far out of town the station was! Since this photograph was taken urban development has obliterated the surrounding fields.

Aerofilms

Frederick Gillingham, the former East Street station master, died aged 67 in retirement at Bath on 15th May, 1934, and the December saw the passing of the last of the old Bridport Railway Company officials when Charles George Nantes died, aged 85. A solicitor by profession (the business still surviving in the town), his many interests included serving as a Town Councillor from 1880 until 1887 when he became Alderman, and Mayor in 1892. Between 1897 and 1919 he served as Town Clerk, and he was active until a few days before his death which closed a chapter in the history of the local railway.

On 13th May, 1935 following a protracted illness, the death occurred at his residence 'Holmlea', Bothenhampton, of Mr Thomas Tuck, who for many years had been in charge of East Street station. He was a staunch supporter of the Baptist Church, and for over 30 years was Superintendent of the Sunday School.

In March 1936 Charles Thomas Widdows, the former Bridport station master, passed away aged 69, having completed 48 years service with the GWR when he retired. His father spent a similar period in the service of the GWR, and his two sons Messrs H.G. and D.R. Widdows were the third generation in the company's employment at Pershore and Bristol respectively. Following his retirement he became a rate collector to the Bridport Local Authority, his district including Litton Cheney, Puncknowle, Swyre, Bradpole, and Chilcombe. He continued in these duties until September 1935. He was also Clerk to the Puncknowle Parish Council. An avid Methodist, he was a lay preacher attached to the Bridport Church.

Finally Mr W.F. Vaughan the last Bridport station master from the days of the Bridport Railway Company, passed away at Yeovil in March 1939, aged 84.

At the same time those still in the service of the railway were making steady progress. At the beginning of 1929 A.S. Chapman was promoted from station master Powerstock to Weyhill, his place being taken by H.E. Cooper of the Bridport platform staff. In 1931 A.J. Mount-Stevens moved to Henbury, near Bristol, his position at Toller being filled by Walter Samways - also from the Bridport platform staff.

John Ralph was presented with a cheque and notecase from the staff and villagers of Maiden Newton by Lord Wynford, prior to his departure to take up the appointment of station master at Yatton in April 1933. His replacement was Mr Walter Edward Ernest Pidding from the Westbury clerical staff. Mr Pidding did not stay long at Maiden Newton, moving to Castle Cary early in 1935, upon which Mr F. Powell from the divisional manager's office Bristol became the Maiden Newton station master.

Again it was 'all change' at Powerstock and Toller. In 1935 H.E. Cooper moved from Powerstock to become station master at Henbury, B.J. Hunt from the Castle Cary platform staff taking over as station master at Powerstock, and early the following year W. Samways went from Toller to Grimstone & Frampton, his place being taken by A.F. Holmes of the Bristol Joint staff. However, had he hardly unpacked his case before he was moved on to station master, Marston Magna, Mr E.W. Marquiss of the Chippenham platform staff becoming station master at Toller.

During the early 1930s the idea of camping coaches had been introduced by the various railway companies, the GWR entering the scene during 1934. Most companies had a policy of placing more than one coach at many locations, but the GWR only ever had one at any given site to give the occupants a degree of privacy. The first camping coach arrived on the Bridport branch for the summer of 1935, and was placed at West Bay. This was an eight-berth vehicle converted from Dean clerestory bogie stock. A second coach was added during 1936, this being a six-berth vehicle formerly a 31 ft 6 in. six-wheel clerestory coach, and this was located at Powerstock.

These coaches were fully equipped with bedclothes, linen, cutlery and crockery. In 1936 the cost of renting a 6-berth coach was £3 a week and a minimum of four rail tickets

Maiden Newton main station buildings were situated on the up side platform, and this view taken in September 1931 clearly shows the knapped flint structure. The signal box of 1885 had stood where the four-wheel barrows are parked on the extreme right. Period adverts, posters, and timetables adorn the up side wall, but for this official photograph the station has been cleared of all signs of life!   *National Railway Museum*

Maiden Newton station looking towards Dorchester from the north end of the layout. An official photograph taken in September 1931, it is full of interesting detail. To the right is the covered train shed of the Bridport branch platform. Owing to the curvature of the track and the footbridge causing sighting problems, the main up starting signal is situated to the left of the picture whilst the down main to branch signal is situated further back on the platform. Clearly shown here is the lack of a connection off the up main line. The ground signal ('dummy') in the foreground is for shunting 'up main to down main'. The branch bay starting signal is to the extreme right.   *National Railway Museum*

A pre-war view of Toller station. On the platform stand the old type 17 gallon milk churns awaiting transport to the dairy at Maiden Newton. Dominating the background is St Peter's church parts of which date back to Norman times. Although the station was simply named 'Toller' the correct name for the village was Toller Porcorum, which means 'The Toller of the Pigs!'   *Lens of Sutton*

A pre-war view of a down branch train standing at Toller station, the train consisting of four-wheeled stock and an elderly pannier tank rebuilt from a saddle tank.   *Lens of Sutton*

Maiden Newton station looking towards Yeovil on 21st August, 1933. Passengers in the dress
of the period wait on the platform as the branch train proceeds to the gravity siding for the run-
round operation.   *Mowat Collection*

Bridport station, looking towards Maiden Newton in 1933. A variety of rolling stock - including
private owner coal wagons - stands in the yard. Nearest to the platform is a 6-wheel Siphon and
an old 4-wheel coach which add to the interest of this historic photograph.
                                                                          National Railway Museum

purchased to travel to the site. An eight-berth coach cost £4 per week with six rail tickets required. It was generally considered that a camp coach holiday cost about half of what would be spent on a conventional holiday and they became very popular. From 1937 an eight-berth coach replaced the original one at Powerstock, a situation that remained until the war caused all the camping coaches to be withdrawn.

The year 1936 was to be a year of minor disasters on the branch. It actually commenced on 27th December, 1935, when a small landslip partially blocked the line between Powerstock and Toller. Then during the year a fault developed on one of the bogies of the branch train whilst it was travelling between Maiden Newton and Bridport, the broken part striking the underside of the coach causing a loud hammering noise. In the compartment above there were two country women, one saying to the other: 'There's something the matter, we better pull the emergency chain', to which the other replied, 'Oh no, don't pull the chain, we'll be fined £5. I can stand it, can't you?'

Upon approaching Bridport station the wheel of the bogie would not go through the pointwork, the coach becoming derailed and damaging the platform edge. Many chairs between Powerstock and Bridport had been broken, 10 tons of new chairs having to be used to replace them.

On 23rd November a van delivering and collecting films from cinemas overturned when it collided with the crossing gates at East Street. To make the incident more incredible the gates were *not* closed across the road at the time!

Mr George Barnby retired from the position of station master at Bridport in May 1938 after 44 years service with the GWR, to spend many years retirement in the town. His replacement was Mr Frederick Joachim Colls from the goods train control office Westbury, who had commenced his railway career at Teignmouth in 1904 and spent his early years in the Exeter Division.

For many years there had been water shortages at Maiden Newton, particularly during the summer months when the well which supplied the water tank ran dry. This necessitated the transportation of water in water tanks (usually old locomotive tenders) from Yeovil. This problem was overcome during 1938 when a water column was erected on the platform at Bridport and new pumping arrangements provided, the work costing £435 including the repositioning of the up starting signal. This relieved the branch engine of having to take water at Maiden Newton on every trip.

In the February of 1938 Bridport Town Council discussed the railway facilities in the town, the Mayor (Councillor A.G. Clapp) who presented the report, said that the General Purposes Committee recommended the Town Clerk be instructed to forward a memorandum to the GWR calling attention to the need for alteration and improvement of the company's services and premises in connection with the Bridport branch, in particular under the following headings.

1. The provision of a crossing loop between Bridport and Maiden Newton to overcome delays which often occur, especially during the Summer months.
2. The rebuilding of Bridport station and the provision of increased siding accommodation for goods traffic there.
3. The provision of one or more through trains daily between Bridport and Weymouth during the summer season.
4. The re-opening of West Bay station to passenger traffic and that a committee be appointed to discuss these proposals with a representative of the company with power to co-opt representatives of the trades of the borough.

Discussing the matter, Alderman Travers said,

'55XX' 2-6-2 tank No. 5521 draws the weed killing train into West Bay during 1938. The train consisted of surplus locomotive tenders, the spray control being mounted on the front of the leading tender. This engine (No. 5521) is fitted with token collection apparatus for use on the Minehead branch, the engine being allocated to Taunton. Having escaped the breaker's yard No. 5521 is at present undergoing restoration at the Dean Forest Railway.   *The late H.T. Hobbs*

The weed killing train stands at West Bay during 1938 hauled by '55XX' 2-6-2 tank No. 5521. The water tanks consist of redundant locomotive tenders. Note the Engineer's Department enclosed brake van No. 403353.   *The late H.T. Hobbs*

It is unfortunate we are just at the end of a branch line, and as a result we do not share the opportunities enjoyed by towns where the main line traffic passes through. There are frequent excursions during the summer months, and by present arrangements the passengers find themselves dumped 2½ miles from West Bay which is the object of the excursion. The same applies to the people who are attracted by the Municipal Camp to spend holidays at West Bay. They are put to considerable expense to reach their destination from the town.

The GWR replied that

... the high cost of re-conditioning the West Bay section and the additional cost of staff and operation could not be justified, and the working of through coaches from Paddington to Bridport could not be arranged. However, commencing on 4th July the 4.25 pm Bristol-Weymouth will call at Maiden Newton where a connection will be made to Bridport, allowing passengers leaving Paddington at 3.30 pm to reach Bridport at 6.48 pm, also allowing passengers leaving Bridport at 8.20 am to spend 5½ hours in Bristol and arrive back at Bridport at 6.48 pm the same day.

The end result was that the GWR had to provide nothing extra, just make a tactical timetable adjustment that looked impressive.

In the same year an express motor coach service between Bristol and Bridport via Wells and Yeovil commenced, but four years earlier Bridport was included on the Royal Blue coach route to the West of England, both these services offering the public useful alternative forms of transport. Southern National again consolidated their ground in 1938 when they took over the 'Bluebird Service' between Bridport and Dorchester operated by C.F.S. Gillham. However, within a year all thoughts of competition were cast aside as many bus services were withdrawn, along with rail services, as both faced a difficult future.

Throughout the year and on into 1939 the international situation had been deteriorating. Although many were taking their holidays as usual and timetables were published for the coming winter, by the end of August the railways and many other organisations were well prepared for the inevitable.

As with many towns in the West Country, Bridport became home to evacuees. On Saturday 2nd September, 1939 two trains arrived at Bridport from Paddington containing children and mothers with babes in arms. Many of the occupants of the second train were conveyed by bus to Lyme Regis. As war was declared on Sunday 3rd two more trains were already on their way, arriving during the afternoon, to bring 850 children and adults to the town.

The Summer timetable prior to the outbreak of war had provided a daily service of 11 trains each way, and six on Sunday; reductions brought about by the National Emergency had an impact on many routes, and the Sunday service on the branch was reduced to one train from Maiden Newton at 2.14 pm returning from Bridport at 3.10 pm, this being an auto-train worked through from Weymouth. From 10th December, 1939 an additional train at 6.50 pm from Maiden Newton, returning from Bridport at 7.15 pm, provided connections on the up main line which gave an arrival at Bristol at 10.10 pm, a boon to servicemen on weekend leave.

The 5th Battalion of the West Kent Regiment moved into the Bridport area to carry out training exercises on 22nd October, a visit being made by His Majesty King George VI on 7th February, 1940. The Royal tour of the area was made from Yeovil by motor car, but the Royal Train passed through Maiden Newton on its way to and from Weymouth for servicing.

During the morning of 5th April, 1940 part of the morning train service was suspended on the branch when special trains took the 5th Battalion to Southampton *en route* to France.

West Bay station during 1938. To the right is camping coach No. 9951. The station building is in use as a dwelling house, and part of the platform is fenced off. Only coal and shingle traffic remained on this section of the line.   *The late H.T. Hobbs*

A pre-1939 view of West Bay viewed from the golf course. In the bottom right stands the camping coach. Behind it stands the resort of West Bay after 50 years of slow development.

K. Bakes Collection

On Sunday April 14th a special conveying relatives of evacuees on a visit arrived at Bridport at 12.40 pm, returning to London at 6.25 pm.

By 1939 the aeroplane had become a sophisticated weapon of war, and attack by air was a major hazard. Following the fall of France invasion was also a real threat. Parts of West Bay were evacuated and the area sealed off, those requiring access being issued with passes. Pill boxes, 'dragons teeth' (tank traps), and other forms of defence were constructed near the railway line. At Maiden Newton a gun emplacement was constructed in a disused quarry alongside the branch in Chilfrome Lane, lined up to fire towards West Bay and Chesil Beach, both possible beach assault landing sites.

In October 1940 the Royal Artillery commenced work on installing rail mounted 12-inch Howitzer guns capable of firing a 750 lb. high explosive shell almost 8 miles. Two sidings connecting onto the branch were constructed for their use; one at Bradpole in an orchard on the up side of Bradpole Crossing and the other further up the line at 7 m. 70 ch., just south of the underbridge to Loders. Constructed by the Railway Construction Company of the Royal Engineers, they had to withstand the weight of the gun and its recoil when fired, anchorage points also being installed to restrain the gun from movement. To conceal the sites from reconnaissance aircraft elaborate camouflage was provided from the points where the siding left the main line, this being in place from the moment construction began.

Work was completed on 4th November and the 15th Super Heavy Battery had been formed to man the positions. Some details had been worked out; for instance, as it was not possible to hold the entire gun train on the sidings only essential wagons would be on site, the remainder of the train being held in a siding at Maiden Newton. In the event of an invasion a 'Fall Back' position was provided at Langport West.

There are eye witness reports of at least one gun being on site, and it is known that training was started and targets 'zeroed in'. However, the defence situation changed and in February 1941 the battery moved to Kent, the sidings remaining for the duration of the war. As for the gun trains themselves; these were self-contained units, usually hauled by a GWR 0-6-0 'Dean Goods' which had been requisitioned by the War Department.

At West Bay defences had been built up, a scrap trawler lay in harbour ready for use as a block ship in the event of invasion, and various Artillery units protected the coastline. From 10th May, 1941 entry to the beach area was prohibited, and on 15th May troops of 1st Batt. The South Lancs. Regiment began unloading scaffolding poles from railway wagons at West Bay to be used as beach obstructions.

West Bay was to feature in the trials for the ill-fated Dieppe Raid. The first exercise codenamed 'Yukon 1', took place on the 12th June, 1942, part of the plan being that 6th Brigade would set up its HQ at West Bay railway station. Although most of the inhabitants of the area had been moved out for the duration of the exercise, the authorities had overlooked the fact that engine driver Peter Miller was living in the station buildings at West Bay, and he recalls one morning getting up, going into the kitchen, and finding a Canadian Brigadier working a wireless set!

A second exercise, 'Yukon 2', later took place, in which the Royal Canadian Engineers went through the motions of destroying the docking and other facilities at West Bay, including locomotives, rolling stock, and railway infrastructure. However, the only official railway involvement in these exercises was the presence of requisitioned Belgium Railway vessels as troop transports and the requisitioned LNER Clyde paddle steamer *Talisman* (HMS *Aristocrat*) which carried 250 Mont Royal Fusiliers.

Whilst exercises had occupied the time at West Bay, the real war was affecting Bridport. At 11.35 pm on 15th April, 1941 two high explosive bombs and 120

BRIDPORT BRANCH.

Single Line, worked by Electric Train Staff between Maiden Newton and Bridport, and by a Train Staff, and one engine in steam at a time, or by Train Staff and two or more engines in steam coupled together between Bridport and West Bay. Crossing Place: Bridport.

Distances Mile Post. M.	C.	DOWN TRAINS. STATIONS.		WEEK DAYS. B Mixed.	B Pass.	B Pass.	B Pass.	B Pass.	B Pass.	B Pass.	B Pass.	B Pass.	B Pass.	SUNDAYS B Weymouth Auto.	B Weymouth Auto.
				a.m.	a.m.	a.m	p.m.	p.m.	p.m.	p.m.	p.m.	p.m.	p.m.	p.m.	p.m.
—	—	**MAID'N N'WT'N**	dep.	**8 5**	**9 40**	**11 15**	**12 35**	**1 50**	**3 10**	**4 50**	**6 0**	**8 5**	**10 25**	**2 30**	**6 52**
2	44	**Toller**	arr.	8 10	9 45	11 20	12 40	1 55	3 15	4 55	6 5	8 10	10 30	2 35	—
			dep.	8 12	9 43½	1120½	1240½	1 55½	3 15½	4 55½	6 5½	8 10½	1030½	2 35½	6 57
3	60	**Stop Board**	,,	P	—	—	—	—	—	—	—	—	—	—	—
5	62	**Powerstock**	arr.	8 18	9 51½	11 26	1246½	2 1½	3 21½	5 1½	6 11½	8 16½	1036½	2 41½	—
			dep.	8 21	9 52	1126½	12 47	2 2	3 22	5 2	6 12	8 17	10 37	2 42	7 4
5	65½	**Stop Board**	,,	P	—	—	—	—	—	—	—	—	—	—	—
9	21	**BRIDPORT**	arr.	**8 32**	**9 58½**	**11 33**	**1253½**	**2 8½**	**3 28½**	**5 8½**	**6 18½**	**8 23½**	**1043½**	**2 48½**	**7 11**
			dep.												
9	54	**East Street**	,,	..	..	..	..	..	..	..	..	..	..	..	..
11	18	**WEST BAY**	arr.	....	....	....	....	....	....	....	....	....	....	....	....

UP TRAINS. STATIONS.		Ruling Gradient 1 in	B Pass.	B Pass.	B Pass.	B Pass.	B Pass.	B Pass.	B Pass.	B Pass.	B Pass.	B Mixed. Th SO	B Weymouth Auto.	B Weymouth Auto.
			a.m.	a.m.	a.m.	a.m.	p.m.	p.m.	p.m.	p.m.	p.m.	p.m.	p.m.	p.m.
WEST BAY	dep.	80 R.	....	....	....	....	....	....	....	....	....	....	....	....
East Street	,,	80 F.	..	..	..	..	..	..	..	..	..	..	..	..
BRIDPORT	arr.	153 R.	....	....	....	....	....	....	....	....	....	....	....	....
	dep.		**6 35**	**8 50**	**10 25**	**11 45**	**1 8**	**2 40**	**3 55**	**5 25**	**6 25**	*8 55*	**3 10**	**7 16**
Powerstock	arr.	52 R.	6 41½	8 56½	1031½	1151½	1 14½	2 46½	4 1½	5 31½	6 31½	*9 5½*	3 16½	7 22½
	dep.		6 42	8 57	10 32	11 52	1 15	2 47	4 2	5 32	6 32	*9 6*	3 17	7 23
Toller	arr.	37 R.	6 48½	9 3½	1038½	1158½	1 21½	2 53½	4 8½	5 38½	6 38½	*9 16½*	3 23½	7 29½
	dep.		6 49	9 4	10 39	11 59	1 22	2 54	4 9	5 39	6 39	*9 17*	3 24	7 30½
MAID'N N'WT'N	arr.	100 R.	**6 54½**	**9 9½**	**1044½**	**12 4½**	**1 27½**	**2 59½**	**4 14½**	**5 44½**	**6 44½**	*9 24*	**3 29½**	**7 35½**

ENGINEERS' OCCUPATION

The Engineers will have occupation of the Bridport Branch every night (Sundays excepted) after last booked train till first booked train for the purpose of working a Ballast Train. See special instructions.

Running times for passenger trains, Maiden Newton to Bridport and vice versa, shewn above, are for maximum load of 90 tons. When this load is exceeded running time to be: 23 minutes Bridport to Maiden Newton and 22 minutes Maiden Newton to Bridport.

ABBOTSBURY BRANCH. Week Days only.

Single Line, Upwey Junction to Abbotsbury, worked by Train Staff, and only one engine in steam at a time, or two coupled.

Mile Post Distances. M.	C.	DOWN TRAINS. STATIONS.		Ruling Gradient 1 in	B Diesel.	B Auto.		B Diesel. SO		B Auto.		B Diesel.		
					a.m.	a.m.		p.m.		p.m.		p.m.		
2	31	**WEYMOUTH**	dep.	—	**7 30**	**9 55**	....	*1 5*	..	**4 55**	....	**8 25**	....	....
1	28	**Radipole**	,,	187 R.	7 34	9 59	..	*1 9*	..	4 59	..	8 29	..	..
0	0	**Upwey Junction Stn.**	,,	74 R.	7 38	10 3	....	*1 13*	....	5 3	....	8 33	....	....
—	12	**Stop Board**	,,	44 F.	—	—	..	—	..	—	..	—	..	..
—	35	**Upwey**	,,	44 F.	7 40	10 5	....	*1 15*	....	5 5	....	8 35	....	....
2	0	**Friar Waddon**	,,	190 R.	—	—	..	—	..	—	..	—	..	..
2	79	**Coryates**	,,	190 R.	7 46	10 11	....	*1 21*	....	5 11	....	8 41	....	....
4	47	**Portesham**	,,	60 R.	7 51	10 16	..	*1 26*	..	5 16	..	8 46	..	..
4	49	**Stop Board**	,,	170 F.	—	—	....	—	....	—	....	—	....	....
6	3	**ABBOTSBURY**	arr.	60 F.	**7 56**	**10 21**	..	*1 31*	..	**5 21**	..	**8 51**	..	..

UP TRAINS. STATIONS.		Ruling Gradient 1 in	B Diesel.	B Auto.		B Mixed. SX		B Diesel. SO		B Auto.		B Diesel.	
			a.m.	a.m.		p.m.		p.m.		p.m.		p.m.	
ABBOTSBURY	dep.	—	**8 2**	**10 30**	....	**12 52**	....	*1 40*	....	**5 30**	....	**8 55**	....
Portesham	,,	60 R.	8 6	10 35	..	1 2	..	*1 45*	..	5 36	..	9 0	..
Coryates	,,	60 F.	8 10	10 40	....	1 7	....	*1 50*	....	5 41	....	9 5	....
Friar Waddon	,,	190 F.	—	—	..	—	..	—	..	—	..	—	..
Upwey	,,	190 F.	8 16	10 46	....	1 24	....	*1 56*	....	5 47	....	9 11	....
Upwey Junction	arr.	—	8 17	10 47	..	1 27	..	—	..	5 49	..	—	..
	dep.	44 R.	8 18	10 52	....	1 30	....	*1 58*	....	5 50	....	9 13	....
Stop Board	,,	—	—	—	..	1P33	..	—	..	—	..	—	..
Radipole	,,	74 F.	8 21	10 56	....	1 34	....	*2 1*	....	5 55	....	9 16	....
WEYMOUTH	arr.	187 F.	**8 25**	**11 0**	..	**1 38**	..	*2 5*	..	**5 59**	..	**9 20**	..

The Engineers will have absolute occupation of the Abbotsbury Branch daily from 5.0 a.m. until fifteen minutes before first train is due to leave Upwey. See Special Instructions.

Working timetable from October 1942 until further notice.

incendiaries fell just 200 yds from Bridport station, fortunately without causing damage. On 6th August, 1942 a raid on the town caused death and destruction when the Star Hotel was destroyed. A second raid on 16th August resulted in houses in East Street and Kings Street being destroyed. Three bombs were dropped, one exploding in a field near East Street station without causing injury.

In the November 488 Battery, 66 Searchlight Regiment, arrived in West Dorset, 'C' troop being based at Toller, doubtless causing much work for the station master as he issued and collected Forces tickets from troops at this rural backwater of the GWR.

Throughout the war traffic was heavy on the branch as the Bridport net industry worked endlessly to supply the forces as they had during the Great War. Train loads of shingle were also hauled from West Bay to various parts of the country to provide materials for the construction of airfields, whilst air raid shelters for the civilian population were brought in by goods train. Coal shortages were another problem during February 1941, the entire coal stocks of Bridport were down to less than 10 tons, and to meet the situation extra wagons of coal were dispatched to the branch. However, at Powerstock stored coal caused a problem. A large amount of small coal had been dumped in the old quarry at the back of the goods yard, and owing to its dust-like nature combustion took place, the fire brigade having to let it burn itself out!

The daily passenger service of 10 trains each way and two on Sundays was well filled as many servicemen were travelling. At the beginning of the war units of the Lincolnshire Regiment were stationed at Maiden Newton, followed by others. A few miles away at Cattistock, units from various regiments were stationed in a hutted camp outside the village, and all this activity required various services from the railway. The approach to D-Day saw the build up of American forces in the area along with their vast quantities of equipment, and in fields south of Maiden Newton station a large stores camp was established.

The country life did not agree with all, a disgruntled American private complaining about his unit being posted from near London to Maiden Newton, was told by a sergeant, 'This is not a one horse town, there are three trains in the station'. Indeed the station was busy at times with hardly standing room on the platforms let alone in the trains, with a large military population and Land Girls and others coming and going. The only bus, run by Messrs Pearce, was to Dorchester on market days, Wednesday and Saturday, otherwise it was the train.

Throughout most of this period the station was under the charge of Mr Leonard Hole, who had replaced F. Powell in late 1941 upon the latter's transfer to Wantage Road. Leonard Hole, who had previously been in the divisional offices at Bristol, moved on in November 1944 to become station master at Yeovil Pen Mill, his place being taken by Mr J. MacMahon, formerly station master at Puxton & Worle.

With the demand for experienced staff there were many such moves. In May 1940 F.J. Colls moved from Bridport to become senior relief station master at Bristol divisional office, his place being taken by Sidney Bray, formerly station master at Badminton. A Plymouth man, he had commenced his career as junior clerk at Yelverton, moving to Codford and Warminster before becoming chief goods clerk at Portland in 1917. His promotion to Badminton came in 1928, and he remained there until 1940 when his place was taken by A.J. Pike, the former Toller station master, who had moved to Easton (Portland) in 1926.

As a starting point for a station master's career, Toller probably held a record for transfers during the war years. In May 1940 Mr E. Marquiss was promoted to Collingbourne, his place being taken by Stanley Purnell, a Bridport parcel porter, who for a while was also responsible for Powerstock. In the Summer of 1942 he moved to

Maiden Newton, viewed from the up platform and looking towards Yeovil on 5th June, 1942. Looking at this wartime view one notes that the station nameboards have been removed following the invasion scare of 1940 and many of the adverts have gone from the walls, those remaining are of a wartime nature such as 'Save Fuel' and others extolling the war effort. The original steps and balustrades on both sides of the footbridge had by this time been replaced by concrete and tubular steel structures. On the right-hand side of the footbridge can be seen the post and gallows into which the oil lamps were raised during darkness, a similar arrangement being shown under the canopy in the foreground. The facilities for winding them into position are shown on the wall pillar to the left. *National Railway Museum*

West Bay station in August 1947, the local coal merchant collecting by horse and cart. To the left is a once familiar sight on our railways - the private owner's wagon - this one bearing the faded lettering of its former owners 'The City of Birmingham Electric Department'.

The late G.W. Puntis

Henbury, and Samuel Rawle from the platform staff at Puxton & Worle took over at Toller. Within six months he had moved to become station master at Grafton & Burbage, his replacement being A.L. Rochester from Marlborough. Rochester went to Weyhill at the end of 1943, when M.E. Maguire arrived from Swindon.

Powerstock - although not having such frequent staff changes - was also a staging point for up and coming staff. Mr E. Ball departed in 1940 to move to Weyhill, then for a while S. Purnell was in charge until the arrival of J.S. Knapp who moved to Edington & Bratton at the end of 1943, C.J. Hendry from the Bridport staff replacing him.

Other members of staff were also on the move, branch fireman C.J. Cave being promoted to driver at Didcot after working the branch for 22 years with driver A.S. Balston. This was thought to be something of a record, a crew working together for such a long period. Porter W. Dunn retired from Maiden Newton in the Summer of 1944 after 43 years service at the same station. Before joining the railway he had been one of Queen Victoria's liveried postillions.

Early in the war many bus services and most express coach services were withdrawn, although the Southern National's Weymouth to Exeter service (No. 47) and a limited Royal Blue Express service still passed through Bridport, mainly to provide connections where railway travel was not available. The rationing of petrol also gave the railway dray horses a renewed lease of life on town deliveries.

Leading up to D-Day many units of the US 1st Infantry Division were camped in the Bridport area for conducting exercises at West Bay. Although mainly equipped with road transport ready for their move up to Weymouth and Portland before sailing to Omaha Beach, the side effects of their presence created more work for the railway, as did the stores and equipment of the various regiments and units that operated in the area during the war years.

With the allied forces advancing through Europe, the tide of war had turned, the last air raid in the Bridport area taking place on 16th June, 1944. The gun sidings at Bradpole and Loders were removed in April 1945, and the following month the war was won, Bridport and the surrounding area having taken a very positive part in the victory, as had the railways on which resources had been stretched to the limit.

During the blackout the work of shunting trains went on, both at main line stations and branch lines, and great credit is due to the men who performed this most difficult work under these conditions.

One night at Bridport the goods shed doors had been closed, the shunter could not see this and when making a shunt into the goods shed road opened them in a rather unorthodox manner, by putting a truck through them.

On another occasion a shunter was putting a string of wagons into a siding and afterwards thought that he had done very well to get so many wagons into the space available. The next afternoon he was walking into the goods yard to report for duty when he saw a set of stop blocks smashed and pushed back into the roadway, a wagon up on end, and coal scattered everywhere. Commenting to a workmate that it appeared the early turn shunter had been busy, he was told that it was not the work of the early turn man, but what he himself had done the night before.

However the goods shed doors and the upturned wagon of coal were nothing compared to the next accident. A goods train was being put into a siding one night ready to be shunted the following morning. The driver asked the fireman to put the train away whilst he went over to the engine shed and attended to some other matter, the driver no doubt thinking that the fireman could handle the engine. The shunter saw the trucks start to roll back and then stop, and although he gave a white light to the fireman nothing happened. Thinking that the fireman could not see the light he walked towards the engine, and arriving at the front truck he found a broken coupling - but no engine! Upon investigation he saw that the engine had gone through the stop blocks at the end of the headshunt and deposited itself in a field and had sunk up to its axles in mud. This accounted for the bang the shunter had heard a little while before.

This caused problems. The signalman asked, 'Is he off all wheels?', to which the reply was 'He's in the b—— field'. It was then discovered that the stop blocks had been catapulted on to the branch line and were causing an obstruction, so detonators were placed on the line according to the rules. These exploded with the arrival of a breakdown train from Weymouth. Within minutes the local Home Guard, ARP wardens and police had arrived, causing a scene not unlike a popular television series. After the excitement had died down and 'Dad's Army' had retired for the night, it took the Weymouth breakdown gang a further 24 hours to put the locomotive back on the track.

Staff shortages had caused several railwaymen to remain after their normal retirement age. B. Russell of Maiden Newton should have retired in 1939, but eventually took his well earned rest in November 1946. Having joined the GWR in 1891 he first went to Maiden Newton two years later before serving at Salisbury and Weymouth, returning in 1919 - first as shunter than as foreman.

However, people were already planning for the future, some in a novel way. Early in 1945 at a meeting of the Western section of the Institute of Transport, a rumoured proposal for the construction of a canal linking Lyme Regis and Bridgwater, to save coastal vessels the difficulty of passing around Land's End, was discussed amid laughter! In March, Councillor Roberts of Bridport told the Council he had seen a proposal in the papers for a canal from Bridport to Bridgwater, which in turn fired his imagination. However, the idea died a natural death. Although West Bay would have been a far more suitable starting point than Lyme Regis, one cannot help recalling the fate of the early railway schemes projected with the same purpose.

A more practical enterprise went ahead at Maiden Newton. To replace the refreshment room of pre-war days, a small tea hut was constructed under the steps of the footbridge on the up platform. It was built and run by Mr Hedley Heyward, a Londoner who had moved to the village during the war years. Something of an entrepreneur, he had it organised so that a tray of confections, carried 'cinema style', was taken to trains standing at the platforms, this supplementing the usual fare available at the hut. Heyward also ran a cafe / fish & chip shop in the village.

It will always remain a mystery why a halt had never been provided at Loders as the village was near to the railway. However, as late as May 1947 it looked like becoming a reality when the *Bridport News* for the 7th carried the following story:

> After a lengthy correspondence with the Ministry of Transport Mr S. Wingfield Digby, the MP for West Dorset, was informed some weeks ago that the provision of a halt on the GWR line at Loders had been approved.
> He has now heard further from the Ministry to the effect that there has been some difficulty in obtaining possession of the land required for the approach to the new halt, which may necessitate an alteration in the position of the platform.
> In the circumstances, he has been told it has not been possible for work on the site to commence, but good progress has been made with the manufacture of the pre-cast concrete units which will be used for the construction of the platform.

There the matter rested until the November, when Wingfield Digby asked the Minister of Transport, Albert Barnes, a question in the Commons concerning the halt. Mr Barnes replied: 'I am informed that the provision of a halt on the GWR line at Loders has been approved in principle and a scheme is in the course of preparation'.

The fact that there appears to be the only two reports of the proposals gives rise to the suspicion that the whole affair was never pursued with any great vigour. The subsidence of an embankment between Powerstock and Toller caused the suspension of train services on the branch on Monday 23rd December. The 6.30 am train left Bridport, but returned when it was found that the embankment was sloping precariously. A lorry was dispatched to collect fish and other perishable goods and newspapers from Maiden Newton, and a bus service calling at Powerstock and Toller was brought into operation. The slip was quickly repaired, however, and services were resumed at 2.30 pm the same day. Indeed there was so little fuss or delay that a letter appeared in the *Bridport News* thanking the railway staff and in particular station master Bray:

> Arriving at Bridport station on Monday morning, a couple of score of us were hailed with an unruffled and courteous 'Sorry but there is no railway service this morning, but other arrangements have been made for everyone'. Sure enough commodious buses were already marshalled in the adjacent station yard waiting to convey passengers to Maiden Newton, where connections were picked up with the least possible delay, while a small fleet of lorries had been pressed into service for the purpose of dealing with incoming and outgoing mails, luggage and general goods. No confusion, no hurry, the whole affair seemingly taken as a matter of regular service by everyone concerned.

Praise indeed, and how different from the situation 50 years later when there is a problem!

As we come to the end of ownership of the line by the GWR, it is noteworthy that the discipline of the old company was still being upheld. A goods porter, admitting the theft of two jellies valued at 1*s*. 3*d*., the property of the GWR, was bound over for one year by the Bridport Court. The defendant had been in the employ of the GWR only since March (1947) at a weekly wage of £4 5*s*. When the Chairman of the bench asked what his future position with the company would be, Inspector Perry of the Transport Police replied, 'He has got his cards sir'. Perhaps if he had known the fate of the engine cleaners at the turn of the century he would have considered himself a lucky man!

Petrol was still rationed and for most the family car was still a far-off dream, but although bus services were slowly being restored fuel and vehicle shortages made this difficult. In July 1945 Mr Craven, who had taken over the station bus service, obtained a new vehicle, a Bedford OWB 32-seat utility bus (BJT 34). Unfortunately this was larger than the pre-war Ford AA, so an appeal appeared in the *Bridport News* for anybody who had space to garage it!

The Summer timetable for 1947 gave a service of 11 trains each way and four on Sundays. It was to be the last summer of travelling on the GWR. The Transport Bill had received its Royal Assent on 6th August, and from the first of January 1948 the GWR became the Western Region of British Railways, part of the British Transport Commission.

It is interesting to note that as early as the mid-1840s there had been suggestions in Parliament that the developing railway system be nationalised. In 1894 the various railway unions had campaigned for the same. A Bill before Parliament in 1919 was an attempt to nationalise the system, but under opposition the Bill was dropped in favour of the plan to group the railways into four main companies. The subsequent Act of 1921 resulted in their formation in 1923, the GWR being the least affected and keeping its own name. Now in 1948, 92 years after its formation as a local company, the Bridport branch had become the property of the nation.

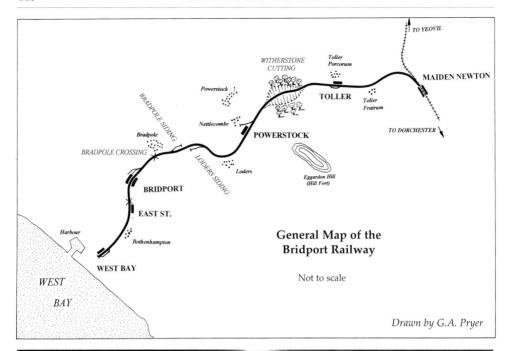

TO YEOVIL

MAIDEN NEWTON

WITHERSTONE CUTTING

Toller Porcorum

Powerstock

TOLLER

Toller Fratrum

TO DORCHESTER

BRADPOLE SIDING

Nettlecombe

POWERSTOCK

Bradpole

BRADPOLE CROSSING

LODERS SIDING

Loders

Eggardon Hill (Hill Fort)

BRIDPORT

EAST ST.

Harbour

Bothenhampton

General Map of the Bridport Railway

Not to scale

WEST BAY

WEST BAY

Drawn by G.A. Pryer

The branch train shed at Maiden Newton, showing the interior detail. Note the generous clearance between the track and the back wall, a legacy from broad gauge days.   *Roger Holmes*

Chapter Six
The Route Described

No branch line book can be complete without a description of the line. The period chosen for the run is during the late 1940s, before any great changes were made to the route. All trains were hauled by steam, and the railway was really a railway.

The line passed through some of the most beautiful countryside in West Dorset, but unfortunately in these steam days the small carriage windows did little to give the best views; it was the engine crews travelling towards Bridport who saw most of the scenery.

The journey starts from the covered branch bay situated on the up side of Maiden Newton. The station has two main line platforms plus one for the branch; the station buildings are of knapped flint construction. Originally the main line at Maiden Newton, during the days of the WS&W, was constructed as a single track, and the station was of some importance as a crossing place. The goods shed is situated on the Dorchester side of the station close to the up line. It is a structure which dates back to the broad gauge days and is built of stone, flint and timber. The signal box, standing at the Dorchester end of the down platform, is of GWR design and is constructed of brick with a hip roof.

Passengers aboard, the guard's whistle blows, and the branch train slowly leaves Maiden Newton on its 9¼ mile journey to Bridport.

Leaving Maiden Newton station, the branch runs for the first hundred yards parallel with the main line and then turns sharply left under the Yeovil road bridge, dropping down a gradient of 1 in 100. The line still curving away left, then passes under five road bridges in quick succession and there are several sets of concrete tank traps left over from World War II.

The gradient now eases to 1 in 90 and the track curves right and passes the Maiden Newton up distant signal. Reaching the ¾ mile post the gradient changes to a climb of 1 in 150, levels out for about ¼ mile and then climbs again at 1 in 200 towards Toller. On the left is the hamlet of Toller Fratrum, where on the hillside can be seen one of only three churches in England dedicated to Basil the Great.

Just after the 2½ mile post the train slows and stops at Toller station. The station is part of the village which is dominated by its church and tower dating back over 500 years. The full name of the village is Toller Porcorum, derived from the Latin, and means 'Toller of the pigs', so named because of the large number of pigs that were bred in this part of Dorset. The station itself is a typical small GWR wayside station constructed of wood with a brick base. Included in the normal platform furniture is a corrugated iron lamp room, and a cast-iron gents' toilet at the Maiden Newton end of the platform. The goods facilities here consist of a loop line and a small loading dock. The gate leading to the dock has a notice 'Goods Station'. A considerable amount of goods traffic has been handled here over the years.

The train leaving Toller passes under a road bridge, and the engine now starts to work as the gradient changes to 1 in 85 for about ¾ mile, then eases to 1 in 270 until the summit is reached at the 3¾ mile post. Here is a sign board 'All goods and mineral trains must stop dead here'. This is for the brakes to be pinned down before the descent of 1 in 50 through Witherstone cutting, the scene of many of the early difficulties on the line. The sides of the cutting are not steep and are well cut back, although evidence of earth movement can still be seen at this point.

At the 5¼ mile post the gradient eases to 1 in 75, the line now passing through Powerstock Common and along a short section of level track before the train stops at Powerstock station. The platform is situated on the up side of the line and is more than

Maiden Newton signal box photographed in May 1965 when it still had the traditional cast GWR style nameplate displayed below the windows.   *C.L. Caddy*

An interior view of Maiden Newton signal box during the 1950s. To the right can be seen the 'Webb & Thompson' Electric Train Staff machine used to control the Bridport branch.

The late P. Sims

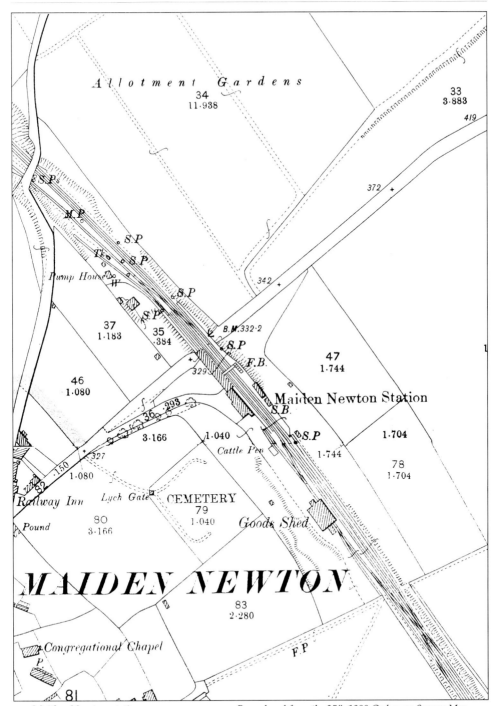

Maiden Newton station. *Reproduced from the 25", 1900 Ordnance Survey Map*

Maiden Newton goods shed. The wide entrance clearly shows its broad gauge origin dating back to 1857. The inner home signal is mounted on a bracket to allow it to be viewed by drivers of up trains.   *C.L. Caddy*

Class '2' 2-6-2 tank No. 41305 runs into Maiden Newton with a one-coach train from Bridport during the period when there was just one steam working a day. The main line service to Yeovil can be seen disappearing into the mist in the distance.   *David Lawrence*

Single unit railcar No. W55032 departs from Maiden Newton with the branch train on 18th
April, 1975, as No. D1072 *Western Glory* departs with 10.05 am Weymouth-Bristol train.
B.L. Jackson

A Swindon-built two-coach unit approaches Maiden Newton with a train from Bridport shortly
after the introduction of diesel units in 1959.   *The late J.D. Blackburn*

Class '45XX' 2-6-2 tank No. 4507 rounds the curve towards the Chilfrome road bridge after leaving Maiden Newton with a Bridport-bound train. To the right the wartime tank traps (Dragons Teeth) still stand as a reminder of the invasion threat of 1940. Engine No. 4507 was the last surviving Wolverhampton-built locomotive on British Railways, this view being taken in May 1959 just before the end of regular steam working on the branch.   *I.D. Beale*

Class '57XX' 0-6-0PT No. 3737 in the Dorset countryside between Toller and Maiden Newton with an up train on 13th July, 1957.   *J. Spencer Gilks*

Toller station, viewed from the road overbridge on 27th April, 1963. Although still staffed at that time, the goods siding had already been removed.   *C.L. Caddy*

Toller station, looking towards Bridport. At the time the station was still staffed, the fire buckets in position, the station seat and all other fittings in place. In the foreground stands the ubiquitous cast-iron gents, once a feature of many railway stations.   *Lens of Sutton*

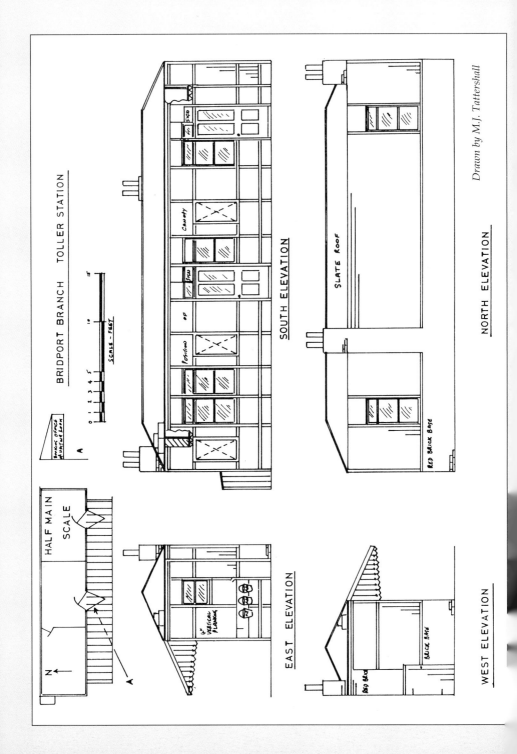

BRIDPORT BRANCH   TOLLER STATION

SOUTH ELEVATION

NORTH ELEVATION

EAST ELEVATION

WEST ELEVATION

HALF MAIN SCALE

SCALE - FEET

SLATE ROOF

RED BRICK BASE

Drawn by M.J. Tattershall

Class '4575' 2-6-2 tank No. 5548 departs from Toller with an up train for Maiden Newton on 31st March, 1956. To the right is the cast-iron gents' toilet. In the siding to the left a wagon stands in the loop siding awaiting loading with the products of Galpin's sawmill. *C.L. Caddy*

On the last day of operation an extra train was run from Maiden Newton at 5 pm and is here seen standing at Toller station. Within hours, Dorset's last passenger branch will have closed. *B.L. Jackson*

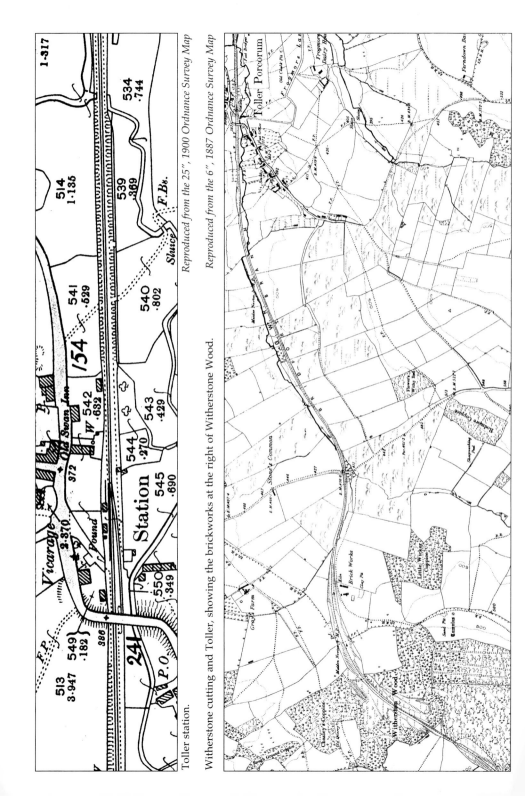

Reproduced from the 25", 1900 Ordnance Survey Map

Toller station.

Reproduced from the 6", 1887 Ordnance Survey Map

Witherstone cutting and Toller, showing the brickworks at the right of Witherstone Wood.

Powerstock station looking towards Bridport on 21st August, 1933. The 1910 extension to the platform can be clearly seen. To the right goods wagons occupy the yard. *Mowat Collection*

A scene from a past age, deep in rural Dorset. With roses around the door, the back entrance to Powerstock station looks more like a country cottage. Only the loading dock, loading gauge, and sidings in the garden detract from this idyllic view! *D.M. Habgood Collection*

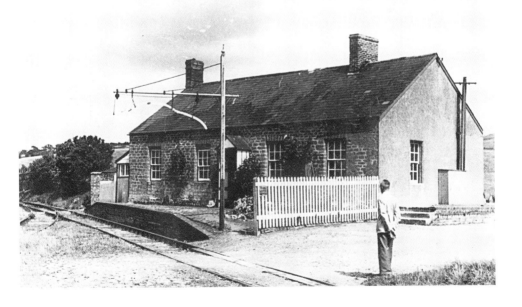

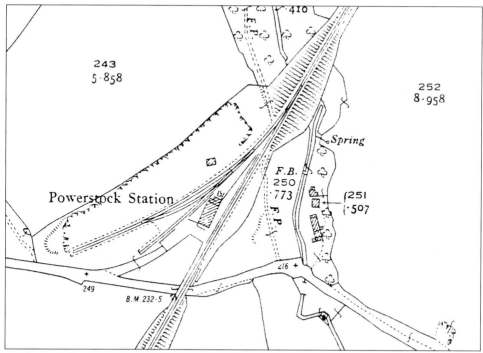

Powerstock station.   *Reproduced from the 25", 1900 Ordnance Survey Map*

Powerstock station viewed from the 8.7 am Maiden Newton-Bridport train on 20th January, 1956. Little changed at this remote outpost of the GWR - but there was life, and a box van stands in the loading dock.   *The late H.C. Casserley*

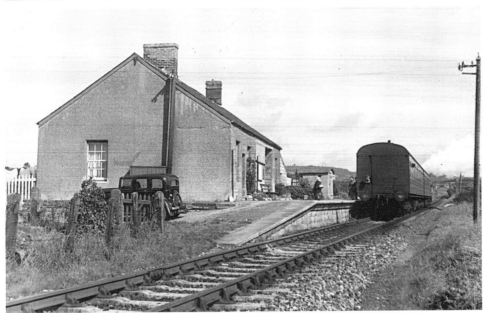

A Maiden Newton-bound train stands at Powerstock, shortly before the end of steam operation on the branch. Apart from the iron lamp hut on the platform and the GWR 'B set' forming the train, there is little else to suggest that this station once belonged to the GWR. It has been described by one railway historian as 'a rail-connected crofter's cottage!'   *Lens of Sutton*

A Swindon-built unit waits at Powerstock with a train bound for Bridport on 23rd September, 1959.   *Stations Merseyside*

Bradpole Crossing.   In this pre-war view the crossing keeper holds the gate open as the
maintenance man checks the gate lock.   *M.J. Tattershall Collection*

Bradpole Crossing, showing the results of a train failing to stop before the gates were open!
                                                         Miss E. Fox

a mile distant from the village of that name. The station itself stands in the small hamlet of Nettlecombe. The station buildings are constructed of stone, the main part of the building being the station master's house. Behind is the goods yard, part of which was quarried out and is served by two sidings. The only other item provided is a small loading platform. The station is dominated by Egardon Hill, which was an ancient camp site in the days before history was recorded, and later used by the Romans. Egardon stands 820 ft high and is protected by ramparts of 30 ft.

The train pulls out of the station and crosses a road bridge and reaches another stop sign before a steep gradient of 1 in 75 for a distance of ½ mile, then easing off again to 1 in 62. It's downhill all the way now to Bridport. The line curves away to the right, and passes the village of Loders. Towering behind the village is Boarsbarrow, a hill with a cluster of trees on the top. This was a burial site in the days of the very early settlers.

At the 7¾ mile post the gradient eases off to 1 in 130, and just before Boarsbarrow farm occupation crossing the train passes the site of a wartime gun siding. The Bradpole Crossing distant signal stands here as a warning to train crews that the crossing is soon to be reached. Another gun siding was situated here during World War II. The engine whistles up to inform the crossing keeper at Bradpole of its approach in time for him to open the gates. There is a friendly wave from the children waiting to see the train go by the crossing keeper's hut on the up side of the line. Now it's a short level run through to Bridport, passing on the way to its left 'Happy Island', the site of many a picnic party and Sunday school treat.

The train now starts to slow up for the approach to Bridport and to the right of the line timber is stacked high in the lineside yards. The platforms at Bridport are on a sharp left hand curve, this being caused by the extension of the line to West Bay. The main station buildings are original and stand as built, being in line with the original track, which was a dead end. The down platform was added in 1894 and is provided with a waiting shelter constructed of wood and corrugated iron. To the rear of the platform stands the engine shed built to broad gauge dimensions and constructed of stone, as are the rest of the station buildings and goods shed.

The goods yard is situated on the up side of the track, and is fairly large for a branch line. The goods shed is also large, built to handle most types of goods and traffic.

Bridport station is the end of the line for passengers and only one train a day now travels on the West Bay extension which is for goods traffic only.

Continuing our journey on the goods train to West Bay, we leave Bridport station travelling on the extension opened in 1884. At the end of the down platform an occupation crossing is passed, serving a petroleum store on the down side of the line. To the right of the crossing are the station stables where the railway cartage horses were kept and now motor lorries are garaged. A slight downhill gradient of 1 in 153, across an iron bridge spanning the River Asker and through the crossing gates at East Street, which stops the traffic on the main A35 road. To the right the town of Bridport stands looking down on the railway, and on the other side is the station master's house. Coming to a halt at East Street station we notice that both the brick-built house and the station buildings are now deserted; the last passenger to be picked up here was in September 1930.

The track now levels out for a ¼ mile. On our right the town can be clearly seen, and a time check can be made with the clock on the Town Hall. To the left is the village of Bothenhampton. The track starts a short climb of 1 in 80 over the Bothenhampton road bridge, and through the Wanderwell cutting, which has steep sides, under the brick road bridge which carries the road to Burton Bradstock and the coast road to Weymouth.

The line now descends at 1 in 80 for another ½ mile then levels out for the final stretch to the West Bay terminus which is only a few feet above sea level.

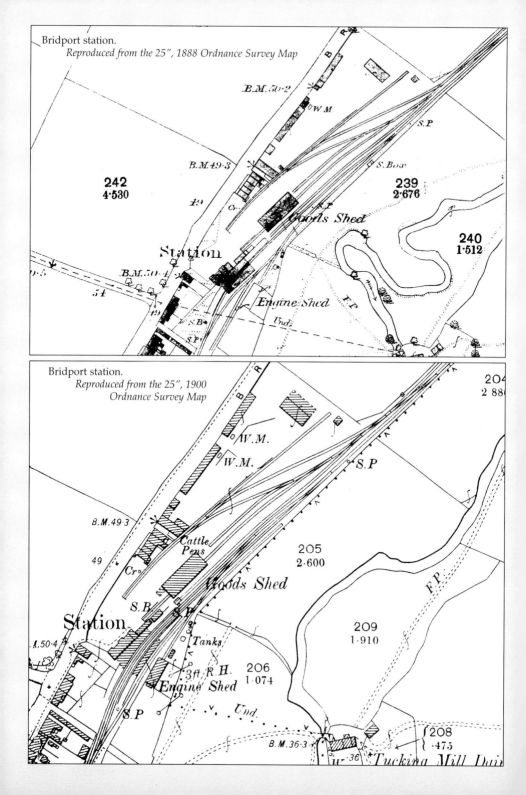

Bridport station.
Reproduced from the 25", 1888 Ordnance Survey Map

B.M.50·2

W.M.

B.M.49·3

242
4·530

239
2·676

240
1·512

S.P.

S.Box

Station

Goods Shed

B.M.50·4

54

Engine Shed

F.P.

Und.

S.B.

S.P.

Bridport station.
*Reproduced from the 25", 1900
Ordnance Survey Map*

204
2 88

W.M.

W.M.

S.P

B.M.49·3

49

Cattle
Pens

205
2·600

Cr.

Goods Shed

F.P.

S.B.

S.P.

209
1·910

Station

A.50·4

Tanks

206
1·074

3ft R.H.

Engine Shed

Und.

S.P.

B.M.36·3

36

208
·475

Tucking Mill Dair

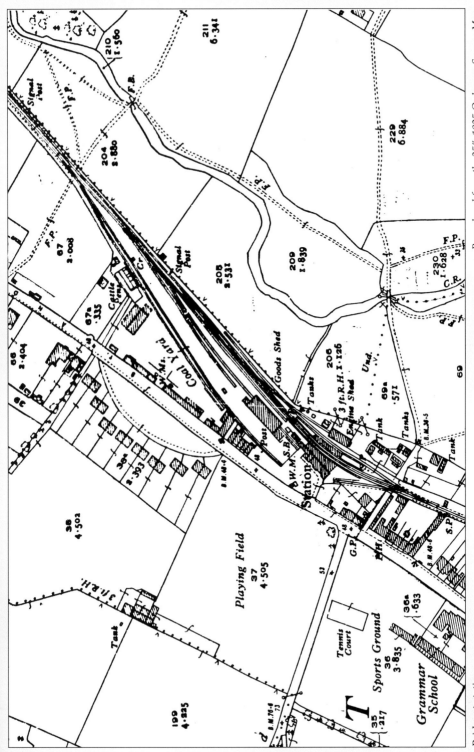

Bridport station.

Reproduced from the 25″, 1925 Ordnance Survey Map

An exterior view of Bridport station taken during the early 1960s. The photograph clearly shows the 'local' design of the station, which - apart from the signal box and other later additions - looked very un-Great Western.   *R.K. Blencowe Collection*

Bridport station in August 1933. The curvature of the track and platform to accommodate the extension to West Bay is very obvious.   *Mowat Collection*

Bridport, looking towards Maiden Newton on 4th September, 1958. A '45XX' class tank stands outside the engine shed and a good selection of wagons fill the yard. Posters on the down platform proclaim the benefits of a visit to such exotic places as New Milton or Aberystwyth!

Derek Phillips Collection

When compared with a similar view of Bridport station taken from the same angle in 1906 (*see page 70*), little had changed in 50 years! The rolling stock had improved, and some of the signals were rail-built Southern replacements, but the station was still one of those odd arrangements so often found on branch lines. *S.C. Nash*

'57XX class' 0-6-0 PT No. 7780 stands at Bridport station with a Maiden Newton train. The coaches appear to have a shine to them; Bridport was known for the clean condition in which coaching stock was kept. The engine is facing down the line, but usually engines employed on branch duty worked chimney towards Maiden Newton.   *I.D. Beale*

'45XX' class 2-6-2 tank No. 4562 awaits departure from Bridport with the 8.55 am to Maiden Newton on 20th January, 1956. To the left can be seen the brake van and one box van of the 8.7 am mixed train which has just arrived from Maiden Newton.   *The late H.C. Casserley*

Bridport on a wet day. Steam from the carriage heating seeps out, and puddles on the platform say it all. Not even a GWR 'B' set and a '45XX' tank could make travel a joy on a wet winter's day!   *R.S. Carpenter*

A scene in 1947, the final year of the Great Western Railway. A pannier tank stands outside Bridport shed, and there is a 'B' set in the back loop. To the right is the canopy of the down platform, added in 1894.   *National Railway Museum*

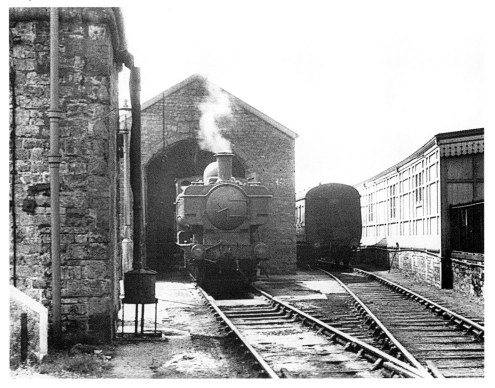

'45XX' class 2-6-2 tank No. 4507 stands outside Bridport shed on 5th May, 1959, when the branch had only a few weeks left of regular steam operation.   *S.C. Nash*

'45XX' class 2-6-2 tank No. 4507 takes coal from the electric coal hoist at Bridport shed in May 1959, this luxury only being installed in the last few years of steam operation. The inspection pit at the bottom right marks the site of the original broad gauge turntable.   *S.C. Nash*

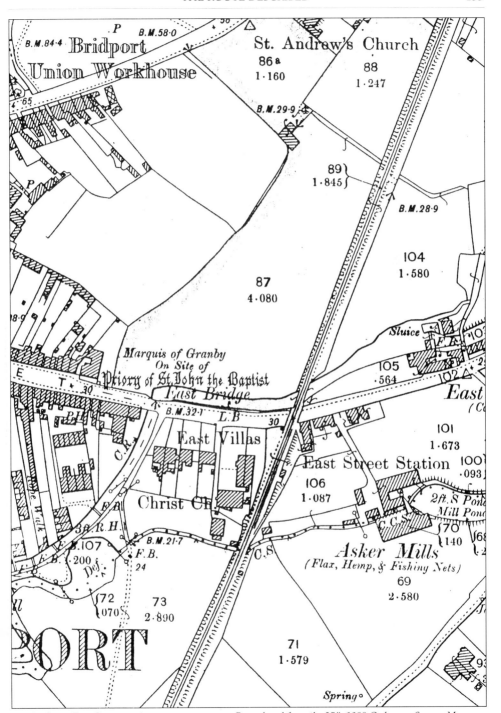

Bridport East Street station.

Reproduced from the 25", 1900 Ordnance Survey Map

The original Bridport East Street station, a thatched cottage that just happened to be near the point where the line crossed the road! It was a minor miracle that it was not destroyed by a spark from a passing train, and it survived until 1904. To the right is the end of the platform.

M.J. Tattershall Collection

East Street station, looking through the level crossing towards Bridport station, which is just visible in the distance. On the platform stands a cast-iron gents' and a waiting shelter, behind which can be seen the roof of the thatched cottage that served as a station office and house. The platform seats, adverts, and gas lamps add to this interesting scene.   *I.D. Beale*

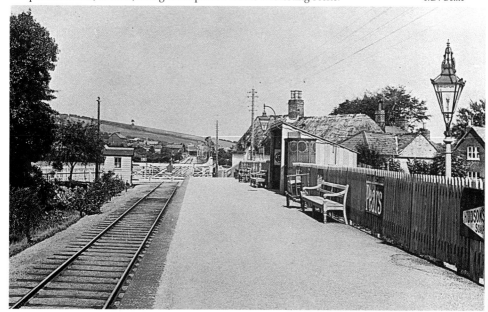

East Street, looking along the main road towards Dorchester. On the left stands a signal supplied by the Gloucester Carriage & Wagon Company and to the right is the station master's house and ground frame hut. An approaching Aveling & Porter roller adds to this period scene.
K. Bakes Collection

East Street station in use as a house, photographed on 7th June, 1958. Its occupant Bridport shunter, 'Snowy' Belben, looks on as the Railway Enthusiasts Club special heads back towards Bridport. *R.M. Casserley*

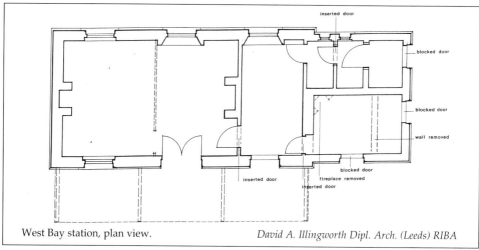

West Bay station, plan view.   *David A. Illingworth Dipl. Arch. (Leeds) RIBA*

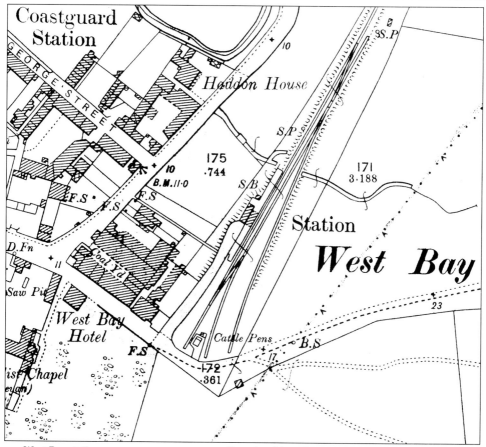

West Bay station.   *Reproduced from the 25", 1900 Ordnance Survey Map*

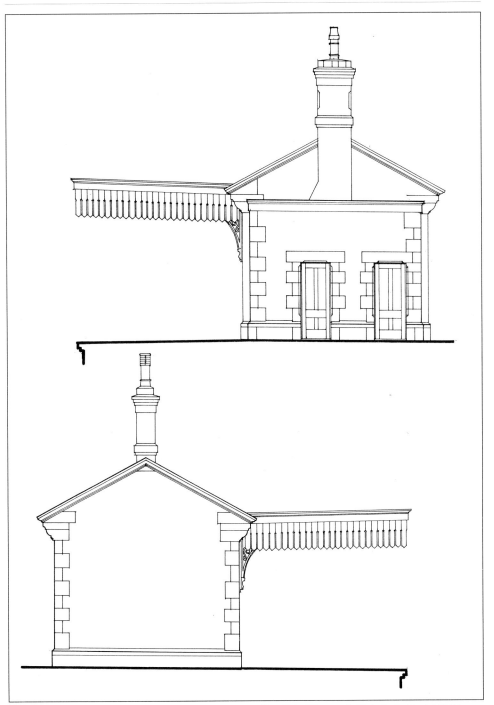

West Bay station, end elevations.   *David A. Illingworth Dipl. Arch. (Leeds) RIBA*

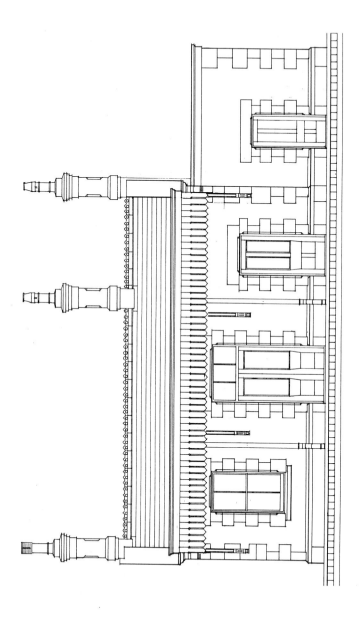

West Bay station, East elevation.

David A. Illingworth Dipl. Arch. (Leeds)

West Bay station, West elevation.

David A. Illingworth Dipl. Arch. (Leeds)

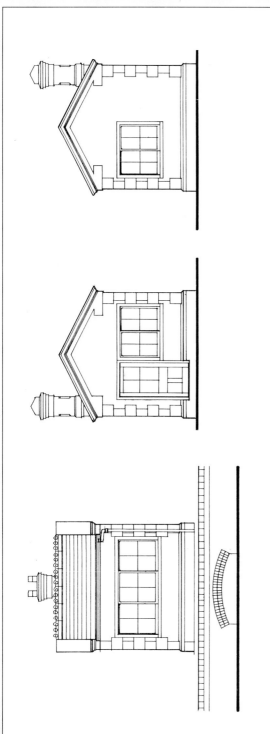

West Bay signal box.
David A. Illingworth Dipl. Arch. (Leeds) RIBA

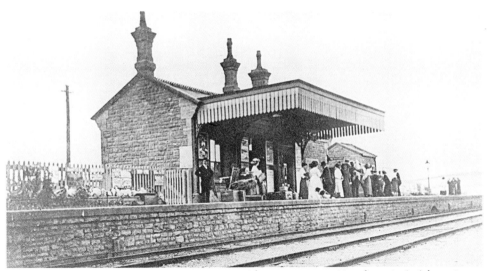

A pre-World War I scene at West Bay station, with passengers awaiting the arrival of the train from Bridport. However the gentleman on the left seems to be expecting it to arrive from the buffer stops end! The luggage on the platform and the Vignoles 75lb. rail, with which the extension was laid, complete this Edwardian scene.

By permission of the Bridport Museum Service

West Bay station viewed from East Cliff during the early 1920s. The signalling is still in use and the motor vehicle has arrived, although the local carter is still employing horse and cart in the goods yard. Looking along the road towards Bridport, there was practically no housing development at that time. *By permission of the Bridport Museum Service*

The station is of stone construction, and to a design that is to be seen all over the GWR system. On the platform is the signal box, and apart from one siding and a short spur to a cattle dock, facilities are non-existent. No sign can be seen of the large seaside resort that was to rival Bournemouth and Weymouth.

So the journey along the Bridport and West Bay branch ends, just over 11 miles of railway having been traversed. It only remains to climb aboard the train and make the return journey back from whence we came.

Goods Traffic

To evaluate the usefulness of the Bridport branch to the people living in the district, one has to return to the early 1800s when the roads of West Dorset were little more than cart tracks. Through fair weather and foul, people and goods were transported across the county, and when one takes into account the hilly nature of West Dorset, it could take as long as half a day to travel between Bridport and Dorchester (the County town), a distance of only 15 miles! The only other means of transport was by sea to Bridport Harbour, not the easiest harbour to enter unless weather conditions were perfect.

A closer look at Bridport in pre-railway days finds very little unemployment, thanks mainly to the town's industrial base. Factories in the town and surrounding district manufactured ropes, twines, all kinds of fishing and sporting nets, sail cloth, and even shoe thread, both for the home and export markets. Amongst the many products were the nets for Wembley Stadium, the Wimbledon Courts, and the Hangman's rope(!) - hence the saying 'Stabbed by the Bridport Dagger' which meant to be hung. In the early years the principal raw material was flax, the strongest natural fibre obtainable, which was grown in the surrounding countryside, and what could not be obtained locally was imported from as far away as Russia through Bridport Harbour.

To process this raw material several large Flax Mills stood alongside the River Brit, water wheels being used to provide the power. With the introduction of the steam engine to power the mills coal had to be shipped in from South Wales and the North Somerset coalfields involving the treacherous sea journey down the Bristol Channel, around Land's End, and up the English Channel. Bridport Harbour was a very difficult place to enter - particularly with a sailing vessel -and a ship's captain who misjudged the weather and tide could soon find his vessel wrecked on the notorious Chesil Beach.

Bridport Harbour, like many other small ports before the arrival of railways, was thriving, but the local ship-building trade diminished as the change from timber to steel construction took place, and the yards that had built many sailing vessels, including ships for the Royal Navy, disappeared.

The building of the railway caused both headache and heartache, and no fortunes were made from it, but it brought an unrivalled method of travel for both passengers and goods. Until then to travel at a speed of 40 mph was unheard of. Bridport station became the gateway to the remainder of the country in connection with the other railways then being constructed. As a result the town prospered, and the inhabitants enjoyed the benefits that the railway brought.

Coal could now be brought direct from the coalfields of Somerset and South Wales; during the first year of operation 6,000 tons of it travelled over the branch. In return a local product, pit props, were transported back to the mines instead of returning empty wagons. The materials required by the net and twine factories could be brought in and the finished products could be quickly dispatched all over the country and indeed the world.

Not everybody, however, was well pleased with the services the railway could provide, a complaint being received in December 1875 concerning a hamper and two bags consigned from Bridport to Manchester which took eight days to make the journey. Added to this, two rabbits from the hamper were pilfered *en route*, the complainant adding that previously a 12 lb. piece of pork had been stolen.

The only part of the district that did not benefit from the arrival of the railway in Bridport was the harbour, at which business sharply declined, the sea-going trade there no longer being needed for the principal imports and exports of the town. The fact that there were two turnpike gates between Bridport Harbour and Bridport station also gave the railway a considerable advantage, although for many years timber continued to be imported, and a large proportion of the sand and gravel continued to be shipped out.

It would be impossible to name all the companies who benefited from the railway over the years, whether they were situated in Bridport, Powerstock, Toller or Maiden Newton, or which company was the railway's best customer, although the net and twine industry must have been top of the league. Coal merchants received their stocks by rail, and they were stored in the railway yards to await delivery to the various customers. Amongst the many merchants were John Hoare of South Street, Dan Stembridge, South Street; J. Brownson, North Allington; Henry Good, West Bay; and the Wallsend Coal Company which was owned by Monteith & Alford of South Street. Two other merchants set up business in the station yard at Bridport, these being Bradford & Sons and the Somerset Trading Company, later to become Ralls & Son who became agents for the Westlake sack hiring company. In later years with the coal trade in decline only Bradfords and Ralls remained of the original traders. Although new traders in the form of J. Gurd & Sons, R.J.B. Cox & Sons and the Co-operative Society arrived, there were then just two who were from outside the town.

Following the Great War, the availability of the motor vehicle initiated the first moves away from the railway for the conveyance of goods traffic. However 1923 was considered a good year, 47,083 tons of goods being handled at Bridport together with 469 cattle wagons, whilst on the passenger side 39,634 tickets were issued.

Where the coal trade declined owing to its discontinuance as the main provider of power and heat, the rope and net industry changed to keep abreast of the changing customer market. Once the principal provider of employment for the town's people and those in the surrounding district, it operated from many small factories which were scattered around the town, between houses and in various nooks and crannies, in a fashion that would not be tolerated today by either the planning regulations or Health & Safety laws. In recent years, both the industry and work force have declined. Among the smaller companies were Ewens & Turner, George Kenway, Walter Tucker, Herbert Hounsell Ltd, William Hounsell & Co., R. Budden & Son, and S. Whetham & Sons Ltd. The larger firms consisted of J. Gundry & Co, who had been manufacturing flax products since the reign of Charles II, William James, of Pymore Mill, Rendel & Coombes, William Edwards, William James and William Gale. As time went by the smaller firms were swallowed up by the larger, Hounsell's works becoming Hounsell's (Bridport) Ltd.

All had accounts with the railway company, receiving raw materials and sending large quantities of finished products daily, and as rope is heavy and freight was charged by a combination of weight plus mileage it was a substantial source of income for the railway company.

During the 1940s the remaining small companies amalgamated to become Bridport Industries, whilst Joseph Gundry remained a separate unit until recent times when they and Bridport Industries merged to form Bridport Gundry's (Holding) Ltd. Today, with the advancement of man made fibres, there is very little left of a once thriving industry. With recent company sell-outs and mergers, only Gundry's name survives in Gundry Netting (Bridport) Ltd.

At the East Street end of Bridport station there was a petrol and oil store operated by the Anglo-American Oil Company and Shell Mex & BP Ltd, the bulk supplies being brought in by rail tanker and discharged through a standpipe situated just beyond the engine shed. Despite its close proximity to the steam operated railway there were never any accidents!

Many years ago Maiden Newton possessed a cattle market, which later developed into an annual sheep fair, this event providing the railway with traffic in cattle and sheep. There were several large pig farms in the area, the products of which were destined to make the journey to the large sausage and pie factory at Calne in Wiltshire. Bridport also had a cattle market in those days, and often the results of the day's dealings would be transported by train. There was also occasional cattle traffic from both Powerstock and Toller to the larger markets.

Maiden Newton has in years past provided much traffic for the railway. Prior to the Great War there were several corn mills and a small iron foundry in the village, and there were the usual arrangements for local coal merchants and other traders whose goods were transported by rail. During the early 1890s George Whitty was the local coal merchant and agent for the West of England Sack Hiring Company. By 1898 Bishop was an established coal merchant, and Charles Read ran the White Hart Hotel and the railway refreshment rooms and was also the agent for the GWR. The Mearns family had taken over the White Hart by 1907, although there is no mention of the refreshment rooms, but were also agents for the GWR, and by the outbreak of the Great War had expanded to become coal merchants and haulage contractors, a trade they continued for many years after.

In November 1918 Albert Pearce took over the carrier and coal merchant's business of Shorto of Cattistock, and he also collected his supplies from Maiden Newton yard. Pearce expanded the business, purchasing his first motor bus during 1923. Like many buses operated by local carriers it offered only a market day service for many years, a daily service not commencing until the mid-1950s, shortly after which the bus service of Legg of Evershot was acquired to expand the business further. As with Mearn's, the coal side of the business declined and was sold to Bryer Ash Ltd in the mid-1960s, by which time all supplies had to be collected from Dorchester owing to the closure of Maiden Newton yard.

By 1912 R.C. Carter had established a wholesale dairy at Maiden Newton, later known as Carter's & Dorset Modern Dairies. It became part of the United Dairies group during the 1920s. Before the days of collecting milk direct from the farms by road vehicle it was transported from Bridport, Powerstock, Toller and various stations on the main line in churns to Maiden Newton for processing before being dispatched to the London bottling plant. However milk in churns loaded into Siphon vans was labour intensive and required a vast amount of rolling stock, particularily in the days of the original tapered 17 gallon churns, although the introduction of the later 10 gallon type made the work a little easier. It was, however, the introduction of milk tank wagons on the railway that improved the transit of bulk supplies.

On 26th January, 1933 the first road-rail tanks left Maiden Newton for the London Depot. The road-rail tank was a compromise for locations where the dairy was not situated alongside the railway, the tanks being towed to the station by tractor and loaded onto special flat-bed wagons at a loading dock. At its peak four tanks a day in Summer and three in Winter were dispatched from Maiden Newton, each tank holding 2,000 gallons - the equivalent of 200, 10 gallon churns.

Galpin's sawmill at Toller provided a steady traffic in pit props and wooden boxes for the fruit trade, which at times could amount to four or five wagons a day. In season the Watercress trade was heavy, boxes being consigned to many towns across the county, a majority of this being forwarded by passenger train.

Although the railway hastened the decline of Bridport Harbour as a commercial enterprise, and the promised holiday resort under the name of 'West Bay' failed to develop, the harbour retained some trade, in particular the importation of timber from European countries. Much of this traffic was handled by Messrs Burt, Bolton & Haywood, who, before the age of the heavy lorry, relied on the goods yard at West Bay to load wagons for dispatch to various destinations.

The famous Chesil Beach which stretches from Portland in the east to West Bay was also a provider of traffic, the sand and gravel from the West Bay end being of particular value to the building and other specialised trades. The haulage of this material from the beach was at one time a substantial business and was mainly handled by Messrs Norman Good and Phillips & Sons. This sand and shingle was sent far and wide, one retired railwayman remembering shingle being sent to Egypt of all places!

Back in 1887 in an attempt to attract business from the agricultural community, cattle pens were erected at West Bay station, but this scheme was not a great success. Following the withdrawal of passenger services over the extension, the goods yard with its close proximity to the beach with its shingle trade and the harbour for timber, and a small amount of coal for the local merchant, remained a necessity - if not a profitable one - for many years.

Today West Bay has developed as a holiday resort, albeit nothing like the dream of 1884! The commercial trade has all but gone, a very few small ships now entering the harbour, and the trade in shingle from the beach has been banned for environmental reasons.

The war years restricted the use of road transport until the end of fuel rationing in January 1951, however, there was a decline in the milk traffic handled by the branch. Motor lorries had started to collect from the farms and transport direct to the dairies, but at that time the outward traffic of milk from Maiden Newton to London still flourished.

The general agricultural traffic handled was still extremely heavy. Both the firms of Silcox and Lever's sent cattle cake and other animal feeds by rail, these being stored in warehouses at Bridport station and delivered by railway lorry when required by the farmer. During the early 1950s there were seven railway lorries employed collecting and delivering in Bridport and the surrounding countryside, and in 1953 it was estimated that the Bridport vehicles had covered 38,000 miles and handled 12,000 tons of goods during the year.

Industrial unrest in the railway industry, particularly the strike of 1955, undermined goods traffic, many good customers turning to the road haulage industry which could offer more competitive rates and a flexible service. The decline continued - at first slowly but then gathering pace.

During the Great Freeze of 1963 Bridport was cut off to the outside world and again the branch became the town's lifeline - although this was the final fling. From 5th April, 1965 goods facilities were withdrawn from the branch and Weymouth became the area goods depot for South and West Dorset.

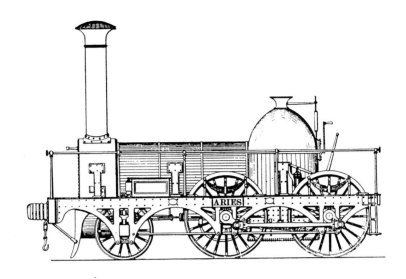

Leo Class **"ARIES"** *1841*

Line drawings of GWR broad gauge locomotive classes
known to have worked over the Bridport branch.

Bogie Class **"HESIOD"** *1849*

Motive Power

Motive power for the branch was supplied by Weymouth Depot, engines being changed with the sub-shed at Bridport when maintenance or repairs were required. At times Yeovil supplied a locomotive; during the early 1900s, and there were frequent exchanges of engines between Weymouth, Yeovil and other depots in the area, this to a degree continuing until the end of steam.

As the branch allocation could be any of Weymouth's locomotives suitable for the work, many over the years took their turn, therefore the following account only covers part of the known allocation and engines of a particular historic interest, as full class histories are covered in the RCTS series, *Locomotives of the GWR*, and other publications.

History does not record the details of the locomotive that hauled the first train, although 'Bogie' class 4-4-0 saddle tank *Hesiod* was recorded as working on the branch during its opening month, *Theocritus* of the same class was also employed on the branch at various times. Both locomotives were members of a class of 15 built by R. & W. Hawthorn & Company of Newcastle, *Theocritus* in December 1854, maker's No. 883, and *Hesiod* in March 1855, maker's No. 886.

Constructed with inside sandwich frames which extended only from the back buffer beam to the front driving wheels, there was no main frames to support the cylinders and bogie, these being fixed to a gusset plate on the underside of the boiler. The bogie swivelled on a ball and socket joint! The driving wheels, the leading set being flangeless, were 5 ft 9 in. diameter and the bogie wheels 3 ft 6 in. The cylinder diameter was 17 in. and the stroke 24 in. the crankshaft also being supported by a centre bearing, whilst the saddle tank held 9,630 gallons.

Hesiod was withdrawn from service in February 1872, *Theocritus* following in December 1873, the following February being sold to the Staveley Iron & Coal Company. However, as the Staveley company had no broad gauge lines, the use to which *Theocritus* and another broad gauge engine were put is not recorded.

In November 1860 a member of the 'Leo' class of 2-4-0 saddle tanks was recorded as being in use on the branch. Designed by Gooch and built by three different contractors, the 18 locomotives in the class were the first goods locomotives on the GWR. They were originally tender engines, but owing to adhesion problems were quickly converted to saddle tanks, the frames being extended to accommodate the coal bunker, their weight in rebuilt form being 25 ton 14½ cwt. The driving wheels were 5 ft diameter and the leading wheels 3 ft 6 in.

In June 1862, *Aries* and *Virgo* were working the branch, *Aries* (builder's No. 66) and *Virgo* (builder's No. 71) were constructed by Rothwell & Company of Bolton in June and December 1841, and were withdrawn from service exactly 30 years later in June and December 1871.

Although agreed with the Board of Trade before opening that only tank locomotives would be employed owing to the lack of a turntable at Maiden Newton, this agreement appears to have lapsed. A Gooch 'Standard Goods' 0-6-0 tender engine *Psyche* was reported being at Bridport on 8th December, 1873, one of a class of 102 locomotives built at Swindon having 5 ft diameter wheels and weighing 32 tons 5 cwt. (without tender). *Psyche* was constructed in October 1853 and withdrawn in June 1874.

The only known photographic evidence of a broad gauge engine on the branch shows 'Victoria' class 2-4-0 *Brindley* at Bridport. *Brindley* was the last of a class of 18 engines built at Swindon, and entered service in May 1864. The view at Bridport was taken in the first part of the engine's life as the 'Iron Coffin' guard's lookout is still mounted on the back of the tender, and in later years the locomotive was fitted with a cab to protect the crew. The 'Victoria' class had 6 ft 6 in. diameter driving wheels and

The only known photograph of a broad gauge engine on the Bridport branch. Taken about 1866, it shows 'Victoria' class 2-4-0 *Brindley* standing at Bridport station. The gentleman standing on the footplate (marked with a cross) is thought to be Mr Albert Hart, later divisional supt Paddington. Note the 'Iron Coffin' guard's lookout on the rear of the tender. In the foreground is part of a wheel of the Bridport turntable.

Gerry Beale Collection

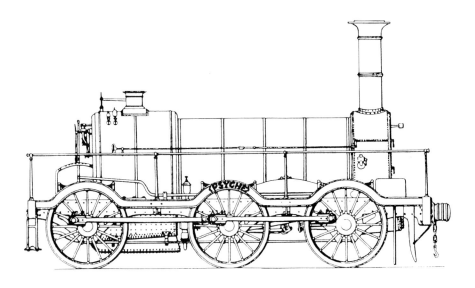

Standard Class **"PSYCHE"** *1853*

Line drawings of GWR broad gauge locomotive classes
known to have worked over the Bridport branch.

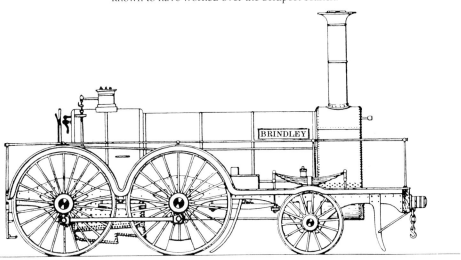

Victoria Class **"BRINDLEY"** *1864*

Ex-Monmouthshire Railway & Canal Co. 4-4-0 tank No. 1305 stands at West Bay, having just arrived with a train from Maiden Newton in June 1900.   *I.D. Beale*

No. 1305, photographed at Weymouth *circa* 1900 in her rebuilt form as a side tank.
                    National Railway Museum

4 ft leading wheels with cylinders of 16 in. diameter and 24 in. stroke, the locomotive weighing 30 tons 13 cwt. (without tender), *Brindley* was withdrawn in March 1879.

It is obvious that other unrecorded broad gauge engines worked over the branch - including tender locomotives. Several of the Gooch 'Standard Goods' class were allocated to the Weymouth line, and members of the 'Victoria' class were well represented, all locomotives only having a name, numbers not being introduced until after the broad gauge had been removed from the area.

Following the gauge change various 0-6-0 saddle tanks became the principal motive power on the branch. The '1016' class had appeared on the line by the opening of the West Bay extension. Several members of the 'Metropolitan' class 2-4-0 tanks allocated to Weymouth also appeared on the branch. No. 6, a 'Small Metro', is recorded as having failed at Maiden Newton whilst working the 5 pm West Bay-Weymouth service on Saturday 15th September, 1894.

Various members of the '517' class 0-4-2 tanks allocated to Weymouth for working branch and local services also appeared at Bridport. By 1916 the practice of Weymouth operating the Sunday service over the branch - particularly during the winter months - using the '517' class and auto-trailers became established and continued until the end of steam. This utilised spare stock on a Sunday and kept Weymouth crews' knowledge of the branch up to date.

In 1932 the '48XX' class 0-4-2 tanks were introduced, (renumbered into the 14XX series in 1946); by June 1936 No. 4803 had appeared on the branch, the new engines gradually replacing the veteran '517' class, the last disappearing from the Weymouth allocation during 1946. As the '517' class worked local services from Weymouth after 1905 as auto-trains assisted for a period by GWR steam railmotors, the question is, did a steam railmotor reach Bridport? As these would probably been classed as auto-trains in the working timetable, there is no definite answer, although there is a veiled reference to one working a train crewed by volunteers during a strike.

On 1st August, 1880 the GWR acquired the Monmouthshire Railway & Canal Co., taking over a total of 54 locomotives, 7 of which were later to work the Bridport branch at various times. These engines left the Newport area about 1890/91 and some were working at Bridport by 1894.

Renumbered into GWR stock, Nos. 1304 to 1307 were 4-4-0 side tank locomotives which had been built by the Monmouthshire company at Newport. Each weighed 41 tons 3 cwt. They were fitted with side tanks having a capacity of 750 gallons of water, but after being rebuilt by the GWR the water capacity was reduced to 650 gallons. Their driving wheels - originally 5 ft diameter - were replaced by larger ones of 5 ft 2 in., although the bogie wheels remained at 2 ft 8 in. diameter. Alterations were made to the cab, offering the crew better protection from the elements. The modifications carried out to the locomotives increased their weight to 42 tons 4 cwt.

The other engines, Nos. 1308 to 1310, were outside-framed 0-4-4 tanks built by the Avonside Engine Co. of Bristol. Of these No. 1308 (Works No. 976) was not fitted with a saddle tank and only carried 900 gallons of water in a back tank, whereas Nos. 1309 and 1310 (Works Nos. 1057/8) were both fitted with short saddle tanks and could each carry 1,000 gallons of water. These two locomotives weighed 49 tons 18 cwt each. When rebuilt all three engines were fitted with a full length saddle tank which increased their water capacity to 1,366 gallons and they also had their 5 ft diameter driving wheels replaced by larger ones of 5 ft 2 in.

Ex-Monmouthshire Railway & Canal Company engine No. 1308. Although this photograph was taken at Newport, the engine is in the condition in which she first appeared on the Bridport branch, before her reconstruction in 1898.   *Locomotive Publishing Co.*

No. 1308, photographed at Weymouth *circa* 1900 in her rebuilt form with a full length saddle tank.   *National Railway Museum*

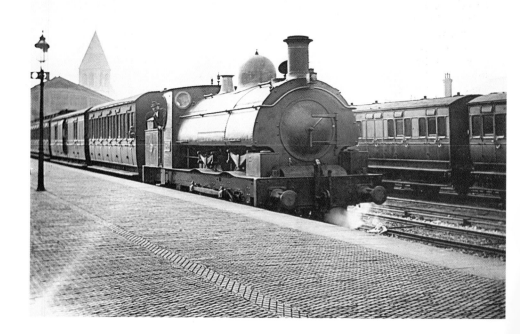

GWR No.	Monmouth No.	Builder	Year built	Year rebuilt	Withdrawn	Type
1304	14	Monmouth Rly	1870	Sep. 1893	Nov. 1905	4-4-0T
1305	41	Monmouth Rly	1871	Jul. 1895	Jan. 1905	4-4-0T
1306	15	Monmouth Rly	1872	Jun. 1896	Oct. 1904	4-4-0T
1307	10a	Monmouth Rly	1875	May 1898	Nov. 1905	4-4-0T
1308	47	Avonside	1873	Oct. 1898	May 1904	0-4-4T
1309	5	Avonside	1874	Mar. 1897	Sep. 1903	0-4-4ST
1310	51	Avonside	1875	Feb. 1899	Apr. 1908	0-4-4ST

Although associated with the Bridport branch, these tanks also carried out pilot duties at Weymouth and sometimes worked the Abbotsbury branch. During the late 1890s the average failure rate of locomotives per month on the GWR was 30-35 ranging from complete mechanical failure to just running out of steam. Unfortunately the Monmouth tanks and the Bridport branch are conspicuous in the breakdown reports that have survived.

No. 1304 suffered four tube failures between May 1894 and July 1898, a broken slide valve in May 1894, and a broken axle box the following April. No. 1305 had a tube failure on 16th May, 1897 and was brought to a halt on three different trains on 16th July with the same problem, and in the August of the following year. In April 1895 she suffered a valve gear failure and a cylinder cover blew off at Toller in January 1896, Toller also being the scene of a broken motion block in November the following year.

No. 1306 had a tube failure in 1897 and a second the following year, whilst No. 1308 came to a halt with a defective steam pipe in May 1895. There were also five failures with these locomotives on the Abbotsbury branch during this period!

Just after the turn of the century there appeared to be an upheaval in the GWR motive power department. During 1902 the entire batch of 'Monmouth Tanks' (1304 excepted) appeared on the branch, in between periods at Weymouth and Yeovil. No. 1310 saw the New Year in on the branch, to be replaced in the middle of the month by No. 1309, the changes proceeding throughout the year. No. 1309 put in the highest mileage on the branch, followed by No. 1307, whilst No. 1310 only appeared at the beginning of the year followed by a visit to Swindon Works and allocation to Yeovil. The principal supporting engines were the '1076' 'Buffalo' class, Nos. 729, 1586, 1654 and 1730, assisted by No. 904 of the '645' class and No. 1135 of the '1034' class.

By 1904 the '2021' class were dominating the scene, No. 2031 obtaining the highest mileage and working seven months on the branch, whilst Nos. 2125 and 2126 worked the branch for two months. A member of the '645' class, No. 904 put in three months, whilst '2854' class No. 1730 only spent from 25th June to 23rd July here. The significant change was the demise of the 'Monmouth Tanks'. Whilst No. 1310 spent the year at Weymouth, only No. 1304 appeared at Bridport between the 23rd June and 20th August. Following her return to Weymouth she was dispatched to Swindon Works on 15th October and subsequently condemned.

During 1905 three members of the '2021' class, usually a very reliable engine, suffered failures. On 5th April No. 2125 was about to depart from Bridport with the 7.17 pm to West Bay when the boiler lagging caught fire, thereby pre-empting a Bulleid light pacific party trick by almost 40 years! She then failed for reasons not recorded on 26th August at Powerstock. No. 2126 had tube failure in March, whilst No. 2147 stopped at Toller on 18th August with a broken eccentric strap bolt. On 9th August, 1906 No. 2086 was stopped at Grimstone & Frampton with a broken cylinder whilst working the 11.5 am West Bay-Dorchester through train.

Two years later the branch was operated entirely by the '2021' class tanks, except for an appearance of '1076' 'Buffalo' class No. 1586 during June. Of the eight locomotives

Class '1076' 'Buffalo' class No. 1641 runs around its train at West Bay during the September of 1929. Note the original 1884 Vignoles 75lb. rail still in use.   *The late Dr. Ian C. Allan*

'14XX' class auto tank No. 1453 departs from Maiden Newton for Bridport with a Sunday train on 22nd September, 1951. Within a short period of time the wooden post GWR signals were replaced by rail-built ones of Southern design.   *R.A. Lumber*

officially recorded as covering branch duties during the year Nos. 2125 and 2147 were allocated during January, No. 2125 had the highest mileage, working eight months on the branch, No. 2038 working six months, and No. 2086 five months. Nos. 2031, 2032, and 2147 only achieved two months, No. 2126 only spent part of January at Bridport before returning to Weymouth and later moving to Swindon. The '2021' class remained the branch engine throughout the period. In 1910 Nos. 2038 and 2044 attained the highest mileage, despite No. 2044 failing at Toller on 29th March with a broken slide valve. She was also one of the few of the class to be fitted at the time with an extended smokebox. No. 2017 was the third highest mileage engine whilst '645' class No. 902 appeared in January and February, and '1076' class No. 750 went to Bridport at the end of December.

The '2021' class were represented by Nos. 2113 and 2119 during 1921. Later the class were to disappear from the area. A versatile engine, many in later years were rebuilt as pannier tanks and had a long life. Of the former Bridport engines No. 2125 survived until August 1925, although No. 2038, condemned in April 1953, had a reprieve as a stationary boiler until July 1956. Nos. 2031 and 2147 went during 1953 and Nos. 2032 and 2044 in the Summer of 1951.

In 1928 the 'Buffalo' '1076' class was the principal branch engine, No. 2042 running the highest mileage, followed by No. 966, whilst No. 1171 only worked the branch early in the year, with '645' class No. 1804 putting in a short spell during May.

The year 1935 saw the last of the 'Buffalo' '1076' class. During the previous year Nos. 1239, 1281 and 1289 had worked the branch at various times, No. 1289 being withdrawn during the July. No. 1281 was withdrawn in May 1935, No. 1039 following in October, these being the last outside-framed locomotives to work over the line. They were very smooth-running engines and had a good reputation for work. Of special mention Nos. 1239 and 1242, built in 1876, were converted to work on the broad gauge in the West Country in 1887 and following the abolition of the broad gauge in 1892 were rebuilt to standard gauge. Like many others in the class they were converted from saddle to pannier tank in later life.

In September 1936 No. 7408, of the new '74XX' 0-6-0 pannier tank class, was covering branch services, and during 1937 '655' class 0-6-0 tanks Nos. 1775, 1782 and 2710 with '1813' class No. 1831 mainly worked the branch, although No. 7415 of Yeovil Shed was engaged on branch duties during September. By 1938 usually two '74XX' were available for branch work, assisted by members of the '655' class.

The first recorded visit of a heavier locomotive was during 1938 when '55XX' 2-6-2 No. 5521 - a Taunton based engine - visited the branch with the divisional weed killing train. In July 1939 '45XX' class 2-6-2 tank No. 4536 and '4575' class Nos. 5509 and 5558 were reported as working at Weymouth on local services, but as their stay in the area was short it is not known if the branch was included in their employment. However, No. 7404 was allocated to Bridport at the end of the year, and with the use of this class the crews had the opportunity to work new locomotives instead of the usual time-worn specimens that they had on many occasions.

During 1941 '4575' class No. 5555 and '655' class No. 2702 were active on the branch. That December Nos. 2702 and 2703 were the normal branch engines with No. 7408 standing in if either of the other two were not available. By February 1942 Nos. 2702 and 2720 were alternately employed on the branch with No. 5555 which was changed for No. 5511. According to Swindon records, three members of the '48XX' class 0-4-2 tanks were allocated to Bridport for short periods during the war: No. 4854 in July 1941; No. 4815 during February 1942 ; and No. 4867 in May 1945.

Little information is recorded for the remainder of the war, but there was one wartime instance of a tender engine arriving at Bridport with a troop train. Retired branch driver

'57XX' class 0-6-0PT No. 7780 approaches Bridport station with a train from Maiden Newton. To the left is the the goods yard headshunt and buffer stops, the scene of a wartime shunting incident when the fireman put the engine through the stop blocks!   *I.D. Beale*

'45XX' 2-6-2 No. 4562 stands at Bridport between duties. Of the various members of the class to work the branch No. 4562 stayed the longest and was the most popular.   *I.D. Beale*

Peter Miller recalled how upon its arrival Bridport staff telephoned control to inform them that this engine should not have been on the branch, the simple reply being 'It got down there, so it will go back out!'

After the war the '74XX' class saw very little service on the branch. From then until the end of regular steam-hauled passenger trains the motive power ranged between two '57XX' or two '45XX' locomotives, or one of each.

In mid-1946, Nos. 4527, 4536, 4660, 7782 and 9628 were available from Weymouth to cover the duties. On the night of 31st December, 1947 Nos. 4562 and 4660 worked the last GWR trains and became the first engines to work the line for British Railways.

Early 1950 saw one pannier tank, No. 9642, and '45XX' tanks Nos. 4520, 4527 and 4562 available for branch work. In March 1953 No. 4507 was allocated to Weymouth and spent a considerable time on the branch until that August when she was moved to Yeovil. During 1956 '4575' class No. 5548 was allocated to Weymouth and carried out branch duties, as did '57XX' No. 9601, a Yeovil based engine.

Following heavy repairs at Swindon, No. 4507 returned to Weymouth in February 1958 resplendent in lined green livery, and returned immediately to branch duties. The motive power depots at Weymouth and Yeovil Pen Mill were handed over to the Southern Region in February 1958. As the Southern already had operational control of the lines within the area it made little difference apart from administration, the former GWR locomotives being handed over to the Southern Region.

With the introduction of the 1959 summer timetable local services in the area were taken over by diesel multiple units, this including certain workings between Bristol and Weymouth, the Weymouth-Yeovil local service and the Bridport branch, which was served by units based at Weymouth, the sub-shed at Bridport being closed.

The last two steam locomotives to leave Bridport shed on the morning of Monday 15th June were '45XX' class Nos. 4507 and 4562, coupled together with No. 4507, driven by Peter Miller, leading. At Weymouth they lay in store until the following March, when No. 4562 (built at Swindon in 1924) was sent for scrap. No. 4507 went to Swindon for light repairs. Of the various '45XXs' employed on the branch No. 4507 deserves special mention as the last engine built at Wolverhampton Stafford Road Works to be in service with British Railways. Built as No. 2168, she was completed in May 1907. Under the general renumbering scheme of 1912 she became No. 4507, serving her early days in Devon and Cornwall. She entered the Bristol Division in 1929 and worked in the North Somerset area. Ten years later she was based at Swindon, and early in the war was shedded at Andover for working over the MSWJR. The early 1950s saw her in the Taunton area before her move to Weymouth

Following repairs at Swindon Works in 1959 she was allocated to Yeovil Town shed where she remained until towed to Swindon in October 1963, by which time it was estimated she had travelled 1,198,165 miles, and was also the oldest locomotive in regular service on the Western Region. The local Wolverhampton press suggested that a fund should be started to purchase her for preservation, but unfortunately the idea was not taken up. On 15th July, 1964 she entered Bird's yard at Pontymister, and by the end of the month a unique engine had gone!

Two other '45XX' class tanks that worked the branch also held records. No. 4508 ran an estimated 1,244,723 miles, the highest recorded for the class, whilst No. 4539 ran the lowest mileage, a mere 748,890 - which was strange, as most of the class exceeded over a million miles.

Of the pannier tanks working the branch in the post-war period, only two call for special mention. No. 7780 was withdrawn in 1963 following a spectacular collision with another engine within the confines of Weymouth engine shed! No. 9642 appeared on

Class '2' 2-6-2 tank No. 41305 waits to depart from Bridport with a one-coach train during the period when only one steam-hauled passenger train daily operated over the branch following the introduction of diesel units. *David Lawrence*

Pressed Steel single unit No. W55032 has just arrived at Bridport on 3rd April, 1965. Eight weeks later the down platform and all other sidings would be taken out of use. *D.M. Habgood*

the branch between 1947 and 1953, and following withdrawal she was sold for scrap in January 1965 to R.S. Hayes of Bridgend, who used the engine in their yard for three years. She was subsequently purchased for preservation, and now fully restored she resides at the Swansea Vale Railway.

After the arrival of the diesel units, only the goods service and the one remaining steam-hauled passenger train were hauled by '57XX' class tanks. At the end of 1963 these were replaced at Weymouth by Ivatt class '2' 2-6-2 tanks Nos. 41261, 41284, 41295, 41298, 41305 and 41320. The only special mention of these locomotives is that Nos. 41295 and 41320 hauled the last steam train over the branch - the LCGB special on 22nd January, 1967 - No. 41295 being the rear engine on the return journey was the last engine on the branch! No. 41298 passed into preservation with the Ivatt Locomotive Trust, and today resides at the Buckinghamshire Railway Centre, Quainton Road.

Of the multiple unit replacements there is little to record. When first introduced two-car units were employed, but latterly a 65-seat single car - referred to as a 'Bubble Car' - sufficed. Of these, No. W55033, built by Pressed Steel in 1960, after finally running in the West Midlands in WMPTE Midline livery, is now preserved on the Colne Valley Railway at Castle Headingham.

Rolling Stock

Most types of goods wagon were to be seen on the branch over the years. Pre-war, private owner coal wagons were common, both those owned by the colliery companies and coal merchants. Four of the local coal and building material distributors had their own wagons, Sullys of Bridgwater, The Somerset Trading Company, Ralls & Son, and Bradford the coal merchant. Wagons belonging to Messrs Bryer Ash, who had depots in the Dorset area, could also be seen delivering coal to the smaller merchants they supplied. The Somerset Trading Company wagons were the most colourful, being bright red with white lettering shaded in black, whilst Bradford's, who operated over 200 wagons, were black with white lettering. Originally wagons owned by Ralls were in a lead colour, with white lettering shaded in black. In later years a livery of black with white lettering was adopted. (Bryer Ash had always had a livery of black with white lettering.) Pre-1915 many of the older private owner wagons had only dumb buffers, and some had no hand brakes fitted!

There were also the tank wagons belonging to the petroleum companies who operated the fuel depot at Bridport.

Owing to the gradients on the branch a heavy guard's van was always used. Of particular interest was a 24 ton six-wheel van, No. 56943, which was used for a period. The regular branch van was fitted with both vacuum brake and steam heating pipes to enable it to be used with mixed trains.

Of the passenger stock, the usual branch line practice of using older vehicles cascaded down from main line work prevailed up to at least 1930, which in practice meant that the newer coaches were just a little less decrepit than the oldest! Four-wheelers served on the branch up to the closure of the West Bay section, apart from the occasional bogie coach that was used to strengthen trains. The most comfortable coaches seen on the branch were the auto-trailers, which ran when Weymouth provided the Sunday service.

The first 'quality' stock were the ubiquitous 'B sets' which had first been introduced by the GWR during the mid-1920s, and these became the standard stock for the branch from the early 1930s. Non-corridor, and having small windows, they could not be described as the most elegant design to come out of Swindon, but they were far superior

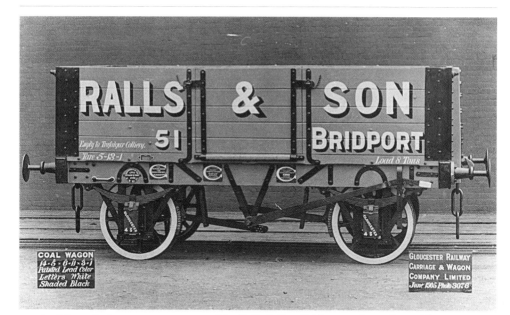

An 8 ton private owner wagon owned by Ralls & Son, Bridport coal merchant. This wagon constructed by the Gloucester Railway Carriage & Wagon Co. in 1905 was painted in a lead colour, with white letters shaded black.   *By permission of Gloucestershire County Records Office*

A 10 ton private owner wagon owned by Ralls & Son, Bridport coal merchant. This wagon constructed by the Gloucester Railway Carriage & Wagon Co. in 1916, was no doubt to wartime economy painted in a plain black livery with white lettering.
By permission of Gloucestershire County Records Office

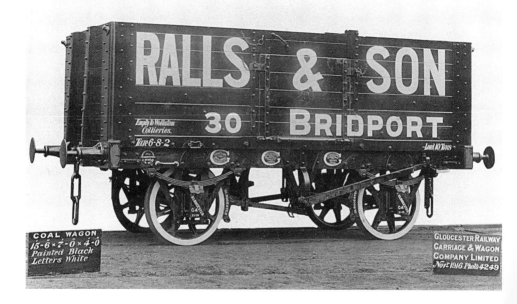

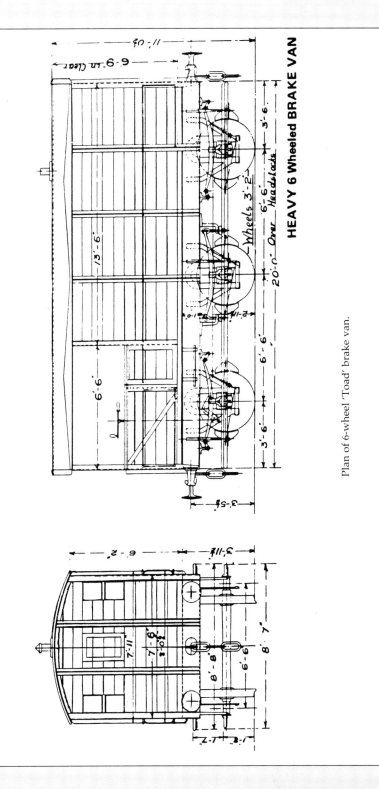

HEAVY 6 Wheeled BRAKE VAN

Plan of 6-wheel 'Toad' brake van.

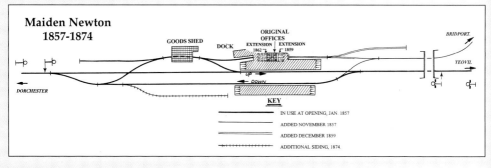

**Maiden Newton
1857-1874**

GOODS SHED   DOCK   ORIGINAL OFFICES

EXTENSION 1862 — EXTENSION 1859

BRIDPORT.

YEOVIL

UP

DOWN

DORCHESTER

KEY

IN USE AT OPENING, JAN. 1857

ADDED NOVEMBER 1857

ADDED DECEMBER 1859

ADDITIONAL SIDING, 1874.

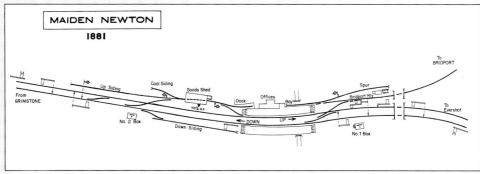

MAIDEN NEWTON

1881

To BRIDPORT

M

Up Siding   Coal Siding   Goods Shed   Spur   Water Tank

Dock   Offices   Box   Bridport Rly

From GRIMSTONE

To Evershot

No. 2 Box   Down Siding   DOWN   UP   No. 1 Box

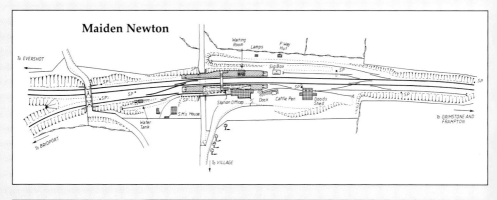

Maiden Newton

Waiting Room   Lamps   P. Way Hut

To EVERSHOT

SP   Sig Box   SP   SP

SP   SP   SP   SP   SP

Station Offices   Dock   Cattle Pen   Goods Shed

S.M's House

Water Tank

To GRIMSTONE AND FRAMPTON

To BRIDPORT

To VILLAGE

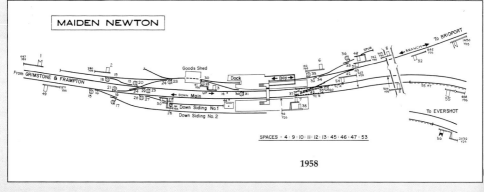

MAIDEN NEWTON

To BRIDPORT

BRANCH

From GRIMSTONE & FRAMPTON

Goods Shed   Dock   Box   SPUR

Down Main

Down Siding No.1

Down Siding No.2

To EVERSHOT

SPACES · 4 : 9 : 10 : 11 : 12 : 13 : 45 : 46 : 47 : 53

1958

to the previous 'boneshakers' and gave good reliable service until the end of steam-hauled passenger trains.

Before World War II a brake third was kept at Bridport for strengthening purposes, and during the summer service one was also kept at Maiden Newton for use on either the branch or main line as required. Since the war only the Bridport coach was kept, this being known as the 'night coach'. One of the last vehicles used for this job was No. W6991, a brake composite built in 1936 that had been converted into a slip coach. However, with the reduction of slip coach working, it was relegated to branch work like many others of its kind.

The only restriction for passenger stock was that coaches (including rail motors and trailers) 70 ft long and over were prohibited from the entire branch.

Signalling and Train Working

When first opened the Wilts, Somerset & Weymouth Railway was mainly single line, the section between Yeovil and Dorchester having crossing loops at Evershot and Maiden Newton. However, owing to the telegraph being incomplete at the opening, Maiden Newton could not be used as a crossing place until 7th May, 1857, by which time the telegraph was in operation. Until then trains were worked by pilotman.

The signalling of trains over many sections of the line was controlled by the 'Telegraph Permissive Block System'. This included the Evershot to Maiden Newton and Dorchester sections. With this system trains were worked strictly to the timetable which gave details of the places where certain trains crossed. When trains were delayed or running out of sequence the double needle telegraph was employed to send messages to revise the crossing orders, which were issued by the station in rear. The trains were signalled forward but not 'blocked back'. At a later date a report suggests that a following train was allowed to enter the section, the driver being given a Caution note.

The original signalling at Maiden Newton consisted of the usual GWR disc and crossbar signals, two at each end, the outer one acting as a distant signal. All signals and points were hand operated.

The double needle telegraphs on the Weymouth line were replaced by the simpler single needle version after 1863, these being used on the single track sections between Evershot and Maiden Newton and Maiden Newton to Dorchester, although these instruments were not interlocked with any points or signals. At least with the code system developed with the 'needle' station staff could find out what was happening along the line, and before a train set out the station clerk could be reasonably sure that another had not been sent off from the other end of the single line section to meet it head on. The 'needle' was used in conjunction with crossing order forms, these being a written reminder of the movements taking place.

Operation of the single line sections required great care, and special regulations were laid down. The station clerk was officially the only person allowed to operate the telegraph, whilst the policeman walked about the station working points and signals. When using the telegraph the clerk also had to write down the message, and it had to be repeated at the receiving station. Just before the departure of a train a description of the train and 'line clear' signal was sent. The station clerk had to have a clear understanding of the movements taking place and ensure the trains were issued with the correct crossing orders.

This system was superseded in 1868 on the Evershot-Dorchester sections by Train Staff and Ticket, this being used in conjunction with the 'needle'.

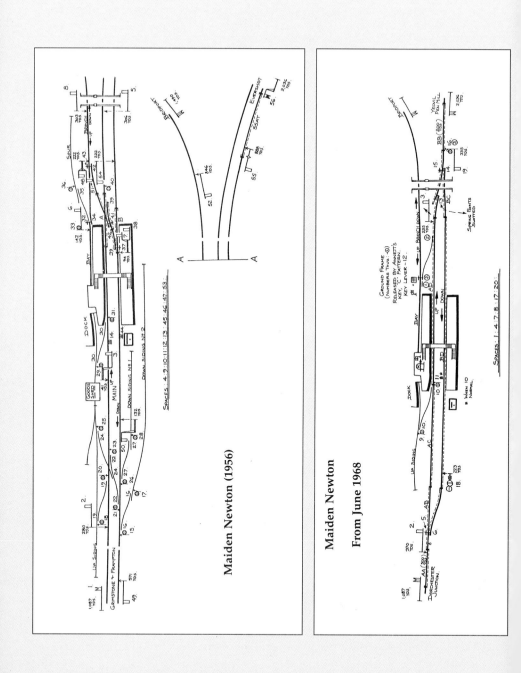

Maiden Newton (1956)

Maiden Newton
From June 1968

The staff consisted of a length of wood with the name of the section it protected marked on it. As there was only one of these, a driver could not enter a section until he had possession of it or a written ticket giving authority to proceed having been shown the staff.

In 1873 the needle telegraph was replaced by the disc block instrument between Thingley Junction and Dorchester Junction, and Absolute Block working introduced.

During 1877 two signal boxes were opened at Maiden Newton. No. 1 box (later renamed North Box) contained 22 levers of which 16 were in use, and No. 2 box (later renamed South Box) had 14 levers of which 12 were used. The earlier disc and crossbar signals were replaced by semaphores. In 1879 the electric train staff was in operation on the single line sections either side of Maiden Newton, but this was short lived, as by the 10th June, 1881 the Evershot-Maiden Newton section had been doubled, and likewise southwards to Grimstone & Frampton in May 1884. In July the following year the Grimstone to Dorchester section was completed, thus removing the last single line section on the line to Weymouth.

Spagnoletti's Absolute Block instruments were introduced. The two signal boxes at Maiden Newton were replaced by one box situated at the Dorchester end of the down platform during 1885. This was of timber construction, with 30 levers (all in use), in which form the signalling at Maiden Newton was to remain for many years.

From the outset the Bridport branch had been worked by a simple train staff. The first signal box was erected at Bridport in 1882, but as the line was only worked by one train at a time, it could control very little. Its main function was to operate points and signals at the station, which in 1881 had been described as 'partially interlocked'.

The West Bay extension of 1883 cost £400 19s. 5d. to equip with signalling, the work being carried out by the Gloucester Wagon Company, who for a while carried out signalling work on a limited scale. Very little remains of the signalling department records, except for entries in the company Minute books giving a limited account of transactions. At the following meetings only the value of the contracts was recorded.

12th June, 1883.	Bridport Railway Company	£240
10th July, 1883	Bridport Railway Company	£15
9th October, 1883	Bridport Railway Company	£16 5s.
13th November, 1883	Bridport Railway Company	£133

These are slightly at variance with the Bridport company figures! It also seemss strange to involve four separate contracts for such a small amount of work.

The signal box at West Bay was a small structure situated on the platform. The signals supplied were the usual semaphore type of the period, having a single spectacle glass showing red. When the signal dropped to 'clear', the signal lamp was uncovered to display a 'white light'. It was not until 1892 that green replaced the white light as an 'Alright' night indication in signals.

With the alterations needed to Bridport station for the extension, a ground frame was built at the West Bay end, and alterations made to the existing Bridport box.

At East Street the crossing gates were provided with protection by signals, which together with a wicket gate for pedestrians, were locked from a ground frame situated nearby. Although this signalling equipment had been added, only one train could work between Maiden Newton and West Bay at a time with a train staff, under the 'one engine in steam' (or two or more coupled) method of working (the staff at the time being coloured red).

The necessity of working more than one train on the branch was resolved with alterations carried out at Bridport during 1893, the Electric Train Staff being introduced between Maiden Newton-Bridport-West Bay on 19th November, 1893. The instruments were

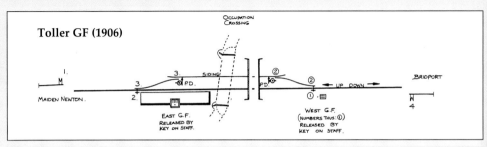

Toller GF (1906)

Occupation Crossing

MAIDEN NEWTON.

SIDING

P.D.

EAST G.F.
RELEASED BY
KEY ON STAFF.

P.D.

UP DOWN

WEST G.F.
(NUMBERS THUS: ①)
RELEASED BY
KEY ON STAFF.

BRIDPORT

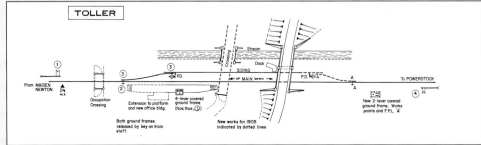

TOLLER

From MAIDEN NEWTON

Occupation Crossing

Extension to platform
and new office bldg.

Both ground frames
released by key on train
staff.

Crossing

Stream

Dock

SIDING

P.D.

UP MAIN DOWN

4-lever covered
ground frame.
(Nos. thus ①)

New works for 1905
indicated by dotted lines

P.D. 'A'

To POWERSTOCK

New 2-lever covered
ground frame. Works
points and F.P.L. 'A'

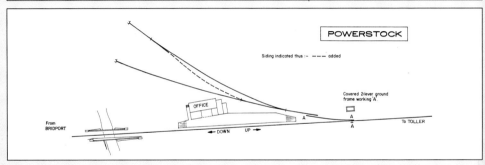

POWERSTOCK

Siding indicated thus :- --- added

OFFICE

Covered 2-lever ground
frame working 'A'.

From
BRIDPORT

DOWN UP

To TOLLER

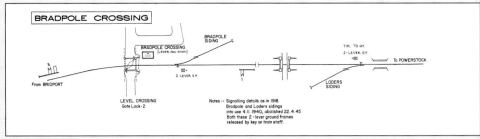

BRADPOLE CROSSING

BRADPOLE CROSSING
(LEVER Nos. GIVEN)

BRADPOLE
SIDING

2-LEVER G.F.

From BRIDPORT

LEVEL CROSSING
Gate Lock-2

Notes :- Signalling details as in 1918.
Bradpole and Loders sidings
into use 4.11.1940, abolished 22.4.45
Both these 2-lever ground frames
released by key on train staff.

T.M. 70 CH.
2-LEVER G.F.

To POWERSTOCK

LODERS
SIDING

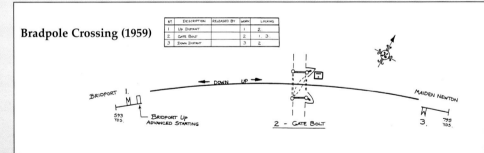

Bradpole Crossing (1959)

N°	DESCRIPTION	RELEASED BY	WORK	LOCKING
1.	Up Distant		1	2.
2.	Gate Bolt		2	1, 3.
3.	Down Distant		3	2.

BRIDPORT

DOWN UP

593 YDS.

BRIDPORT UP
ADVANCED STARTING

2 - GATE BOLT

MAIDEN NEWTON

795 YDS.

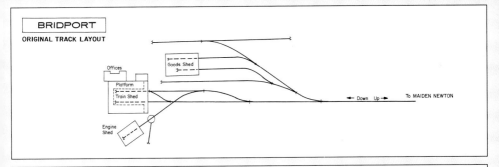

BRIDPORT

ORIGINAL TRACK LAYOUT

Offices
Platform
Train Shed
Goods Shed
Engine Shed

← Down   Up →   To MAIDEN NEWTON

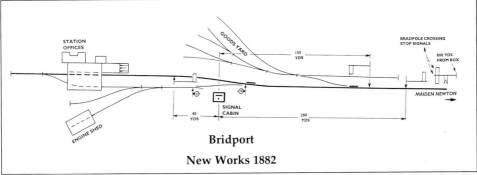

STATION OFFICES

GOODS YARD

155 YDS

BRADPOLE CROSSING STOP SIGNALS

800 YDS FROM BOX

MAIDEN NEWTON →

40 YDS

SIGNAL CABIN

280 YDS

ENGINE SHED

Bridport

New Works 1882

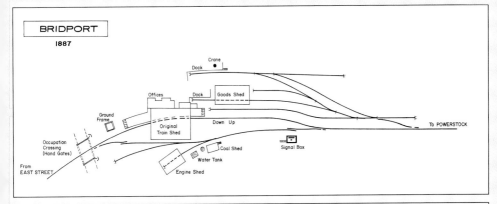

BRIDPORT

1887

Crane
Dock
Dock
Offices
Goods Shed
Ground Frame
Original Train Shed
Down Up
Coal Shed
Signal Box
Water Tank
Engine Shed

Occupation Crossing (Hand Gates)

From EAST STREET

To POWERSTOCK

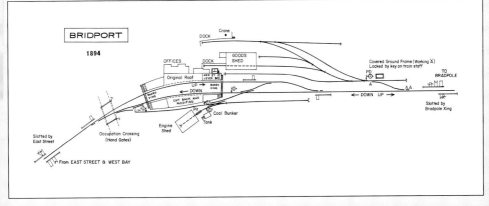

BRIDPORT

1894

DOCK
Crane
DOCK
GOODS SHED
OFFICES
Original Roof
NEW 21 LEVER BOX
BOARD XING
UP
DOWN
CUT BACK AND MODIFIED
Pit
Coal Bunker
Engine Shed
Tank

Covered Ground Frame (Working 'A')
Locked by key on train staff
PD
A
A.A
← DOWN UP →
TO BRADPOLE
Slotted by Bradpole Xing

Slotted by East Street

Occupation Crossing (Hand Gates)

From EAST STREET & WEST BAY

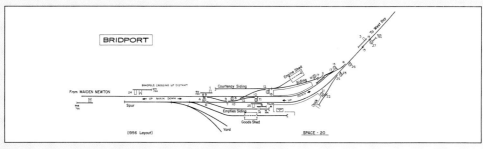

BRIDPORT

From MAIDEN NEWTON

BRADPOLE CROSSING UP DISTANT

Courtenay Siding

Engine Shed

Siding

To West Bay

UP MAIN DOWN

UP

Spur

Empties Siding

Goods Shed

Yard

(1956 Layout)

SPACE - 20

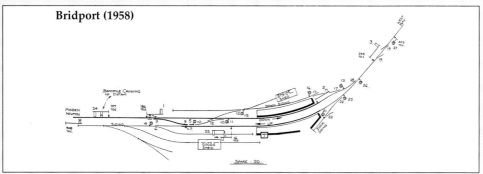

Bridport (1958)

BRADPOLE CROSSING
UP DISTANT

MAIDEN
NEWTON

SIDING

DOWN SIDING

UP

GOODS
SHED

SPARE : 20

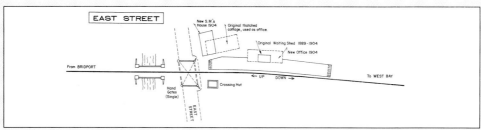

EAST STREET

New S.M.'s House 1904

Original thatched cottage, used as office.

Original Waiting Shed 1889-1904

New Office 1904

From BRIDPORT

UP   DOWN

To WEST BAY

Hand Gates (Single)

Crossing Hut

EAST STREET

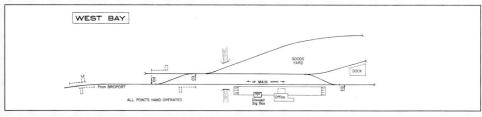

WEST BAY

GOODS YARD

DOCK

M   From BRIDPORT

UP MAIN DOWN

ALL POINTS HAND OPERATED

Disused Sig. Box

Office

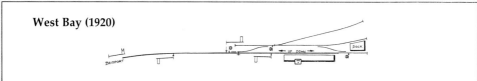

West Bay (1920)

M

BRIDPORT

UP   DOWN

DOCK

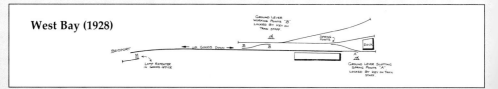

West Bay (1928)

GROUND LEVER WORKING POINTS "B" LOCKED BY KEY ON TRAIN STAFF

SPRING POINTS

BRIDPORT

UP GOODS DOWN

B   B

DOCK

M   LAMP REPEATER IN GOODS OFFICE

A

GROUND LEVER SLOTTING SPRING POINTS "A" LOCKED BY KEY ON TRAIN STAFF

subsequently moved to the new signal box which opened on 2nd July, 1894, this being equipped with a standard Great Western stud locking frame with levers at 5¼ inch centres and sweeps on the quadrant plates. The latter arrangement formed a foot-rest for use when pulling the levers. The frame had 27 levers, of which 21 were in use at the opening. There was a ground frame at the Maiden Newton end of the layout controlling the entrance to the goods yard, this being locked by the key on the train staff. The entire branch was then operated on the Webb & Thompson train staff system, assisted by disc block telegraph.

The branch was divided into two sections, Maiden Newton-Bridport and Bridport-West Bay, this giving much greater flexibility in the operation of the train service.

With the alterations at Bridport, the old signal box - a wooden structure on the down side near the entrance to the goods yard - was removed, as was the ground frame at the West Bay end of the station.

In 1905 a second connection to the siding at Toller (at the Bridport end) was added, this like all other ground frames on the branch, being released by the key on the train staff.

Returning to Maiden Newton, the signal box of 1885 was replaced in 1921 by a 56-lever structure fitted with a standard GWR vertical tappet frame with levers at 4 inch centres. This was situated just beyond the end of the down platform at the Dorchester end, and formed the final signalling layout of the branch. However, equipment exposed to the elements and subject to wear and tear requires renewing at regular intervals, some examples follow. During 1911 Bradpole Crossing gates and locking had to be replaced, as did the point connections at Bridport signal box. The crossing gates and ground frame at East Street required replacement during 1915, and a section of telegraph wires along the branch were replaced during 1928, for which 21 miles of wire were required! Over the years many signals and other equipment were replaced, largely unnoticed until the 1950s, when some of the signals at Maiden Newton and Bridport were renewed. The line was then under the control of the Southern Region, which erected its standard rail-built upper quadrant signals and single disc ground signals of the Westinghouse pattern.

Like many other GWR branch lines, the 'economic' system of maintenance was employed, using a ganger's occupation key. This saved the ganger having to send two men to protect a trolley when placed on the line, so he could cut his work force by half. By the removal of his ganger's key from its instrument he would lock the electric train staff instrument so that no trains could enter the section.

From 8th June, 1965 the signal box at Bridport was closed, and within a short while all track, except a single line into the platform, had been removed. The branch was then worked by a wooden train staff, using the 'one engine in steam' system. Until then Bridport had been one of the few branches to retain the electric train staff, many lines having gone over to the lighter and much smaller electric key token many years before.

The severe reduction in traffic over the main line resulted in it being converted to single line between Castle Cary and Dorchester West, with passing loops at Yeovil Pen Mill and Maiden Newton. The first section to be converted was between Castle Cary and Yeovil on 12th May, 1968, Yeovil to Maiden Newton followed on the 26th, and the remaining section to Dorchester West on 9th June. The latter section is operated by tokenless block, in which the block instrument is fully locked with the signals as well as the track circuits. The Dorchester end was controlled by Dorchester Junction signal box, as was the point where the line became single at the north end of Dorchester West station. The other two sections were controlled by the electric key token system.

With the singling of the line, a colour light signal was brought into use as a down starter at Maiden Newton, this being a Ministry of Transport requirement for a signal controlling entry into a tokenless block section, although all other signals at the station remained semaphore.

Maiden Newton: the branch 'B set' under the control of the guard, rolls back into the bay platform, whilst '45XX' class 2-6-2 tank No. 4562 waits on the branch approach. When the coaches have come to rest the engine will rejoin the train ready for the return journey to Bridport.   *M.E.J. Deane*

Change-over time at Maiden Newton on 13th July, 1957. '57XX' class 0-6-0PT No. 3746 arrives with the 11.5 am from Bridport, whilst No. 3737 stands with a set of stock on the gravity siding.
                                                                                                                            J. Spencer Gilks

The simplification of the layout included alterations to the branch connection, trains having to reverse from the up loop into the branch bay to gain access to the branch, the connecting points being controlled from a 3-lever ground frame released from the signal box and unlocked by an Annett's key from a release instrument housed with a telephone in a cabinet near the ground frame.

In the signal box itself, the 56-lever frame was shortened to a mere 20 levers. The only remaining signals on the branch were the fixed distants at Bradpole Crossing and on the approach to Maiden Newton, the latter being the only GWR wooden post signal left standing in the area.

Further economies have also taken place at the Dorchester end of the single line section, Dorchester Junction signal box closed on 5th July, 1986, control of the junction with its simplified layout and the tokenless block instruments being taken over by Dorchester South box, which with its panel, also took over the operation of Weymouth on 19th September, 1987.

In the on-going efforts to reduce the operating cost of the Yeovil-Dorchester line, Maiden Newton signal box closed on 15th May, 1988, thus bringing to an end the history of GWR signalling in the county, although the box survived in use by the permanent way department as a mess room for a while, but is now derelict. To allow continued use of the passing loop the points at each end are hydraulic, and set to lie normally for the respective loops. A speed restriction of 20 mph is in place whilst within the station limits. On both the up and down platforms a small hut houses the key token machines for the Yeovil-Maiden Newton section. Upon arrival with a train from either direction the driver unlocks the hut and telephones the Yeovil Pen Mill signalman, who then gives him permission to either replace or withdraw a token from the machine. This done, the driver locks the hut and proceeds on his journey.

Working Methods

When both the Bridport branch and the main line opened in 1857, the entire system of working was far more simplistic than in later years when various regulations were introduced to ensure a high degree of safety for both passengers and staff.

The crossing stations on the Wilts, Somerset & Weymouth line were of a standard layout, and as finances were stretched these were somewhat basic and consisted of a passing loop on the down side and a goods siding on the up side, which with its associated pointwork, created a loop for shunting purposes.

When the Bridport branch first opened there was no bay platform, the branch train having to operate from the down loop platform - a situation that involved the branch train either remaining on, or retreating to the branch approach if a passing or shunting move had to be made on the main line.

By the end of 1859 this situation had been rectified by the provision of a bay platform on the up side and a gravity siding to allow the engine to be released from the end of the bay platform. Although not unique to Maiden Newton, there were few examples of this system in use. After unloading in the branch bay a train that had arrived from Bridport would shunt back onto the steeply graded siding, brakes would be applied to the coaches, the engine then uncoupled and returned to the branch bay. The points would then be changed allowing the engine to proceed back onto the branch approach to the rear of the points, which would again be changed for the gravity siding. The brakes of the coaches would be released, and under control of the guard would be allowed to run back into the bay platform. The points would again be changed, and the engine moved

Maiden Newton, and '45XX' class 2-6-2 tank No. 4562 rejoins the stock after the gravity shunt move.
Note the volume of parcel traffic being unloaded from the branch train.   *I.D. Beale*

forward to join the train for the return journey down the branch, the entire operation
requiring 37 lever movements in the signal box.

If the guard was a little premature in applying the handbrake on the descent, the
coaches could come to a halt before clearing the points. It then required some work with
a pinch bar against the wheels to get them moving, or a nudge from the engine (not
necessarily on the buffers) to remedy the situation.

The fact there was no facing connection off the up main line onto the branch made it
difficult for trains from the Weymouth direction to enter the branch, the only connection
being a trailing one off the down main line (having a single slip making a crossover onto
the up main). This arrangement caused many shunting movements that blocked both
main lines, a situation that was to continue until the simplified layout of 1968. Ironically,
just prior to the Great War there was a plan to extend the north end of both platforms and
incorporate a facing connection in the new works, but unfortunately these plans were
never proceeded with.

The method of working the branch was dictated by the signalling system employed -
or the lack of it - and until the improvements at Bridport in 1894 only one train could
occupy the branch at any given time. Although this difficulty was overcome, the fact
that no crossing place was ever established between Maiden Newton and Bridport
meant that the Electric Train Staff system was never used to its full potential.

A Board of Trade requirement was that the branch would only be worked by tank
locomotives (an exception being made in the case of the divisional engineer travelling with
his inspection train). However, how strictly this ruling was upheld is open to question. An
original requirement was for a turntable to be installed at both Bridport and Maiden
Newton, and whilst the former was installed there is no evidence of one ever being installed
at Maiden Newton. But there is evidence that tender engines, worked over the line at least
in broad gauge days.

The early arrangements at Bridport left much to be desired. The lack of a run-round
loop within the platform area required the train to be pulled the final few yards by

horses after the engine had been released, or propelled in from the back end by the engine after it ran round in the station approach, a situation well demonstrated in the fatal accident of January 1882.

Although mixed trains had always been a feature of the branch, in the early days goods wagons marshalled between the engine and passenger stock were quite common to allow easy picking up and dropping off at sidings along the route. The fact that the wagons of the period were not 'vacuum fitted' was immaterial, as neither were the coaches employed - a situation that persisted well into the late 1880s!

Originally the speed of passenger trains was not to exceed 30 mph and goods trains 15 mph, although in later years the speeds were raised to 40 and 20 miles per hour respectively. There were also several other local instructions to enable the safe working of the branch.

At Powerstock no wagon or truck was to be moved from the sidings to the main line unless it was coupled to an engine. At Bridport no shunting was to be performed at the East Street end of the station unless the engine was on the East Street side of the wagons. This was owing to the falling gradient towards East Street level crossing gates. A clear example of the dangers here was demonstrated in July 1950 with a ballast train! (*See Chapter Seven.*)

Double-heading of trains was not uncommon over the branch. The first recorded evidence of this practice was on the opening of the West Bay extension in 1884. On 11th September, 1937 Nos. 7408 and 7415 double-headed a nine-coach train of campers from Bridport to Maiden Newton, and the Southern Counties Touring Society special on 25th August, 1963 was also double-headed by Nos. 7782 and 4689. It is certain that other special trains, particularly during both wars, were also double-headed on account of weight.

However on the Bridport branch the main reason for double-heading was not because of the load of the train, but as a means of moving two locomotives at the same time. A regular example of this was the 8.07 am Maiden Newton to Bridport. This was a mixed train of both passenger stock and goods vehicles. This situation was created by the working in one direction only of the 6.30 am passenger train from Bridport. This was worked by a locomotive and one coach known to the local railwaymen as the 'night coach'. Upon arrival at Maiden Newton this coach was propelled to the top of the gravity siding where it stayed all day. The engine would then shunt Maiden Newton yard and collect the freight for Bridport. In the meantime the 7.35 am train from Bridport would arrive at Maiden Newton consisting of the usual 'B' set. The train made a connection with the 7.17 am Weymouth-Chippenham service and after the up Weymouth train had cleared the station the goods vehicles would be attached to the rear of the 'B' set which formed the 8.07 am down train. This would then be double-headed by the branch engines to Bridport, where upon arrival, one engine would shunt the yard and the other operate the passenger service. With this unbalanced working, every two weeks the Signal and Telegraph department had to transfer a dozen staves from Maiden Newton to Bridport to prevent Bridport running out of them.

On Thursdays and Saturdays the 'night coach' returned to Bridport on the 4.30 pm train, but on other days of the week it returned on the 9.45 pm down train, this connecting with the 6 pm Paddington-Weymouth service. The guard's van for the mixed train in the morning would stay at Maiden Newton overnight, having worked up with the 7.42 pm freight train from Bridport, the engine working back to Bridport later in the evening. If the freight traffic was heavy an extra train would run, usually after the 9.45 pm passenger train, also an extra freight train ran at midday if required.

With the introduction of diesel units in 1959 one steam-hauled passenger train survived. The engine and brake van would work up from Weymouth with any traffic for the branch, and after shunting at Maiden Newton would proceed to Bridport with the goods train. The engine would then be attached to the 'B' set which was stabled behind the down platform and work the 7.30 am up train. Upon arrival at Maiden Newton the coaches would be shunted into the down siding behind the signal box and left. The engine would then shunt on the main line and on the branch, returning to Bridport with the 'B' set in the afternoon.

By the time the goods facilities on the branch were withdrawn, the steam working of the extra passenger train had ended. From then the first down train departed Maiden Newton at 7 am, having commenced as the 6.35 am from Weymouth. Likewise the last up train, 8.48 pm from Bridport, ran through to Weymouth arriving at 9.38 pm. This through working off the branch came to an end on 4th May, 1968, after which Westbury motive power depot supplied the branch diesel unit. The procedure was then for a Westbury driver and guard to bring the unit to Maiden Newton in the morning and work the first branch trains of the day, until a crew from Weymouth arrived to operate the middle part of the days working. The Westbury crew returned home as passengers on an up main line train. Later a Westbury crew would travel down to relieve the Weymouth crew and complete the branch duties before returning to Westbury with the diesel unit.

In earlier steam days Bridport had employed four locomotive crews and a spare driver/fireman, plus a night shedman who cleaned and coaled the engines, but latterly the spare driver/fireman was not employed.

Bridport crews only worked Sundays on the branch during the summer service, as Weymouth usually covered the winter Sundays with a Weymouth based auto-train.

Between trips, the branch engine would sometimes be used at Maiden Newton for shunting duties, typical moves being as follows. The down Kensington ro-rail milk empties would be put back in the 'Bridport Siding' by the train engine. Later the branch engine would shunt them over to the end loading dock on the goods shed spur, ready for the tanks to be drawn off and taken to the dairy by tractor. In the afternoon after the loaded ro-rail tanks had been returned to their wagons and shackled down, the branch engine would pull them forward towards the goods shed, ready for the up Weymouth-Kensington milk train to set back off the up main and collect them.

Particularly in the days before tank wagons, milk traffic was a labour intensive occupation as the churns were moved around the station and loaded into vans. There was also considerable paperwork, as all churns had to be covered by consignment notes. Fish traffic was also heavy in more senses than one. The boxes of fish off the down early train had to be wheeled from the down platform to the up for loading into the branch train, and the hauling of the trolley up the platform ramp after crossing the board walk called for all available hands!

Another traffic once common on branch lines was the transport of rabbits to various butchers etc., these being packed in wicker baskets.

A considerable revenue was earned, particularly in pre-war days, with excursion and special cheap day tickets. Passengers travelled by specified normal service trains over the branch and on the main line. There were also facilities for excursionists to travel to Bridport. For instance, during the summer of 1931 passengers from the Bristol-Frome branch and the Wells-Witham branch could have a day in Bridport by making three changes of train in each direction. In earlier days when paddle steamers called at West Bay it was possible to make an evening sea trip to Weymouth and return by train, there also being other one-way railway journeys on various sailings.

Chapter Seven

Nationalisation to Closure

Britain's railways now belonged to the state. At first there was very little alteration on the branch and the GWR atmosphere still prevailed. Gradually, however, new posters, printed paperwork, and uniform badges arrived, although stocks of GWR tickets lasted many years to places where there was not a great demand. Coaches and other stock remained in the old GWR livery until a repaint was needed, a 'B Set' in GWR livery was still operating over the branch during 1950.

Staff changes again dominated the picture. Early in 1948 Toller station master F.G. Thomas moved to Heytesbury, his replacement being F. Hayward from the platform staff at Weston-Super-Mare. Like many at Toller his stay was short and by late the following year he had moved to Grimstone & Frampton. In August 1948 the Powerstock station master, C.H. Hendry, moved to Bridport as a clerk, Ernest Bray moving from Bridport as his replacement. In October Mr S.W. Bray, the Bridport station master, was promoted to Devizes - a class 1 position - and he later moved to Bath Spa before retirement. Mr O.P. Marston, formerly of Shirley near Birmingham, then took up the vacant position at Bridport.

In 1950 Ernest Bray had the distinction of being the last station master at Powerstock. Upon his moving to Thornbury his position was not filled; the first changes were taking place on the branch!

In April 1950 the branch, and also the main line between Weymouth and Sparkford, was handed over to the Southern Region of British Railways under a scheme involving changes in regional boundaries, although the motive power depot at Weymouth still remained the responsibility of the Western Region, retaining the shed code of 82F.

On 23rd July, 1950 an incident happened that shattered the peace and quiet of a Sunday lunch at Bridport East Street when a brake van and wagon crashed through the level crossing and came to rest just past East Street station with the remains of the two gates festooned over them. They had become detached from a ballast train during shunting operations at Bridport station and had run down the slight gradient and through the gates. Fortunately there was a lull in the traffic on this busy road and apart from the newly painted gates being shattered there was no other damage.

The next morning early passers-by saw a card pinned to the remains of the gates with the following verse inscribed on it:

We have a goods train once a day,
From Saturday to Monday
But see the stately carriages,
A battering ram on Sundays.

During 1949 it was reported that the average number of persons using the branch daily was 137 in winter and 340 in summer. The summer timetable for 1951 still gave 11 trains each way daily, although the Sunday service had been reduced to three. Although the railways were the property of the State the idea that they were sacrosanct was soon dispelled by reductions in services at many places and a spate of branch line closures, locally both the Portland and Abbotsbury branches closing shortly after.

On 27th January, 1951 petrol rationing ended, which gave greater freedom of movement on the roads. Bus services had also returned to normal by that time and Southern National, like other companies in which the railways held shares, had become the property of the State. It was also the final run for the independent operators in the

Mr Sidney Bray, the last GWR station master at Bridport. *Nigel Bray*

In November 1957, the Bridport station staff were photographed with the signal box as the background to celebrate the Centenary of the branch opening. Station master George Gover is seated, front row centre.

M.J. Tattershall Collection

area. The 'Greyhound Bus' bus service was sold to Chard & District Motor Services in August 1951, which in turn sold their local services to Southern National that December, thus ending an era in local transport.

On 2nd July, 1952 the Queen visited Dorchester, and this brought a great deal of activity to Maiden Newton station with the arrival of the Royal Train during the evening. It had been decided that the former LMS Royal Train should be stabled overnight in the down siding at Maiden Newton before proceeding to Dorchester the next morning, when it was hauled by No. 6977 *Grundisburgh Hall* and No. 6978 *Haroldstone Hall* driven by drivers S. Puckett and T. Balston of Weymouth.

That year also saw the Bridport permanent way gang win the prize for the best kept length of track in class 'D'. The same gang were also awarded the prize for the following two years.

It seemed that 1952 was an eventful year for the branch, for near the end of that year the canopy on the down platform at Bridport station was in need of major repairs and it was decided to dismantle it.

As there was now no passenger service to West Bay it was not replaced - although a small bus shelter type hut was placed on the platform, no doubt for the benefit of anybody waiting to meet passengers off the train.

During 1952 the Western Region reintroduced the popular pre-war camping coaches, but now the branch came under the commercial control of the Southern Region. Although they had reintroduced their camping coaches as early as 1947, sadly the opportunity was not taken to site any vehicles on the branch.

The year 1953 saw the closure of the tea hut at Maiden Newton station, Ron Copp who had managed it leaving to join the railway at Weymouth, and by this time Mr Hayward was developing his building and other business interests in the area.

In the Summer of 1953 Bridport celebrated the 700th anniversary of the granting of a Royal Charter by Henry III. A pageant was held in the Borough playing fields and during the week many people came to view the spectacle. According to the *Bridport News*, Mr Richard Hawkins of Christchurch, a retired schoolmaster and a Bridportian, was planning a special through train for Pageant visitors, starting at Christchurch and calling at Bournemouth and Poole to terminate at East Street station, but the matter proceeded no further.

During 1953 Mr Marston was replaced at Bridport by Mr Gover, the first Southern Region station master appointed to the branch. Previously station master at Grateley, a position he had held since 1943, and before that a clerk at Bournemouth, he had commenced his career with the LSWR at Plymouth.

Just as the Summer season was commencing, the ASLEF strike of June 1955 was to close the branch for 18 days. As all six footplate staff at Bridport were ASLEF members the strike completely stopped the service, the 36 other railwaymen employed on the railway reporting for work but having little to do. However, on the main line a few trains were running. The *Bridport News* reported: 'Rail strike brought golden harvest for West Bay at Whitsun. Extra buses carried big crowds from Yeovil and East Somerset'. On that Monday evening, between 5 and 7.30 pm, 12 buses left West Bay for Yeovil. The net industry delivered using their own vehicles, and road transport in general covered most requirements

It was the road hauliers and bus companies who won the day, indeed it was the turning point for many who had previously used the railways in finding alternative transport suitable for their purposes. Many, forced to use long distance coach transport for the first time, enjoyed the comfort of a guaranteed seat and the lower fares. On 17th June, following the settling of the strike, '57XX' 0-6-0 tank No. 9620 left Bridport driven

A busy time at Maiden Newton on 19th July, 1948. A pannier tank awaits departure with the branch train from the bay platform, whilst both up and down trains stand on the main line. A porter wheels a truck of parcels along the down platform and empty milk churns once a common sight at Maiden Newton-await collection.   *G.W. Puntis*

Maiden Newton on 1st April, 1959. '43XX' class 2-6-0 No. 5384 stands at the up platform, whilst barrows loaded with parcels off the branch train await transfer. In the background is watercress from Toller, and in the foreground parcels of nets from Bridport. Shunter Charlie Woodland stands on the footplate of '45XX' class 2-6-2 No. 4562 as the stock is propelled back onto the gravity siding.   *Lens of Sutton*

'Castle' class No. 5074 *Hampden* approaches Maiden Newton with a Weymouth-Bristol train on Sunday 23rd September, 1951. On Bridport Siding, to the left stands a spare ro-ro milk tank wagon, and on the right in the goods shed entrance stands another loaded with a road tank, awaiting collection by the up milk train. *R.A. Lumber*

'Castle' class No. 5034 *Corfe Castle* passes through Maiden Newton with the down 'Channel Islands Boat Express' on 4th September. It was the beginning of the end, at the end of that summer service the boat train would cease to use the Western route, and the Castle Cary-Weymouth section of the old Wilts Somerset & Weymouth line would lose its only named express. Already diesel units had taken over the Bridport branch working, and within a few years steam would disappear from the scene. *Derek Phillips Collection*

'57XX' class 0-6-0PT No. 3746 stands at Toller station with a Bridport-bound train on 13th July, 1957.
J. Spencer Gilks

Witherstone cutting on 20th January, 1956, viewed from the 8.7 am mixed train from Maiden Newton to Bridport, the goods vehicles being visible at the rear of the train. The earthworks on the right were still of an unstable nature. *The late H.C. Casserley*

'57XX' class 0-6-0PT No. 3746 heads towards Bridport down through Witherstone cutting on 13th July 1957. The cut back formation clearly shows the problems of past years.
J. Spencer Gilks

'57XX' class 0-6-0PT No. 7780 near Bradpole crossing with the 7.30 am from Bridport to Maiden
Newton.   *I.D. Beale*

'57XX' class 0-6-0PT No. 7780 heads through the delightful Dorset countryside with a Bridport-
Maiden Newton train.   *I.D. Beale*

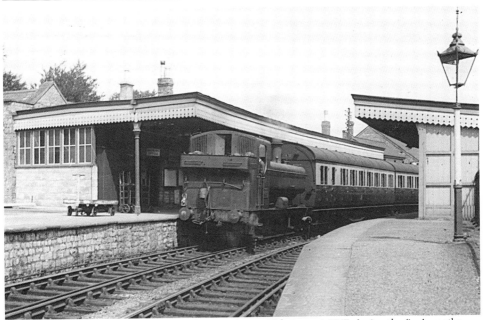

'57XX' 0-6-0PT No. 4660 stands at Bridport station on 19th August, 1947, during the final months of the GWR. The 'B' set in the well loved chocolate and cream livery of that company.

L&GRP

'57XX' class 0-6-0PT No. 4624 waits to depart from Bridport with a Maiden Newton train during 1954.   *I.D. Beale*

'57XX' class 0-6-0PT No. 4689 approaches Loders with a Bridport-bound freight consisting mainly of mineral wagons.   *I.D. Beale*

West Bay station in the summer of 1960, with '57XX' 0-6-0PT No. 7780 arriving on the goods train. Mrs Graves, who then occupied the station as a dwelling, has her washing hanging out, whilst hanging over the gate in the foreground is a young Gerry Beale watching history in the making. It was good training; Gerry is now an accomplished railway historian.   *I.D. Beale*

by A. Bonny and fired by D.J. Bonny, the unusual combination of father and son forming a footplate crew.

The Suez crisis of 1956 and the subsequent fuel rationing for a short while brought back a small amount of trade to the railway, including the Cattistock Hunt who brought horses and hounds to Bridport in horse boxes attached to the 10.08 am Maiden Newton-Bridport.

Holding the record as the longest serving Maiden Newton station master, Mr J.H. MacMahon retired in September 1957. During his time in the village he had become a member of the Parish Council, Vice-Chairman of Maiden Newton Garden & Allotment Society and a member of the British Legion, whilst Mrs MacMahon was Treasurer of the Garden & Allotment Society and President of Maiden Newton Women's Institute. At a retirement presentation he was presented with a silver tea service, a coffee table and a leather notecase containing money.

Mr MacMahon said that, 'looking back, the 13 years seemed like an eternity and he felt that the time had come for him to make way for someone else. He had been blessed with an extremely good staff at Maiden Newton on whose support he had always been able to rely'.

'I have found the people of Maiden Newton a very friendly lot', he continued, 'They are nice people, they take you into the fold. I have fallen out with practically everyone in the village, but I have fallen in again and there has never been any bad feeling'.

The vacancy at Maiden Newton was filled by Mr W.E. Wrattenbury, formerly station master at Topsham, previous to which he had occupied various clerks' positions on the Southern Region in Devon. At Maiden Newton he was to have the distinction of being the last station master.

The year 1957 saw the last appointment of a station master at Toller, when T.W. Benney moved to Hollingbourne (on the South Eastern section of the Southern Region) and his place was taken by F.G. Barrett, formerly a relief signalman in the Southampton area.

November 1957 was the centenary of the opening of the branch, and thoughts were turned to marking the event with some form of celebration. The idea of running a special train to West Bay was discussed but did not materialise, and the only record of the event was a photograph of the station staff taken on the platform at Bridport.

Although the special train did not travel to West Bay to celebrate the centenary, Sunday 7th June, 1958 saw the first passenger train at West Bay for 28 years, when a group of about 80 from the Railway Enthusiasts Club toured the Dorset branch lines with ex-Southern Railway 'M7' class locomotive No. 30107 and a two-coach push-pull unit. Before arriving on the Bridport branch the special had travelled over the Hamworthy goods branch, and climbed to Easton on the Portland line. As far as the records show, this was the only visit to the Bridport branch by a Southern Railway locomotive.

Although by then the motor coach had captured most of the party travel traffic, 150 members of Bridport Congregational Church travelled in two additional coaches attached to the afternoon train for their Sunday School outing to Powerstock in August 1958.

November was a busy month for the station staff at Bridport. On 27th Sir Robert Fossett's Circus visited the town and the problem of six elephants lost on the Bridport branch arose. Their keeper arrived at midday at the station expecting to find the elephants just arriving on the train so that he could unload and parade them through the town, but to his consternation he was told that no one at the station knew anything about any elephants arriving at Bridport station. The keeper was very perplexed, but the

Southern Railway 'M7' class 0-4-4 tank No. 30107 stands at Bridport station whilst working a special over the branch for 'The Railway Enthusiasts Club' on 7th June, 1958. This was probably the only occasion that a Southern Railway engine ever ran over the branch.   *C.L. Caddy*

Southern push-pull unit No. 738 propelled by 'M7' 0-4-4 tank No. 30107 waits to depart from the down platform at Bridport for West Bay on 7th June, 1958. Note the detail in this photograph that makes up the railway scene; to the right is the corrugated extension of the engine shed, and to the left the once-familiar Scammel delivery lorry.   *R.M. Casserley*

Southern push-pull unit No. 738 propelled by 'M7' class 0-4-4 No. 30107 passes under Wanderwell Bridge between East Street and West Bay, on 7th June, 1958 with the Railway Enthusiasts Club special to West Bay. *J. Spencer Gilks*

Southern 'M7' class 0-4-4 tank No. 30107 stands at West Bay with push-pull unit No. 738 after arrival with the first passenger train for 28 years, the Railway Enthusiasts Club special on 7th June, 1958. The fireman has climbed onto the engine to attend to the Westinghouse pump, whilst to the right the long disused West Bay signal box is gradually taken over by ivy. Although the station was to one of William Clarke's oft-repeated designs, the signal box was a pure one off! *J. Spencer Gilks*

'45XX' class 2-6-2 tank No. 4562 waits to depart from Bridport during May 1952.

National Railway Museum

'14XX' class 0-4-2T No. 1402 is seen at Bridport in 1956.   *C.J. Gammell*

station foreman assured him most firmly that no elephants could arrive without his knowing it! The keeper then went into the office where he was told that not even the station master knew anything about six elephants. By now crowds had gathered outside and three police officers had arrived to escort the animals through the streets. The trainer - now in a state of mild hysteria - was shouting 'I must have my elephants'. By this time the station staff had been on the telephone to other stations seeking the lost elephants and news was eventually received that they would be arriving on a later train. With the arrival of the next train the elephants appeared, and their wagons were quickly shunted into the unloading bay where they were unloaded and taken away by a very relieved keeper.

By 1959 Weymouth Motive Power Depot had been handed over to the Southern Region and coded 71G. On 16th February of that year a three-car diesel unit arrived at Weymouth for crew training purposes, as the local services between Weymouth and Bristol (together with the Bridport branch) were to be dieselised as part of the Bristol area diesel scheme. On 6th April regular diesel working by three trains daily started on the main line. With the introduction of the summer service on 15th June, the diesel units replaced steam to a great extent on the Weymouth to Bristol service, and there was complete dieselisation of the passenger service on the Bridport branch except for the 7.40 am Bridport to Maiden Newton and the 4 pm Maiden Newport to Bridport. These were worked by the branch goods engine then supplied by Weymouth as the Bridport shed had closed.

On the introduction of the diesel units, they were being supplied by Weymouth who also supplied the crews for their working. The Bridport motive power staff and guards had been transferred to Weymouth, where some of them worked trains over the main line and up the former Southern line to Bournemouth for the first time in their careers.

With the start of diesel train services the branch looked as if it had a secure future. The *Bridport News* featuring the event said: 'A new epoch in the life of Bridport started on Monday when diesel trains ran into the town for the first time'. How true were those words to become during the next 10 years, as at the time the passenger service was good, as was the amount of freight traffic handled. In the summer of 1960 there were 13 trains daily each way and eight on Sundays.

Early 1960 also saw the transformation of West Bay station buildings. Although having previously been used as living accommodation for railway staff, they had been allowed to fall into disrepair. Mr and Mrs Graves purchased the dilapidated building and refurbished it as their new home, the ticket office becoming the bedroom, the parcel office the drawing room, and the dining room was situated in the old waiting room. The porter's room was transformed into a kitchen whilst the station toilets was converted into a bathroom. Unfortunately the Graves' stay was short, and the building returned to a semi-derelict state.

The first notable reduction in facilities on the branch came in 1960, when Frederick Barrett, the last station master, left Toller in the April to become station inspector at Bournemouth Central, from which date goods traffic ceased to be handled at Toller. This was followed by the withdrawal of goods facilities at Powerstock from 13th March, 1961. Although the goods services had been cut from these two stations, the passenger service remained at 13 trains daily.   In May 1961 station master Gover retired from Bridport and went to spend his retirement at Torquay. There was no hurry to replace him as the position was covered by area relief staff until early 1962, when R.H. Leigh - previously station master at Pevensey & Westham in Sussex - was appointed to become the final station master in the town.

The year 1962 saw the retirement of Mr Leonard Hole, who had been the wartime station master at Maiden Newton until moving to Yeovil Pen Mill in 1944, a position he

All bright and new, a two-car diesel unit stands at Bridport station shortly after their introduction to the branch in 1959. *M.J. Tattershall*

Table 70 — MAIDEN NEWTON and BRIDPORT

WEEK DAYS

Miles		am	am	am S	am E		pm	pm S	pm E	pm S	pm E	pm S	pm E	pm S	pm E	pm E	pm S	pm S	pm E	pm S	pm E	pm	pm
	Maiden Newton .. dep	8 15	1012	1125	1130	.	1216	1 10	1 30	2 21	2 44	3 20	3 34	4 13	4 50	5 15	5 18	6 35	6 36	8 12	8 17	9 17	10 9
2	Toller	8 20	1017	1130	1135	...	1221	1 15	1 35	2 26	2 49	3 25	3 39	4 18	4 55	5 20	5 23	6 40	6 41	8 17	8 22	9 22	1014
5¾	Powerstock	8 26	1023	1136	1141	.	1226	1 21	1 41	2 32	2 55	3 31	3 45	4 24	5 2	5 26	5 29	6 46	6 47	8 23	8 28	9 28	1020
9¼	**Bridport** .... arr	8 33	1030	1143	1148	...	1234	1 28	1 48	2 39	3 2	3 38	3 52	4 31	5 10	5 33	5 36	6 53	6 54	8 30	8 35	9 35	1027

WEEK DAYS

Miles		am	am	am E	am S	am S	am E	pm S	pm E	pm S	pm E	pm S	pm E	pm S	pm E	pm S	pm		pm	pm		pm	pm
	Bridport .. .. .. dep	7 30	9 7	1036	1045	1148	1152	1240	1 0	1 35	2 10	2 55	3 8	3 47	4 25	4 40	5 58	..	7 40	8 50	..	9 40	1032
3½	Powerstock	7 36	9 13	1042	1051	1154	1158	1246	1 6	1 41	2 16	3 1	3 14	3 53	4 31	4 46	6 4	....	7 46	8 56	....	9 46	1038
6¾	Toller	7 43	9 20	1049	1058	12 1	12 5	1253	1 13	1 48	2 23	3 8	3 21	4 0	4 38	4 53	6 11	..	7 53	9 3	..	9 53	1045
9¼	**Maiden Newton** ... arr	7 50	9 25	1054	11 3	12 6	1210	1258	1 18	1 53	2 28	3 13	3 26	4 5	4 43	4 58	6 16	....	7 58	9 8	....	9 58	1050

SUNDAYS

	pm	pm		pm	pm	pm	pm	pm	
Maiden Newton .. dep	1259	2 16	..	4 0	4 55	6 40	7 25	8 12	..
Toller	1 4	2 21	....	4 5	5 0	6 45	7 30	8 17	....
Powerstock	1 10	2 27	..	4 11	5 6	6 51	7 36	8 23	..
Bridport .... arr	1 17	2 34	....	4 18	5 13	6 58	7 43	8 28	....

SUNDAYS

	pm		pm	pm	pm	pm	pm	pm
Bridport .. .. .. dep	1 45	..	3 30	4 30	5 30	7 2	7 48	8 32
Powerstock	1 51	....	3 36	4 36	5 36	7 8	7 54	8 38
Toller	1 58	..	3 43	4 43	5 43	7 15	8 1	8 45
Maiden Newton ... arr	2 3	....	3 48	4 48	5 48	7 20	8 6	8 50

E Except Saturdays. **S** Saturdays only.

Timetable for 18th June to 9th September, 1962.

Timetable for 17th June to 3rd September, 1963.

Table 70 — MAIDEN NEWTON and BRIDPORT

WEEK DAYS ONLY

Miles		am	am	am S	am E		pm	pm S	pm E	pm S	pm E	pm S	pm E	pm S		pm E	pm S	pm S	pm E	pm S	pm E	pm	pm
	Maiden Newton .. dep	8 15	1012	1125	1130	.	1216	1 10	1 30	2 21	2 44	3 20	3 38	4 13	..	5 15	5 18	6 35	6 36	8 12	8 17	9 17	10 9
2	Toller	8 20	1017	1130	1135	...	1221	1 15	1 35	2 26	2 49	3 25	3 43	4 18	....	5 20	5 23	6 40	6 41	8 17	8 22	9 22	1014
5¼	Powerstock	8 26	1023	1136	1141	.	1227	1 21	1 41	2 32	2 55	3 31	3 49	4 24	..	5 26	5 29	6 46	6 47	8 23	8 28	9 28	1020
9¼	**Bridport** .... arr	8 33	1030	1143	1148	...	1234	1 28	1 48	2 39	3 2	3 38	3 56	4 31	....	5 33	5 36	6 53	6 54	8 30	8 35	9 35	1027

Miles		am	am	am E	am S	am S	am E	pm S	pm E	pm S	pm E	pm S	pm E	pm S	pm E	pm S	pm		pm	pm		pm	pm
	Bridport .. .. .. dep	7 30	9 7	1036	1045	1148	1152	1240	1 0	1 35	2 10	2 55	3 8	3 47	4 25	4 40	5 58	..	7 40	8 50	..	9 40	1032
3½	Powerstock	7 36	9 13	1042	1051	1154	1158	1246	1 6	1 41	2 16	3 1	3 14	3 53	4 31	4 46	6 4	....	7 46	8 56	....	9 46	1038
6¾	Toller	7 43	9 20	1049	1058	12 1	12 5	1253	1 13	1 48	2 23	3 8	3 21	4 0	4 38	4 53	6 11	..	7 53	9 3	..	9 53	1045
9¼	**Maiden Newton** ... arr	7 50	9 25	1054	11 3	12 6	1210	1258	1 18	1 53	2 28	3 13	3 26	4 5	4 43	4 58	6 16	....	7 58	9 8	....	9 58	1050

E Except Saturdays. **S** Saturdays only.

held until his retirement and a record 18 years as station master at that station. Upon retirement he entered the local council and became Yeovil's 50th Mayor during 1970.

During the Summer of 1962 the Sunday service was reduced by one train to seven each way, and with the introduction of the winter service on 10th September, the Sunday service was withdrawn altogether from the branch and the daily service reduced to 11 trains each way.

A letter in the *Bridport News* in April 1962 suggested that the section of line between East Street and West Bay be converted into a road, this idea receiving a mixed reception. The local Council planning officers' preference was for a bypass running east to west, and not north to south. Little did the writer know at the time that the railway route would eventually form a major part of the town's bypass!

The following week a reader suggested that parking facilities be provided at East Street and a miniature railway laid thence to West Bay, with the novel feature of the narrow gauge track being laid in the centre of the existing rails so that the present use of the railway (for goods) could continue!

From 3rd December, 1962 the extension to West Bay was closed to goods traffic. This had declined to a few wagon loads of coal and a little traffic in shingle from the beach.

It is ironic to recall at this point that West Bay had now partially developed - although 30 years after the passenger service was withdrawn. The original West Bay Land and Building Co. had made a start by building a terrace of houses in 1885 and completing the esplanade in 1887, but now a new type of development had taken place in the past few years with the creation of a bungalow estate on the west side of the harbour. The tourist trade had also been built up in recent years, too late for the railway to benefit or the speculators of the 1880s who had envisaged a complete town, but at last West Bay was firmly on the map, albeit not the railway map.

January 1963 saw Britain paralysed by the worst winter blizzards that had been seen for many years, and the town of Bridport, situated as it is with steep hills to the west, narrow roads to the north and the road to Dorchester exposed to all weathers, found itself cut off except for the railway. During that time every item needed for the town was carried by the railway. Some traffic it had not carried for years returned and there was traffic that it had never handled before, such as the town's daily bread.

At a Town Council meeting held shortly after, the Mayor, Councillor Harold Smith, speaking of the great value of the railway to Bridport during the past fortnight, said 'I express appreciation of the good work British Railways have done in getting through the necessities of life. I think we should record our approval of the work of the local branch of British Railways. It will strengthen our claim that the line should remain open'.

Although the Beeching report was yet to be published, there were fears locally as to the future of the branch, it being known that the Beeching plan was drastically to remould the existing railway system.

In January that year the branch was transferred back to the control of the Western Region, as was the main line between the north end of Poundbury tunnel, Dorchester, and Sparkford. This was in a scheme which handed over all Southern Region-controlled lines and former Southern Railway lines west of Salisbury over to the Western Region. In the case of the Bridport branch the locomotives, diesel units, drivers and guards were still supplied by the Southern Region from Weymouth.

On Wednesday 27th March, 1963 the Beeching plan was published. In all, 2,300 passenger stations and halts were to be closed, and in the county of Dorset, 24 stations and halts were listed for closure. The Bridport branch was to close completely and on the main line all stations between Yeovil Pen Mill and Dorchester West, including the latter, were to close. During August the Dorchester Rural District Council undertook to support any

The final passenger train to West Bay on Sunday 25th August, 1963. Pannier tanks Nos. 4689 and 7782 stand here with the Southern Counties Touring Society special. Seventy-nine years earlier the Railway Company had such great hopes for the tourist trade at this small resort, but the last tourists to arrive were rail enthusiasts who wished to travel over little-used branch lines.

B.L. Jackson Collection

Class '2' 2-6-2 tank No. 41284 leading and No. 41301 at the rear, the first LCGB 'Bridport Belle

fight to keep Maiden Newton station open. At this time there was still a service of 12 trains daily during the summer on the branch and on Easter Monday of that year between 30 and 40 passengers travelled on the 3.8 pm train from Bridport to Maiden Newton.

In the afternoon of 25th August, 1963 the sound of a train was again heard on a Sunday - and it was also a steam train! Two pannier tank locomotives, Nos. 7782 and 4689, hauled the 7-coach special train chartered by the Southern Counties Touring Society. As with a previous special run in 1958 this train had travelled over the Hamworthy Goods branch and the Portland branch before arriving on the Bridport line. There was a 20 minute stop at West Bay before returning to Maiden Newton, where the train was handed over to former London & North Eastern Railway 'A3' class locomotive No. 60112 *St Simon* for the return journey to London.

The first actions towards keeping the branch open were taken by the local authorities early in 1964, but the future of the Salisbury-Exeter line, the Castle Cary-Dorchester line and the Lyme Regis branch were also causes of concern. By the end of February it was announced that the Salisbury-Exeter line would be kept, albeit in a simplified form. The West Dorset MP, Mr Simon Wingfield Digby, stated in the *Bridport News* of 28th February, 'I am hoping that the Axminster-Lyme Regis line will be retained. But I am afraid the Maiden Newton-Bridport line will inevitably be proposed for closure'.

From 6th April, 1964 the passenger service was reduced to 8 trains each way daily instead of the previous 12 down trains and 13 in the up direction. In a letter from British Railways (Western Region) to the Bridport Rural District Council it was stated that the trains taken off ran when traffic was very light and with the revised service the last train from Bridport was 7.40 pm.

Although officially closed, the West Bay extension was to have a final train. On Saturday 11th April the only diesel locomotive ever to run over this section hauled three coaches down to Wanderwell bridge where the Burton Bradstock road crosses the railway. At this point 'Exercise Wessex III' took place. It was assumed that the train had crashed under the bridge. Within seven minutes of the alarm being raised, the Bridport ambulance, fire brigade and local police were on the scene. Seventy members of the civil defence, St John's Ambulance Brigade, and the Red Cross took part with the aid of members of the Casualty Union, who provided the passengers to act as victims for the event. Within 2½ hours all the casualties had been removed to Weymouth and District Hospital. So authentic was the exercise that a number of people nearby went to help thinking it was the real thing.

The Beeching plan had been published and the Bridport branch was listed for closure but no action took place, there being an uneasy silence for all concerned. On 1st September, 1964 a notice was posted for the closure of all intermediate stations between Yeovil Pen Mill and Dorchester West, the latter due for closure on 4th January, 1965. A Public Inquiry was held at Yetminster on 25th November, 1964, and it was argued that it was difficult to see how Maiden Newton could be closed on that date as the Bridport line was still open and no notice of closure had yet been issued. The decision of the Minister of Transport was made known on 22nd April,1965. Maiden Newton and Dorchester West were to stay open, as were Yetminster, Thornford Bridge Halt and Chetnole Halt. The remaining stations and halts, Evershot, Cattistock, Bradford Peverell and Grimstone and Frampton, were to close from 3rd October, 1966.

The old main line was now reduced to the status of a cross-country route. No longer did express trains between Weymouth and Paddington run along its rails. The 'Channel Islands Boat Express' had run to Paddington for the last time on 26th September, 1959. All main services to London out of Weymouth were now operated up the former Southern Railway line, and apart from summer extras, the old WS&W from Castle Cary downwards had become a line for stopping trains and a freight route to the north.

Bridport awaited the worst. With the artery of the main line restricted, what chance of life was there for that small vein running out into the West Dorset countryside?

In March 1965 the rails on the section between Bridport and West Bay, which had not long been relaid with concrete sleepers, were being cut into short lengths by a contractor and removed by lorry for scrap. October 1965 was the tentative date for the closing of the branch according to the Traffic Manager's office of British Railways (Western Region). The *Bridport News* for 7th May stated in the 'Wanderer' column:

> Certain information which has come into my possession gives an interesting picture of the cost involved in maintaining the passenger service between Bridport and Maiden Newton. As I stated last week the closing of the line would mean a saving of £9,315, but it is the breakdown of the figures which is so revealing. On the expenses side, the service costs amount to £16,232 a year, transport movement £3,460, and day to day repair £1,590, making a total of £21,282.
>
> The revenue from the line is £11,450, leaving a balance of £9,832 on the wrong side and from this a further £518 must be deducted for additional road costs. If the line were kept open for another three years there would be an estimated additional loss of £3,510.

The article continues:

> Those who wish to protest against the proposed closure should prepare their case now. If the Minister decides to support the British Rail proposal, it is only by a really determined expression of public opinion that the situation can be saved.

Various suggestions were put forward by the public on how to save costs. One, from County Councillor Mr G.F.M. Best, suggested replacing the trains with a light diesel one-man operated tram, introducing request stops at Toller Fratrum Bridge, Whetley Bridge, Loders Bridge, and Bradpole Crossing. No elaborate platforms would be necessary, and all buildings could be removed to reduce maintenance to a minimum.

A plan also being instigated along with the proposed branch line closures was the concentration of goods traffic at selected stations, the final deliveries being made by road transport. This scheme had not attracted the publicity of the passenger closures, being far less controversial. Freight for Dorchester and West Dorset would be handled at Weymouth, whilst Yeovil dealt with the north of the county, the scheme coming into effect on 5th April, 1965.

Although the scheme could well be argued as a contribution to economical working, it had terminal side effects. Certain traffic was at once lost completely to the road, and coal merchants - dissatisfied in having to travel greater distances to collect supplies - soon arranged direct delivery from the pits by road! Also in the world of railway accountancy the branch lost its goods revenue, having to stand on its passenger traffic alone.

Despite opposition from the local Authorities, there was nothing they could do to prevent the closure. After all, the railway was still delivering the goods, albeit by road from Weymouth! However, in a further round of goods concentration schemes Weymouth yard closed during 1972, goods having to be hauled an even greater distance. It was decline upon decline, and the goods traffic totally disappeared.

All sidings and the signal box at Bridport were taken out of use from the 8th June, 1965, and all surplus trackwork quickly removed. Only a single line into the up platform survived, the most basic layout possible.

Mr R.H. Leigh, the last station master to serve at Bridport had departed, and the branch which the year before had employed 25 staff had now been reduced to three people.

On 3rd October, 1965 British Railways announced the closure date for the branch as 3rd October the following year. It was proposed to introduce a new weekday bus service to meet the main line trains at Maiden Newton and serve the villages of Toller and Powerstock *en route* to Bridport. The reason given for the closure was that the line was showing a loss of £9,314 a year.

Locally the fight to save the line was proceeding, various suggestions being put forward in an effort to find a solution. Mr Ian Forbes from the hotel industry suggested 'That a single deck road-type bus, adapted for use on the railway, should run between Maiden Newton and Bridport'. The *Bridport News* for 22nd October carried a report that there was still a large amount of parcel traffic. amounting to some 4,807 packages outward from Bridport and a staggering 32,924 inwards every year.

At the same time it was revealed that the Town Council had been asked by British Rail if they were interested in purchasing the four railway cottages in Bradpole Road outside the station. Councillor J. Skevington spoke of the advantage of acquiring the railway yard and other premises if the line were to close, but Counsellor Chubb said 'This Council should do nothing to prejudice the keeping open of the railway. If you acquire these houses you are assuming that the railway will be closed, and you will be giving British Rail a big stick to beat us with'.

The only happy story story of the year for the railway was that in fine rain, driven by a high wind, a group of excited children waited on the exposed platform at Bridport railway station for the train bringing Father Christmas to the town. After descending from the train he climbed into his sledge, specially constructed for the occasion, which was then driven to Messrs Cox and Humphries Store in East Street, where he stayed until Christmas Eve.

Indeed the branch was going to need a Father Christmas during the coming year! The failure of British Rail to provide a unit for the 7.37 am from Bridport to Maiden Newton on the 11th January, 1966 made headline news in the local press. A Southern National bus provided a replacement, but although departing Bridport on time it eventually arrived at Maiden Newton 1 hour 33 minutes later having travelled over the slightly snow-covered steep,narrow, and winding roads via Powerstock and Toller. Indeed, this was an omen of things to come!

On 5th April, 1966 a Public Inquiry into the closure of the branch, chaired by Commander M.H. Pugh for the Transport Users' Consultative Committee (TUCC) (South Eastern Area), was held at the Pavilion, West Bay.

At the hearing Mr Marcus Knorpel, the Town Clerk of Bridport, said that during the Great Freeze of 1963, Bridport was virtually cut off from the world, and its sole link was the railway.

Mr R.L.C. Wood, Assistant Clerk to the Dorset County Council, said there were about 100 students in the area affected by the proposed rail closure who attended the South Dorset Technical College at Weymouth. A great many of them travelled by train, and it would be a serious problem to the continuation of their studies if this facility disappeared.

Captain G.F.M. Best of Loders, a private objector, said 'The proposed alternative road just will not carry the traffic. Normal farming activities frequently impede traffic on this road and this situation is aggravated in the summer. A usual speed on this type of road of 12-15 mph is reduced to 5-6 mph. In these circumstances meeting train connections on time at Maiden Newton will be extremely difficult'.

There were other objections on the grounds of the damage the closure of the line could do to the tourist and holiday trade in the summer months and also to the future expansion of the town of Bridport. It was clear that the main objection to the closure of the line hinged on the narrow roads of West Dorset.

Of the road to Maiden Newton a council official said:

It would cost £35,000 to make the surface suitable, and there would have to be 79 passing places. If it were found necessary to strengthen the road surface a further £20,000 would be required. In winter the snow could not be ploughed because of the high banks and would have to be dug out and taken away. At Toller the road was subjected to flooding and at times became impassable, the cost of raising the road above flood level would be £2,000.

Headed by class '2' 2-6-2 tank No. 41320, the LCGB 'Bridport Belle' Rail Tour slips to a standstill in Witherstone cutting on 22nd January, 1967. Photographers at the lineside were handed coffee and sandwiches from the buffet car as Witherstone had its revenge on the last steam train to travel over the branch.   *J. Spencer Gilks*

Class '2' 2-6-2 tanks Nos. 41320 and 41384 steam along the Bridport branch with the LCGB 'Bridport Belle' Rail Tour on 22nd January, 1967. This was the last steam train to travel the branch.   *J. Spencer Gilks*

It was also revealed that Southern National had declined to run a service, on the grounds that it did not wish to increase its fleet and would have to use small vehicles. The Inquiry then closed, the TUCC having to report to the Ministry and a decision would be announced later.

A week after the Inquiry, on 11th April, 1966, Toller and Powerstock stations were reduced to the status of unmanned halts.

The year 1966 was an eventful one for the branch as its fate hung in the balance. On Friday 21st January the gates of Bradpole Crossing were demolished by a train. This had also happened seven months earlier when the same train, the 10.8 am from Maiden Newton, also removed the gates. The normal practice was for the train to stop whilst the guard climbed down and opened the gates for the train to cross the road, the guard then closing the gates and rejoining the train. With both these incidents there were no injuries. Until the cutback in staff on the branch, this crossing had always been manned by a crossing keeper who opened the gates before the arrival of the train. Even so, several demolition jobs had been carried out. Some years before on a dark foggy winter's night, a driver asked his fireman if they were at Bradpole Crossing yet, to which came the reply, 'Yes I think so - the gates are on the front of the engine'. History does not record what form the conversation then took. In any case, it would not be printable.

By the mid-1960s a final fling with steam locomotives was the order of the day up and down the country, with enthusiasts chartering special trains.

The Locomotive Club of Great Britain organised a rail tour to travel over the branch on Sunday 27th January, 1966. Named 'The Bridport Belle' the special was headed by Ivatt class '2' 2-6-2 tank No. 41284 with No. 41301 attached to the rear as run-round facilities had been removed at Bridport. The outward journey was delayed by a points failure at Maiden Newton, and on the return journey the train stalled on Witherstone Bank. However the engines eventually hauled the train clear, and from Maiden Newton it continued along the main line to Yeovil.

A year later, on 22nd January, 1967, another special was organised by the Locomotive Club, again named 'The Bridport Belle'. Departing from Waterloo at 9 am, hauled by 'West Country' class No. 34013 *Okehampton*, it later joined the Western main line to arrive at Maiden Newton via Castle Cary.

It was apparently one of those days when everything went wrong. Shortly after leaving London a passenger was found dead in a toilet, this causing a considerable delay. When the train eventually reached Maiden Newton 70 minutes late the weather had deteriorated to being cold and wet; the main line locomotive was replaced by Ivatt class '2' tanks Nos. 41295 and 41320. At 2.30 pm, with 41295 leading, the final steam working set off down the branch.

After stopping at Bridport where the party alighted and saw history in the making, the special set off again for Maiden Newton. All went well until the climb up Witherstone Bank. The rain had made the rails very slippery and the train eventually came to a halt. They backed away and made several more attempts at climbing the bank. At the rear driver Woods with No. 41295 pushed and driver Baker at the head of the train with No. 41320 pulled, but it was no good, they were stuck. One hundred and ten years after the opening of the line, Witherstone cutting could still cause problems. No. 41320 - by now getting short of water - was uncoupled and proceeded to Maiden Newton to summon assistance, leaving over 400 railway enthusiasts in their nine-coach train to enjoy the view as darkness fell. A diesel-electric locomotive was sent from Weymouth to assist the stranded train. Eventually with the help of type '3' No. D6541 the special reached Maiden Newton where 'West Country' class locomotive No. 34030 *Watersmeet* was waiting to take the train back to Waterloo. Witherstone had again put itself on the pages of history, Bridport's last steam train having to be rescued by a diesel from its slippery banks.

The last steam train waits to depart from Bridport. Class '2' 2-6-2 tank No. 41320 with the 'Bridport Belle Railtour' on Sunday 22nd January, 1967.   *R.A. Panting*

West Bay station on 10th April, 1968. In the foreground the new sewer pipe is ready to be floated out to sea from the station. On the end of the station building is the sighting mark for locating the pipeline. To the right, pipes are stacked on the remains of the cattle dock.

The late R. H. Rickett

At the same time the disused trackbed at West Bay station was being put to use by a new type of line, a pipeline. The pipes for the £340,000 West Bay sewage outfall scheme were assembled on the old trackbed before being towed out to sea and sunk in position.

On the 4th June, 1967 the Minister of Transport said that the Bridport line must stay open. Making this announcement at the National Union of Railwaymen's Branch Secretaries' Conference at Teignmouth, Devon, Mrs Barbara Castle said that if she had agreed to the closure the 100 people who used the line every day would have been put onto buses. The Maiden Newton to Bridport road was little more than a winding country lane and the bus journey would have taken 50 minutes compared with 22 by train. There would have been delays and some hardship, and a lot of money would have had to be spent to get the roads up to standard. In short, it did not make economic or social sense to close the line.

During 1968 the main line had been reduced to a single track, Maiden Newton being a crossing station. The down sidings had been taken out of use, and the gravity siding, not used since 1959, was removed in December 1963.

By the end of 1969 the last railwayman had left Bridport. He was Mr Reg Chester, who for several years had been the only person employed there. The station was then unstaffed at all times of the day, tickets being purchased from the guard of the branch train. The station had received its last coat of paint in 1957, when (with other stations on the branch) it had been painted in Southern Region colours of green and cream. This had now started to fade, and there being no staff to look after the building, all the windows and doors were locked and boarded up. The engine shed and water tower had been demolished, so a general look of desolation had befallen this once thriving country station.

At Maiden Newton the canopy over the bay platform was removed and the steel footbridge replaced by a second-hand concrete structure from a closed station on the Salisbury-Exeter line. The station had also become unstaffed with only a signalman being employed there. As with the branch, all tickets required by passengers were purchased on the trains from the guard. The goods shed was demolished and all trade had gone. The rail borne milk traffic had ceased, and the dairy later closed.

In 1967 the station buildings at Powerstock were put on the property market, and the Read family, who several years before had seen the station and become attracted to it, made enquiries. The asking price was £2,700. However, as other people had offered the same price the sale became a sealed bid auction. Following much red tape, the station was sold to the Read family for £3,250 on 11th November, 1968.

Following the purchase the Read's spent many hours of their weekends and holidays renovating the building. Dormer windows were fitted into the large loft space which was converted into bedrooms, and the former booking office and ground floor accommodation was completely altered. The family moved into this house of character during 1970. Once installed in the house Diane Read found she would become *de facto* station master in the event of a train failing to run. A telephone call from Maiden Newton would ask her to check the waiting shelter, telling the passengers that a taxi or mini bus was on its way, and report the numbers travelling back to Maiden Newton!

Although the Bridport branch remained open it only did so by a slender thread, as all the other closures proposed in the Beeching recommendations had taken place. Further west, the Lyme Regis branch had closed in November 1965, only the Swanage and Bridport branches remaining. Towards the end of 1967 Barbara Castle boasted she had 'Stopped the Beeching butchery'; in truth there was not much left to butcher! The following year she was moved to the Ministry of Labour, and the 1968 Transport Act completely altered the rules of the game.

On 1st January, 1972 the Swanage branch closed - the one Dorset branch not mentioned in the Beeching report. Although general goods traffic had been withdrawn

Having arrived from Maiden Newton, a two-car dmu draws into the up platform, having discharged passengers on the down side and pulled forward onto the West Bay extension. In the background, to the left of the down starting signal, can be seen the small oil depot that supplied the local area.   *R.K. Blencowe Collection*

The basic railway, single unit No. W55033 stands at Bridport station on 21st January, 1967, whilst the once-common Morris Minor Royal Mail van waits as the postman struggles with a sack of mail. Now all has gone except for unit No. W55033 built by Pressed Steel in 1960, which is now preserved on the Colne Valley Railway at Castle Headingham.   *C.L. Caddy*

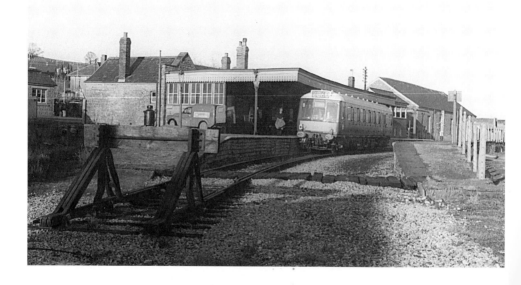

there was still some meat on the carcase, Swanage was a seaside resort, Corfe Castle was the heart of a tourist area, and there was the clay traffic from Furzebrook, but still closure took place. What future, then, for Bridport, now Dorset's only branch line?

On 11th June, 1971 the following notice appeared in the *Bridport News*.

The British Railways Board hereby give advance notice in accordance with Section 54 of the Transport Act 1962 that they plan, subject to Sections 56 of the Act, to withdraw the passenger service between Maiden Newton and Bridport, and to close Toller, Powerstock and Bridport stations.

Again protests and letters to the press appeared - one of the latter to the *Bridport News* suggesting that the branch train be extended through to Dorchester or Weymouth, thus providing a better local service. In the meantime British Rail had claimed that the line was losing £12,000 a year.

At a Council meeting in February 1972 Captain Best revealed he had carried out his own passenger traffic census at Powerstock station, and discovered that 45 villagers regularly used the railway. This included four people who used it to travel to work every day, most of the others travelling at least one day a week. He added 'It must be remembered also that our bus service has been curtailed, so that we only get one bus a week now'.

A Public Inquiry into the closure was held at the Church House, South Street, Bridport on 22nd March, 1972. The 19-strong panel of TUCC listened to objections from 15 persons representing local authorities and other interested parties from West Dorset. The Inquiry, which was attended by about 80 people, lasted only 1½ hours. Mr L.J. Guest, senior assistant solicitor for the Dorset County Council, said: 'The County Council is firmly opposed to the closure of the railway line. It will cause considerable hardship in the area'. He went on to say that to widen the road between Toller and Powerstock would cost £53,000, and an additional £30,000 would be needed to raise certain parts of the road above flood level.

Various figures were presented, it being pointed out that the £4,650 loss of 1965 had now risen to £36,000. In 1965 the average number of passengers carried on the weekday census was 185 when the return fare was 3s. 8d., whilst in 1971 the average number of passengers for the same journeys was 95 when the fare was 28p (4s. 10d.).

After many other objections, the Chairman, Lt-Col Macfarlane, drew the inquiry to a close by asking the British Rail representative for his observations. Now came the bombshell. He said 'British Rail do not want to close the line, it is because the grant aid is being withdrawn that this Hearing is being held. The Ministry wants to know the result of this inquiry before continuing the grant'.

An interim report of April 1972 stated that public transport serving the route of the line was virtually non-existent and the TUCC found that varying degrees of hardship would be suffered by the people who had to use the trains to make necessary journeys. Hardship would result to a small number of daily commuters in particular and would also be suffered by people left isolated from essential contacts in Bridport, Yeovil, Dorchester, Weymouth and beyond.

In December it was announced that a decision to close the Bridport Railway line had been deferred, and the Secretary of State was still considering the matter.

The closure of the line had been scheduled for 1st January, 1973, but trains were still running. In February the Town Clerk of Bridport, Mr Elliot Andrews, was informed that a decision had not yet been made. The Railways Board closure proposal was still being considered and a decision would be made as soon as possible.

Whilst the outcome of the inquiry was awaited there were rumours of plans to re-site Bridport station towards Bradpole, allowing the station area and the trackbed towards East Street to become a bypass for the Beaminster road. Just as the railways and

The last enthusiasts' special to work over the branch, and the only visit by a diesel-electric unit to the line. Unit No. 1130 waits at Bridport station with the 'Wessex Wanderer' on 1st June, 1974.
R.A. Panting

Maiden Newton after a snowstorm on 4th April, 1975, a month before the branch closed. A single car unit waits to depart with the branch train and a Weymouth-Westbury service, worked by a three car unit, stands at the up platform. The small hut on the platform housed an auxiliary token instrument for Yeovil-bound trains.
C.L. Caddy

politicians had been accused of changing the rules to suit their own situation, unfortunately at local council level there was often a farce when officers were protesting about forthcoming closures, whilst in the same building other officers could not get the line closed quickly enough to push through a road scheme!

The railway timetable was also used to downgrade the service. A letter in the *Bridport News* during February 1973 from Mrs Diana Read of Powerstock station exposed the situation.

> In view of road plans for the area, it is obvious that Bridport station must be moved, but on behalf of those who use the train I must protest at any attempt to site the new station as far from the centre of Bridport as Bradpole Crossing. The present station necessitates a long walk to the shops presenting difficulty enough, particularly in bad weather, to the elderly, the infirm and those with small children. The bus service does not connect with the rail service.
>
> The shopping train arrives at Bridport at 10.47 am. If it is on time, the shopper is lucky to reach the town centre by 11 am. Because one walks more slowly when laden with shopping, one must start back no later than 11.55 am to catch the 12.15 pm from Bridport. The next train leaves at 1.47 pm, too late for anyone with lunch to prepare for a family. Some of us are unable to use the afternoon trains to Bridport and back because they cut across both lunchtime and when our children arrive home from school.
>
> In the case of passengers from Powerstock station, most of them walk a mile or more to catch the train and face the same distance on their return. To expect them to walk to and from Bradpole as well is totally unrealistic.

It would appear that the timetable alterations had struck a raw nerve somewhere in the system, for the *Bridport News* during May made the following announcement.

> Shoppers Train Now Runs Again. British Rail has reinstated the lunchtime 'Shoppers train' on the Bridport-Maiden Newton line. When a new timetable came into effect on May 7th, residents in villages on the line noticed that the 12.15 pm service from Bridport had been withdrawn. People coming into town on the mid-morning train had to wait until 1.55 pm before they could leave Bridport.
>
> Faced with having to spend 3 hours in town, villagers wrote to the Area Manager for British Rail and on Monday the timetable was altered to allow a train to leave Bridport at 12.42 pm. The 1.55 pm has now been withdrawn.

On Saturday 1st June, 1974 the last special train ran on the Bridport branch. A three-car Southern Region diesel-electric unit rumbled down the dying line with the 'Wessex Wanderer' whilst making a tour of the area. The *Dorset Evening Echo* for Friday 3rd January, 1975 carried the headline 'The axe falls on Bridport's Line'. The branch was to close on and from the 5th May. The Secretary of State for the Environment had given his consent to the closure of Dorset's last branch line, that British Rail said cost £54,000 a year to keep open. With the news of the closure the Bridport Line Action Group sprang to life and opened a fighting fund to campaign for the retention of the line, but the end had come, there was little they could do.

As the closure date drew nearer the train became busier - particularly on Saturdays when many people took a last ride on the branch. On the day before closure, Friday 2nd May, the single car diesel unit operating the service, No. W55032, had one engine fail during the morning and had to be changed, its last trip being the 1.42 pm Bridport to Maiden Newton. This was the last journey ever operated by a single car train on the branch. At Maiden Newton a 3-car unit was waiting to take over the service for the remainder of the day, and with the large number of people travelling, as well as several parties of school children that joined the train, this accommodation was well filled.

To cope with the anticipated crowds on the last day, a 4-coach train was provided all day consisting of a single car No. W55033 and a 3-car set, Nos. W51387, W59497 and W51345. The normal train service of nine trains each way was extended, there being two

The manager of a famous Maiden Newton Pop Group shaking hands with railway staff before they commence their world tour starting at Bridport? No, the staff of the *Bridport News* on a trip before the line closed. Although we might mock these trendily dressed characters, it was their high class reporting and that of their predecessors that has given us the historical record we have today. The group include, Alison Miller, Gavin Houlgate, Mary Payne, Jennie Jones, Phillip Evans, Roger Bailey, David Couzens (Editor), shaking hands with driver.

Mrs M. Payne

Saturday 3rd May, 1975, and rail enthusiasts alight at Bridport from one of the morning trains to photograph the last day of operation.   *C.L. Caddy*

The last train departs from Bridport at 8.40 pm on Saturday 3rd May, 1975. *M.J. Tattershall*

extra runs - the 2.50 pm from Bridport with a return journey at 3.15 pm and 5 pm from Bridport with a return journey at 5.25 pm.

All day the trains were crowded as local people and railway enthusiasts, who had travelled from all over the country, made their last journeys over the line and photographed it from every conceivable angle. So busy was the last day that two guards were provided on every train to issue the tickets, and to make sure everything went smoothly traffic inspector Cooper from Bristol was present all day travelling with the train. To make a connection with the 2.25 pm from Maiden Newton to Bridport the 'Dorset Dawdler' arrived and decanted its load of enthusiasts into an already well loaded branch train. This special, organised by the Southern Electric Group, had travelled from Southampton visiting the Fawley branch and Weymouth Quay tramway before arriving at Maiden Newton. There were no pathways for the special to travel on the branch, so it was shunted back into the former goods shed siding to await the return of its passengers at 4.27 pm before it returned to Eastleigh via Yeovil and Salisbury.

At 8.15 pm the last train pulled out of Maiden Newton for Bridport. Amongst the many passengers was the Mayor and Mayoress of Bridport, Councillor and Mrs P.C. Norfolk. Upon arrival at Bridport it was greeted by a large crowd who had turned out to see the event. Before departing for the last time a wreath was placed on the front of the train by Paul Smith and David Peel, members of the Dorset Transport Circle, and the Mayor shook hands with the driver, Mr Reg Chappel of Westbury. At 8.40 pm on Saturday 3rd May, 1975 the last train left Bridport station in the twilight to the sound of exploding detonators. Crowds stood by the gates at Bradpole Crossing as it rumbled

Right: The first day of bus replacement Monday 5th May, 1975, following the branch closure. The late Ivor Collins (*on left*) - proprietor of Pearce of Cattistock - stands alongside the first departure from Bridport bus station to Maiden Newton. For the occasion Bedford OB HOD 76 was used, new in 1949 to Western National as No. 597, and purchased by Pearce in 1961. For many years the OB was the mainstay of small country operators. By 1975 the OB was becoming a rare sight in service. HOD 76 was eventually sold for preservation in 1989. *Mrs M.E. Payne*

Above: HOD 76 awaits passengers at Powerstock *en route* to Maiden Newton on Monday 5th May, 1975. *Below:* The once familiar whine of the Bedford 28 hp engine and gearbox - a sound unique to the Bedford - breaks the silence as HOD76 climbs towards Powerstock *en route* to Maiden Newton.

(Both) Mrs M.E. Payne

past, children held out a banner saying 'Farewell to an Era', and large gatherings were also at the wayside stations of Powerstock and Toller.

Just after 9 o'clock the last train came to rest in the bay platform at Maiden Newton. For the Westbury crew, driver Reg Chappel, guard Clifford Sims and assistant guard Alex Fowler, it had been a busy but memorable trip. Shortly afterwards, still with passengers on board for destinations in the direction of Westbury, the train left the bay platform and headed up the main line. Within a minute all that could be seen was a red tail lamp fading away in the distance. With the official closure date of 5th May, 1975, it was exactly 120 years since the incorporation by Act of Parliament of the Bridport Railway Company on 5th May, 1855. Now the last train had gone and the crowds had left Bridport station, someone was heard to say 'I couldn't cheer as it left, there was a lump in my throat'. Another remarked 'Let's leave by the proper exit as a mark of respect', a remark which summed up the feeling of most people at the end of the line.

Conclusion

Within several days of the closure a fine film of rust had formed over the rails. A self-propelled ganger's trolley had made a trip to Bridport and recovered nameboards, notices, and other items required for further use elsewhere. Pearce & Co. of Cattistock, who in former years had been coal merchants at Maiden Newton station, took on the operation of the rail replacement bus service. On the first day of its operation, Monday 5th May, a 29-seat Bedford coach built in 1949 was used. This vehicle - HOD 76 - was formerly No. 597 in the fleet of Western National before being sold by them in 1961. This vehicle was used for the first day of the new service but usually a 17/20 seat minibus is used on the narrow roads that have to be negotiated between Bridport and Maiden Newton.

After remaining untouched for six months, the silence that had descended upon the line was shattered on the morning of 11th November, 1975 when a class '25' diesel locomotive No. 25 164 propelled a 10-ton steam crane down the branch to Bridport, and after removing the buffer stops and placing them upon a wagon, the train returned to the permanent way depot at Yeovil Junction. On Monday 17th the work of recovering the rails started with the aid of a self-propelled ganger's trolley, when men of Yeovil Junction relay gang removed many of the keys and fishplates from the Bridport end of the line. On the morning of the 18th a class '08' diesel shunter No. 08 636 propelled the recovery train to Bridport. This train consisted of a brake van, ballast wagon for the transportation of the recovered keys, a ballast wagon fitted with a diesel powered winch, two bogie bolster wagons, and a ballast wagon fitted with roller gear to guide the rails over when dragging them on to the recovery train.

Before 9 am the rails at Bridport station had been removed, leaving only the sleepers and chairs in position. The rails were being removed from the branch at the rate of two bogie bolster wagon loads per day. In charge of the lifting operation was Peter Morton, who, as a boy in 1939, was one of the evacuees from London who arrived at Bridport station and the safety of the West Country on the very line he was now ripping up. Once all the rails had been removed the sleepers were recovered by contractors. Land and buildings would be eventually handed over to the property department to be disposed of to the best advantage.

On 11th November, 1975 at 11 am the buffer stops were removed at Bridport and track lifting began. Exactly 118 years earlier on 12th November, 1857 Bridport had celebrated the opening of its railway, but unfortunately few mourned its passing!. *Mrs M.E. Payne*

Class '08' diesel shunter No. 08 635 stands just short of Bridport station with the track recovery train on 18th November, 1975. *B. L. Jackson*

Chapter Eight

Conclusion

Having already constructed 'Sea Road South' over the trackbed south of East Street, the closure of the entire branch allowed the Council to acquire the trackbed north of that point and the station site for the construction of a new link road between St Andrews Road and East Road. Bridport station and goods shed were demolished in early April 1977 and the area cleared, and in January 1977 work commenced on the diversion of the River Asker where it passed under the trackbed near East Street. With this work completed the new link road, now named 'Sea Road North', was constructed. It opened to traffic on 20th July, 1978, allowing the narrow Bridport end of Barrack Street to be blocked off. A new road junction on the station site then became the principal entry to St Andrews Road/Barrack Street.

A section of the trackbed north of the station site has been taken over by various warehouses and industrial units, the only surviving railway buildings in 1998 are the former staff cottages and the stable, now a small car repair unit. The public house, the 'Railway Terminus', has been renamed the 'King Charles'. When the station was demolished the platform coping stones were saved, and today form the platform edge of the mock station at Pecorama, at Beer in Devon.

Unlike Bridport, the entire station building of Toller has been saved. Being constructed mainly of timber, it was purchased by the Dart Valley Railway (now known as the South Devon Railway) for £5,000, dismantled into convenient sections during late 1981, and transported to the site of the new Totnes Riverside station (now named Littlehempston) and re-erected. It was completed in July 1988. Along with other buildings it now forms an impressive station at the Totnes terminus of this preserved railway.

The closure of the line and lifting of the track enabled the Read family to purchase the platform and trackbed at Powerstock station for £750 in October 1978. The following year the shelter area of the main building was incorporated into the house, which still functions as a guest house 23 years after the line's closure, having achieved fame for stories of its pipe smoking ghost! So much so that the station appeared on the Television South programme 'Coast to Coast' in March 1982.

The previous year the BBC filmed scenes for its series 'To The Manor Born', starring Penolope Keith and Peter Bowles, at Maiden Newton, the station being renamed 'Marlbury' for the scenes in which the local station faces closure but is eventually saved by the building of a new school that will require transport facilities.

During 1992 a partnership of West Dorset Council, Dorset County Council, The Rural Development Commission, and British Rail put up £100,000 to transform the main building at Maiden Newton into a computer centre. Opened on 23rd April, 1993, Abilities Ltd now train disabled people in office and computer skills.

Along the line the steel underbridges still remain in place at Loders, Powerstock, and Toller, as do bridges over the line along its length. At Bradpole Crossing a section of rail remains embedded in the road, and with a grant from Bradpole Parish Council and West Dorset District Council, the crossing gates have been reconstructed by Bridport joiners John Gale and Bernie Joy - a reminder that a railway once passed where bungalows now stand. Much of the trackbed towards Powerstock now forms a private farm track, as does land on the east side of Powerstock. The notorious Witherstone cutting forms part of the Powerstock nature trail; in Witherstone Woods the remains of the former brick works have been preserved, whilst much of the land towards Maiden Newton has reverted to farm use.

Track recovery taking place near Loders in November 1975. The recovery train is being hauled
by '08' class diesel shunter No. 08 635.   *B.L. Jackson*

Toller station, looking towards Powerstock following removal of the track.   *B.L. Jackson*

At Maiden Newton station a footpath has been made from the old bay platform out along the trackbed of the branch for half-a-mile to the Chilfrome road bridge. The train service now consists mostly of Sprinter units on the Bristol-Weymouth service, although at the time of writing there are still two engine-hauled workings each way daily. In January 1998 the windows of the former signal box were boarded up, as were all doors and windows on the down side waiting shelter - now a common sight at many unstaffed stations.

Apart from in the immediate area at Bridport the remainder of the earthworks in rural Dorset will remain for many years, nature gradually reclaiming them for itself.

The replacement bus service serving Maiden Newton-Toller-Powerstock and Bridport has also changed in the ever evolving world of modern bus operations. Following the deregulation of bus services during 1986, Pearce, Darch, & Willcox, who had operated the service with an 80 per cent subsidy, were replaced by T&T Coaches of Bridport who offered a cheaper tender. Three years later the contract was awarded to Southern National, only to be passed to Mike Halford at the end of the following year.

By 1994 West Bay station had deteriorated to a very poor condition and concern was expressed as to its future. The former signal box had already been demolished during 1988. However the main station structure was not beyond repair, and at the time the £9.3 million West Bay Harbour development project had commenced. It was decided that a visitor centre be opened for which the old station was considered ideal, and with track relaid at the platform, coaches could be used as office accommodation.

Work on restoration commenced late in 1994. The relaying of the track and the supply of two coaches went out to tender and was awarded to the Swanage Railway. On Monday 27th February, 1995 four panels of track were laid by Swanage Railway volunteers, a stop block and GWR tubular starting signal being added. Two coaches were leased from the railway - a former LSWR Ironclad No. 728 and BR Mk I TSO No. 4070 arriving on site early in March. Alongside work on the station restoration went ahead on the coaches, and by 1997 the two restored coaches and a station turned what had become a run down site into an attraction. Most importantly it saw the restoration of one of William Clarke's country stations that were once a familiar part of several GWR branch lines.

During the summer of 1998 the West Bay station site was taken over by a film company for the production of a new BBC prime time drama series entitled 'Harbour Lights', West Bay becoming the fictional village of 'Bridehaven', with former 'Heartbeat' star Nick Berry. Filming commenced on 23rd July, the station building being used as offices for the production company, and the various caravans and equipment being sited in the station yard.

Since closure there have been several suggestions on re-opening the line as a preserved steam railway, these coming to nought. With one preserved steam railway already in the county (the Swanage Railway) it is doubtful if there would ever be an appreciable support for a second!

However, during September 1995 the first proposals for a narrow gauge railway between Bridport and West Bay were discussed at a meeting of interested parties at Bridport. A public exhibition of the proposals was held and outline planning permission from the West Dorset District Council sought. On 19th December another meeting was held at which it was decided to form the 'Brit Valley Railway Limited', the first formal meeting of the new company being held on 31st January, 1996.

A brochure of the intended line was published, the proposal being to build the line in three phases: (1) Bridport-West Bay, (2) Bridport-Crewkerne, and (3) West Bay-Weymouth. In the words of their own literature:

Toller station being dismantled during late 1981 prior to its removal to the South Devon Railway at Totnes.   *B.L. Jackson*

'Rem Alicui Restituere Antecdens Gloria'. Saved for posterity: Toller station rebuilt at Totnes (Littlehempston). Completed in 1988, this restored station is a classic example of a typical GWR small station building from the turn of the century.   *B.L. Jackson*

The Brit Valley Railway is a proposed 2 ft narrow-gauge railway, principally steam hauled, between Bridport and West Bay, on the beautiful West Dorset coast. Future extensions of the railway could go north to link with the designated European strategic rail route at Crewkerne, and also eastwards along the proposed World Heritage Coastline towards Weymouth and Portland.

The Bridport-West Bay scheme is not without merit, given the right circumstances. But one cannot help thinking that phases two and three have a great amount in common with earlier schemes outlined in this book. It was the geographical problems that defeated Castleman's proposal to extend the Southampton & Dorchester Railway west of the county town, and also the westward extension of the Upwey-Abbotsbury branch in the last century.

In a news update in September 1996 the following appeared.

Another exciting development is that we could carry freight (domestic waste in containers) down to West Bay harbour with the railway embedded in the road, ending at the existing coaster berth, or a new berth if the new multi-million pound breakwater is built. The waste could be taken from West Bay by coaster to an incinerator plant at Southampton.

In January 1998 a second scheme for a railway was announced, Aardvark Associates, a locally based public relations company, were planning a feasibility study into setting up a steam railway heritage centre at West Bay station, Aardvark state that just £50,000 would enable half a mile of standard gauge track to be laid, and a small locomotive and stock hired to run pleasure trips and provide engine driving courses!

A leading railway magazine reporting on the matter took a jaundiced view, remarking

Both are the sort of schemes that make seasoned preservationists wake up screaming at 3 am. Not surprisingly, neither has names associated with it that are known in the movement. But I hope that they do not disappear without trace too soon - they could provide railway connoisseurs with a lot of innocent amusement as they fight it out.

The Brit Valley Railway project received a boost when Bridport Town Council planning committee gave their support to the Bridport-West Bay section of the scheme on 16th July, 1998. On 29th July, West Dorset District Council's Western area planning sub-committee gave their support for the scheme subject to certain planning conditions.

The return of the steam locomotive along the route of the former branch is still a dream, but in recent years they have returned occasionally to Maiden Newton through the running of enthusiasts' specials hauled by preserved locomotives. During the Yeovil Steam Festival of 8/9th October, 1994, preserved LSWR 'M7' No. 30053 from Dorset's own preserved railway at Swanage operated a shuttle service between Yeovil and Maiden Newton. It was the first steam train to arrive at Maiden Newton since the final demise of steam in 1967. Ironically the first enthusiasts' special to visit Maiden Newton and travel over the Bridport branch had also been hauled by an 'M7' class in June 1958.

Since 1994 several other steam locomotives have passed through Maiden Newton. On 15th October No. 35028 *Clan Line* worked light engine between Yeovil and Weymouth, and on 12th October, 1997 she again passed through Maiden Newton - this time hauling the first steam railtour through to Weymouth. On 15th November, 1997 preserved LMS '5MT' No. 2968 and GWR '43XX' No. 7325, worked the 'Hardy Flyer' railtour, 140 years after steam first arrived at Maiden Newton and 32 years since the last GWR locomotive stood at the station.

History was to eclipse itself on Saturday 5th September, 1998, when GWR 'King' class No. 6024 *King Edward I*, halted at Maiden Newton whilst working the 'Hardy Express'. In steam days the 'King' class were prohibited from the Castle Cary-Weymouth section of the Wilts, Somerset & Weymouth line.

Restoration work in progress on West Bay station in March 1995. Already the track has been
laid to receive the two coaches.   *M.J. Tattershall*

West Bay station looking towards Bridport in October 1997. In the foreground is BR Mk I No.
4070, and beyond LSWR Ironclad No. 728. At the platform end a GWR tubular post starting
signal has been erected.   *B.L. Jackson*

Appendix One

Chronology

1854	28th September	Report by H.J. Wylie outlining proposed railway
	24th October	Decision to form The Bridport Railway Company
1855	5th May	Bridport Railway Company incorporated
	19th June	First sod cut at Loders by Mr Joseph Gundry
1857	20th January	Main line opened between Yeovil and Weymouth
	29th September	Train makes a trial run over the branch
	5th November	Line passed for opening by the Board of Trade
	12th November	Opening day of the Bridport Railway
1862	31st March	Toller station opened
1874	18th-21st June	Branch converted from broad to standard gauge
1877		First signal boxes erected at Maiden Newton
1879	31st July	Act of Parliament for the West Bay extension
1881	1st July	Branch leased to the GWR
1884	31st March	West Bay extension opened to traffic
1885		Original Maiden Newton signal boxes replaced
1894	July	Station improvements and new signal box Bridport
1900		Company consider sale to the GWR
1901	1st July	Branch bought by the GWR
	25th September	Last meeting of Bridport Railway Company
1902	12th October	Toller station burnt down.
1904		East Street station rebuilt
1905		Toller station rebuilt
1916	1st January	Wartime closure of West Bay extension
1919	7th July	West Bay extension reopened to traffic
1921		New signal box opened at Maiden Newton
1927	January	West Bay signal box closed
1930	22nd September	West Bay extension closed to passenger traffic
1940	4th November	Anti-aircraft gun sidings opened at Loders and Bradpole
1945	22nd April	Anti-aircraft gun sidings taken out
1950	April	Branch under control of Southern Region British Railways
1958	7th June	First passenger train to West Bay in 28 years
1959	15th June	Bridport engine shed closed, diesel passenger trains
1960	4th April	Goods facilities withdrawn from Toller
1961	13th April	Goods facilities withdrawn from Powerstock
1962	September	Withdrawal of Sunday service from the branch
	3rd December	West Bay extension closed to goods traffic
1964	11th April	Last train to travel on West Bay extension
1965	March	Rails removed from West Bay extension
	8th June	Bridport signal box closed, later sidings removed
	7th October	Closure of branch announced
1966	11th April	Toller and Powerstock reduced to unmanned halts
1967	22nd January	Last steam train travels over branch (LCGB)
	June	Line reprieved and will stay open
1968	May/June	Main line reduced to single track
	11th November	Mr & Mrs Read purchased Powerstock station
1969		Bridport becomes unstaffed station
1971	June	Notice of closure of branch
1974	1st June	Last special train travels over branch
1975	3rd January	Closure of branch announced
	3rd May	Last day of operation of branch
	5th May	Branch closed

	17th November	Recovery of track started
1977	April	Bridport station demolished
1981		Toller station dismantled and removed to Devon
1988	1st May	Maiden Newton signal box closed
1994		West Bay station, restoration commenced
1995	March/April	West Bay station track laid, coaches arrive
1996	January	Company formed to build narrow gauge railway
1997	15th November	GWR steam engine returns to Maiden Newton
1998	29th July	Permission to lay narrow gauge railway

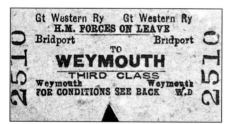
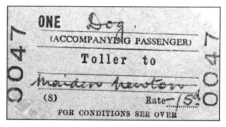

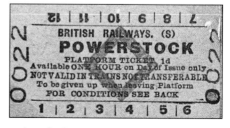

A selection of tickets used on the line.

Appendix Two

Branch Line Staff

Smooth operation depended upon a line's staff structure, from the top management down to the most junior porter or cleaner. The most senior man at local level was the station master, usually a well-respected man in the community who was responsible for the entire operation of his station and expected high standards from those under him.

A few were martinets, although most encouraged staff in their work, but when things went wrong it was the station master who took full responsibility. In the past higher management would soon move a defaulting man to a lesser position, involving both a reduction in his pay and a loss of esteem amongst his peers.

Station masters for all stations except the very smallest usually came from the clerical and booking office staff, and they were graded according to their responsibility - which depended largely on the number of staff under their control. For example, in 1922 Bridport was a class 1, whilst Maiden Newton only warranted a class 3 station master. Originally station masters had either been classed as 'station clerks' or 'booking clerks', although the term 'agent' also sometimes appeared. However, as the railways became more organised the term station master became virtually standard.

At the very small stations such as Toller and Powerstock 'booking porters' or 'inspectors' were employed. They were often the only member of staff, and acted as booking clerk, signalman, porter, and any other job required of them. These were promoted from the better educated members of platform staff, it having to be remembered that in 1850 only 35 per cent of men could sign their name!

The 'booking porter' grade was incorporated into that of inspector in 1890, and following a deputation to Paddington in 1897 the title of station master was bestowed on this lower order which encompassed grades 4, 5, and 6 of station masters' positions. As with the higher grades, any failure to come up to standard resulted in demotion or resignation! Many made good station masters and moved up the grades, whilst others moved around in 'sideways' moves, or stayed put having taken to the local community.

Station Masters at Bridport

	From	To
Daniel Bingham	November 1857	September 1858
Henry Knowles	September 1858	November 1859
John Webber	January 1860	December 1865
Henry Alfred Bond	December 1865	March 1882
Walter Titball	March 1882	October 1885
George Peach	November 1885	May 1895
William Mathews Mitcham	May 1895	August 1900
William Francis Vaugham	September 1900	April 1907
Frederick Weeks	May 1907	December 1922
Charles Widdows	January 1923	September 1926
George Barnby	February 1927	May 1938
Frederick Joachim Colls	May 1938	May 1940
Sidney Bray	May 1940	October 1948
Oliver Marston	October 1948	1953
George Gover	1953	June 1961
R.H. Leigh	January 1962	1965

Station Masters at Maiden Newton

	From	*To*
Frederick Aldrich	January 1857	September 1857
William James	September 1857	June 1858
Frederick Beauchamp	September 1858	January 1860
William Mathews Mitcham	January 1860	April 1862
John Girling	April 1862	January 1866
William Edward Bock	January 1866	November 1869
Henry Yeo	November 1869	January 1876
George Hyrons	January 1876	November 1876
Walter Thompson Gray	November 1876	May 1881
Arthur Dagg	May 1881	August 1882
Alfred Reeve	August 1882	February 1897
Frederick William Cooper	February 1897	December 1897
E.C. Beard	December 1897	May 1899
Arthur John Campfield	May 1899	January 1901
Frank George Dunsford	March 1901	January 1913
Walter G. Stickland	January 1913	January 1919
Sidney Evans	January 1919	November 1925
John Albert Ralph	December 1925	April 1933
Walter Edward Ernest Pidding	April 1933	September 1935
F. Powell	September 1935	November 1941
Len E. Hole	November 1941	November 1944
J.H. Macmahon	November 1944	September 1957
W.E. Wrattenbury	September 1957	1965

Toller

Arthur Henry Woodrow
John Lansdale
Mr Hodder
Frederick William Green
Henry Carter Fisher
Joseph Liddiard
William H. Collins
Samuel Chalk
Edmund Dale
John Ware
John Colwell Brayley
H.S. Hill
John Churchill
Alfred James Pike
Arthur James Mount Stevens
W. Samways
R.F. Holmes
E. Marquis
Stanley C. Purcell
Sam Rawle
A.L. Rochester
M.E. Maguire
W.A.D. Macey
F.G. Thomas
F. Hayward
T.W. Benney
Frederick Barrett

Powerstock

Charles Gardner
Frederick William Green
Edmund Dale
Henry Samuel James
Richmond Roberts
A.F. Wheeler
A.G. Hacker
Arthur Samuel Chapman
H.E. Cooper
B.J. Hunt
E. Ball
S.C.H. Purnell
J.S. Knapp
C.H. Hendry
Ernest Bray

East Street

	From	To
Thomas Tuck	March 1884	January 1921
Frederick Gillingham	January 1921	April 1927

West Bay

William Thomas Moore
Frederick Price
William Chidsey
John Churchill
William J. Glinning
Richmond Roberts
H.E. Toller
William Richard Williams

A selection of Bridport station staff photographed in 1913. Seated centre front row is station master Frederick Weeks.   *M.J. Tattershall Collection*

Listed below is the staff establishment of the Traffic Department during 1922.

Bridport East Street		*West Bay*	
Station master	1	Station master	1
		Porter signalman	1

Toller		*Powerstock*	
Station master	1	Station master	1
Charwoman	1*	Charwoman	1*

Maiden Newton		*Bridport*	
Station master	1	Station master	1
General clerk	1	Booking clerk	1
Leading porter	1	Goods clerks	5
Parcel porter	1	Woman goods clerk	1
Porter signalman	1	General clerk	1
Porters	3	Parcel porters	2
Signalmen	2	Porters	3
Signal lampman	1	Motor parcel vanman	1
		Working foreman	1
Extra staff during		Goods carters	3
Summer 1 Porter grade 2.		Goods checker	1
		Goods porters	6
		Goods shunters	2
		Signalmen	2
		Guards	3
		Crossing Keeper†	1

* Charwoman employed one day a month at each station
† At Bradpole Crossing.

Goodbye Mr Barnby. A photograph of Bridport station staff to mark the retirement of Mr George Barnby on 9th May, 1938.
M.J. Tattershall Collection

Farewell to a Railway

In times of rapid change, it seldom pays
To retrace steps of happy childhood days.
This much I found, when given weather fine
I took a journey on the Bridport line.
The pastoral scene was like in days of yore,
But at the terminus, what shocks lay in store.

I had not been to Bridport for some years,
And what I found there brought me close to tears.
Oh, Bridport, Bridport, what's become of you?
You are but a pale shade of what I knew.
Your sidings gone, your building in decay,
And no line leading onwards to West Bay.

Despite all this, the line retains some charms,
Winding through lush green fields, and past old farms.
Recalling happier, more unhurried days,
When railways were the nation's great highways.
Few people use it now - its pride has gone
And soon tall grass will hide where once rails shone.

But nothing in this world can take from me
Fond memories of the way it used to be.
An engine, simmering quietly in its shed -
Another in the platform - fire being fed
With good Welsh coal, as water fills the tank
To lift the train up dreaded Loders Bank.

Or in the dusk of evening, handlamps gleam
From amidst the sidings, where flanges scream
As trucks of net and twine and cattle foods
Are marshalled up to form the 'Weymouth Goods'
Whilst on the platforms, 'neath the gas lamps glow
The folk of Bridport quickly come and go.

All this has gone. The line has had its day.
It must be closed because it fails to pay.
Now damp, deserted buildings grimly wait
To join most country stations in their fate.
Good men of Bridport, you were asked to use it,
But you declined, and now you're going to lose it.

Who knows, on nights when Autumn moons do peep
Over the brows of Dorset's hillsides steep
To draw up mist's from every pond and stream,
One's ears may catch again the hiss of steam,
And fancy that a train is dashing by,
For though the line be closed, it may refuse to die.

G.A. Pryer, May 1975

Acknowledgements

To assemble a book of this nature, reference has to be made to a great many documents, books, newspapers, and other sources. The principal items include the Bridport Railway Company Minute books and associated documents. Various documents and records of the GWR; *The Great Western Railway Magazine*; *The Bridport News*; *The Dorset County Chronicle*; *The Dorset Evening Echo*; *The Southern Times*, *Signal Box Diagrams of the GW & SR Vol. 1.*

The assistance of the following organisations is gratefully acknowledged; The various departments of the former British Railways; The library services of the Counties of Dorset, Gloucestershire, Somerset, and Fife; The Dorset County Archives Service; Gloucestershire County Record Office, Bridport Museum Services; The Public Record Office Kew; The National Railway Museum, York; Brunel University; The Institution of Civil Engineers; The Imperial War Museum; The Fleet Air Arm Museum Yeovilton; The Royal Artillery Historical Trust; The Queen's Own Royal West Kent Regiment Museum; The Manager Royal Train, Railcare; The Keeper of the Royal Archives Windsor Castle; The Signalling Record Society; Dutch National Railway Museum, Utrecht.

Thanks are also due to George Pryer for his work on the track and signal diagrams and his expert assistance in railway matters, and for checking and correcting the manuscript; Gerry Parkins for notes on early locomotive allocations; Richard Sims for assistance in the early history of the Wilts, Somerset & Weymouth line in particular Maiden Newton; Dr David Evans for information on Operation Yukon; and David Illingworth for the drawings of West Bay station.

And in alphabetical order

K. Bakes, Ivan Beale, Gerry Beale, R.K. Blencowe, Nigel Bray, C.L. Caddy, R.S. Carpenter, R.M. Casserley, N. Collins, M.E.J. Deane, Hugh Davies, M. Esau, A Goodwin, J. Gale, K. Goff, D. Habgood, R. Holmes, D. Hartland, J. Spencer Gilks, D. Lawrence, R.A. Lumber, S.C. Nash, R.A. Panting, D. Phillips, Mrs M.E. Payne, R.C. Riley, A. True, R.E. Toop, Mr & Mrs Young, E. Wilmshurst.

Last but not least the two Jeans, the wives who have for the past eight months put up with much burning of midnight oil and heard no other subject than the Bridport Railway.

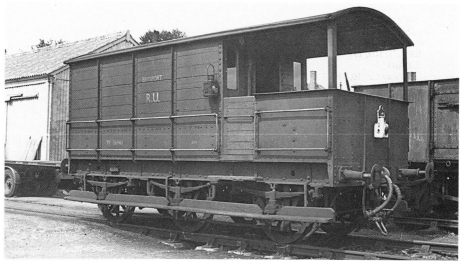

Bridport branch 24 ton six-wheel brake van No. 56943. Note the provision of both vacuum and steam heating pipes to enable the van to be used on the mixed trains that ran over the branch.

I.D.Beale

Index

Abbotsbury 61, 91, 153, 175.
Accidents 16, 18, 39, 44, 47, 48, 53, 56, 59, 61, 71, 77, 83, 85, 99, 107, 109, 175, 197.
Acts of Parliament 7, 8, 10.
Air raids 103, 105.
American Forces 105.
Axminster 7, 8, 14, 35, 61, 66, 67, 89.
Axminster & Lyme Regis Light Rly 67, 73, 89.

Beaminster 35, 44, 73, 89.
Beeching, Dr R. 191, 193.
Berwickshire Rly 39.
Blizzard 46, 47, 57, 65, 145, 191.
Boat Train 57, 193.
Book stalls 57, 65.
Bournemouth 66.
Bradford Peverall 193.
Bradpole 9, 56, 57, 77, 85, 103, 125, 169, 171, 197, 201, 205, 209.
Brickworks 30, 209.
Bridport 1, 7 et seq., 16, 18, 19, 25, 27, 29, 37, 46, 47, 49, 61, 63, 65 et seq., 71, 73, 77, 79, 86, 87, 89, 91, 95, 99, 103, 107, 125, 144, 145, 157, 165 ,169, 171 et seq., 177, 185, 193 et seq., 197, 199, 201, 205, 207, 209, 211.
Bridport Harbour 45, 47, 48, 51, 53 142, 213.
Bridport & Maiden Newton Rly 10.
Bridport News 13 et seq., 21, 23, 25 et seq., 37, 39, 43 et seq., 55, 56, 61, 62, 71 et seq., 85, 91, 108, 109, 177, 189, 191, 193 et seq., 201, 203.
Bridport Railway Co. 10, 11, 13 ., 21, 23, 25 et seq., 29 et seq., 35, 37, 39, 43 et seq., 51, 52, 57, 59, 63, 65, 67, 69, 165, 207.
Bristol & Exeter Rly 7, 8, 14, 34, 35.
Brit Valley Rly 211, 213.
Broad Gauge 39, 43.

Camp coaches 95, 99, 177.
Canal 108.
Castle Cary 7, 169, 193.
Castleman, C. 8.
Cattistock, 193.
Chard 35 et seq., 91.
Charmouth 8, 35, 66, 73, 89.
Chester & Holyhead Rly 13.
Chetnole 193
Cirencester 29.

Clarke, W. 50, 51, 211.
Closures 79, 91, 175, 191, 193, 194, 201, 203, 205.
Coal merchants 143, 144, 159.
Coal Traffic 105, 142, et seq. 194.
Contractors 15, 16, 21, 26, 27, 30, 33 ,49 et seq. 73, 207.
Crewkerne 7, 27, 44, 89, 211.

D-Day 107.
Devenish, Miss 44.
Diesel Units 157, 159, 173, 174, 189, 203.
Dorchester 8, 16, 21, 35, 45, 46, 53, 57, 65, 66, 87, 89, 163, 165, 169, 171, 191, 193.
Dorset County Chronicle 49.
Dunfermline 32.
Dutch Railways 29.

East Street, Bridport; 50 et seq., 56, 57, 59, 61, 73, 86, 89, 99, 125, 165, 169, 173, 177, 191, 209.
Evacuees 101, 103.
Evershot 16, 53, 163, 164, 165.
Exeter 7, 13, 35, 66, 89.
Exercise Wessex 11, 193.
Exercise Yukon 193

Flight, E.G. 9, 10, 17, 21, 23, 27, 29, 30, 31, 35, 37 ,38.
Floods 48, 56.
Frome; 8,65.

Gauge Change 39, 43.
Gerrard, J 15, 16.
Gloucester Wagon Co. 165.
Goods Traffic 142 et seq., 194.
General Post Office 65.
Gravity Siding 171,172.
Grierson, W.W. 45 et seq., 50, 52.
Griffiths, H.R. 87.
Grimstone & Frampton 53, 56, 153, 165, 193.
Gun Sidings 103, 107.
Gundry, J. 10, 13, 14, 21, 25, 27, 32, 44, 45, 49, 51.
GWR 7, 8, 10, 14, 17, 18, 23, 26, 30 et seq., 35, 37, 44, 45, 48 et seq., 57 ,59, 61, 65, 67, 73, 77, 101 ,175, 213.

Hart, W.A. 75.

Indian State Rlys 39.
Industrial Action 50, 85, 87, 145, 177.
Inspection of Line 18, 19.

Kirkcudbright Rly 39.

Legg, W. 66.
Locomotives, 147 et seq.
 Broad Gauge 18, 19, 147, 148, 155.
 Contractors 49 et seq.
 Failures 48, 63, 153, 197.
 LNER 193.
 Monmouth Rly & Canal Co. 151, 153.
 Preserved 157, 159, 213.
 SR 'M7' class 185.
Loders 13, 56, 57, 59, 108, 125.
Loggin, W. 29, 38, 45, 46 ,49 ,52, 53.
LNWR 50.
LSWR 7 et seq., 13, 14, 16, 26, 35, 44, 45, 66 ,67, 73, 74, 89.
Lyme Regis 8, 35, 37, 66, 67, 73, 89, 91, 193, 199.

Maiden Newton; 7,9,14 et seq., 18, 21, 23, 30, 31, 33, 34, 38, 39, 44 et seq., 50, 53, 56, 57, 66, 67, 77, 79, 87, 95, 99, 103, 105, 108, 111, 144, 145, 163, 165, 169, 171 et seq., 177, 193 et seq., 197, 199, 201, 203, 205, 207, 209, 211.
Main line doubling 53.
Mathieson, K. 13, 14, 21, 25 et seq. 31, 32.
Midland Rly 44, 50.
Milk Traffic 144, 145, 174, 199.
Mousley & Lovett 49.
MacDonnell Rail; 10,11,34.

Nantes, C.G. 49, 53, 63, 66, 95.
Narrow Gauge Rly 211.
National Omnibus & Transport Co. 89.
Nepean Lady, 55.

Omnibus Services 19, 27, 66, 73, 85, 87, 89, 91, 99, 103, 107, 109 144, 175, 177, 195, 207, 211.
Opening of line 19, 21.

Paddington 50, 71.
Pole, R.G. 87.
Portland 175, 193.
Powerstock 9, 13, 25, 37, 46, 57, 59, 61, 65, 75, 77, 79, 86, 89, 95, 99, 103, 105, 107, 109, 111, 144, 173, 175, 194 ,195, 197, 199, 201, 203, 209, 211.
Proposed Rlys 7, 8, 13, 14, 35, 37, 44 ,45, 61, 73, 211, 213.
Public Enquiries 193, 195, 201.

Railtours 173, 193, 197, 203, 205, 213.
Railway Times 13.
Refreshment Rooms 44, 108, 144, 177.
Refugees 79.
Rich, Col 51.
Road Transport 83, 144, 145, 177.
Roberts, R.F. 50.
Rolling Stock 57, 99, 159 *et seq.*, 173, 175, 211.
Rope and Net Industry 142, 143.
Royal Artillery 103.
Royal Engineers 103.
Royal Train, 177.

Salisbury 8.
Salisbury & Exeter, 193.
Selkirk & Galashields Rly 9.
Shepperd, J.E. 46, 65.
Ships 8, 51.
  Railway owned 103.
  Paddle steamers 174
Signalling 47, 57, 59, 61, 99, 111, 163 *et seq.*, 173, 194, 199, 211.
Snook, W. 59.
South Devon Rly (DVR) 209.
Southampton 66.
Southampton & Dorchester Rly 7,8.
Southern Times 56, 57.
South Lancs. Regiment 103.
Southern National Omnibus Co. 91, 99, 107, 177, 195, 197.
Southern Region BR 169, 175, 177, 189, 191.
Sparkford 175, 191.
Special Trains 23, 50, 52, 55, 63, 75, 173, 185, 193.
Statts, Forbes J. 29.
Station masters 217 *et seq.*
  Aldritch, F. 16, 128.
  Ball, E. 107, 218.
  Barnby, G. 87, 99, 217.
  Barrett, F.G. 185,189,218.
  Beard, E.C. 66, 67, 218.
  Beauchamp, F. 29, 34, 218.
  Benney, T.W. 185, 218.
  Bingham, D.G. 19, 29, 217.
  Bock, W.E. 37, 38, 218.
  Bond, H.A. 37, 46, 48, 217.
  Bray, E. 175, 219.
  Bray, S.W. 105, 109, 175, 217.
  Brayley, J.C. 71, 218.
  Campfield, A.J. 67, 218
  Chalk, S. 47, 218.
  Chidsey, W. 219.
  Churchill, J. 73, 86, 218, 219.
  Collins, W. 47, 218
  Colls, F.J. 99, 105, 217.

Station masters (cont.)
  Cooper, F.W. 66, 219.
  Cooper, H.E. 95, 219.
  Dagg, A. 47, 48, 218.
  Dale, E. 47, 65, 219.
  Dunsford, F.G. 67, 79, 91, 218.
  Fisher, H.S. 218.
  Evans, S. 85, 91, 218.
  Gardner, C. 37, 219.
  Gillingham, F. 86, 89, 95, 219.
  Girling, J. 35, 218.
  Glunning, W.J. 219.
  Gover, G. 177, 189, 217.
  Gray, W.T. 44, 47, 218.
  Green, F.W. 38, 65, 218, 219.
  Hacker, A.G. 86, 87, 219.
  Hayward, F. 175, 218.
  Hendry, C.J. 107, 175, 219.
  Hill, H.S. 73, 218.
  Hodder 218.
  Hole, L. 105, 189, 218.
  Holmes, A.F. 95, 218.
  Hunt, B.J. 95, 218.
  Hyron,s G. 44, 218.
  James, W. 16, 29, 218.
  Knapp, J.S. 107, 219.
  Knowles, H. 34, 217.
  Lansdale, J. 218.
  Liddiard, J. 38, 218.
  Leigh, R.H. 189, 194, 217.
  Macey, W.A.D. 107, 218.
  MacMahon, J. 105, 185, 218.
  Marquiss, E.W. 95, 105, 218.
  Marston O. 175, 177, 217.
  Moore, W.T. 219.
  Mount Stevens, A.J. 87, 95, 218.
  Peach, G. 55, 59, 65, 217.
  Pidding, W.E.E. 95, 218.
  Pike, A.J., 86, 87, 105, 218.
  Powell, F. 95, 218
  Purnell, S.C. 105, 107, 218.
  Price, F. 219.
  Ralph, J. 95, 218.
  Rawle, S. 107, 218.
  Reeve, A. 48, 53, 66, 218.
  Roberts, R. 79, 86, 87, 219
  Rochester, A.L. 107, 218.
  Samways, W. 95, 218.
  Stickland, W.G. 79, 85, 218.
  Thomas, F.G. 175, 218.
  Titball, W. 48, 55, 217.
  Toller, H. 87, 219
  Tuck, T. 86, 95, 219.
  Vaughan, W.F. 67, 75, 95, 217.
  Ware, J. 218.
  Webber, J. 34, 37, 217.
  Weeks, F. 75, 86, 91, 217.
  Wheeler, A.F. 86, 219.
  Widdows, C. 87, 95, 217.
  Williams, W.R. 89, 219.

Station masters (cont.)
  Woodrow, A.H. 35, 218.
  Wrattenbury, W.E. 185, 218.
  Yeo, H. 38, 39, 44, 218.
Steam Heritage Centre, 213.
Sussex 66.
Swanage 199, 201, 211.
Swatridge, W. 45, 49, 51.

Tasmanian Rlys. 39.
Taylor, G. 85.
Television 208, 209, 211.
Thingley Junction 165.
Thornford Bridge 193.
Thornton, R.D. 57, 59.
The Times 14.
Titball, C.H. 75.
Titfield Thunderbolt 49.
Toller 9, 15, 30, 35, 38, 47, 56, 61, 65, 66, 71, 73, 87, 95, 99, 103, 105, 107, 109, 111, 144, 145, 153, 169, 175, 185, 189, 194, 195, 197, 209, 211.
Totnes (SDR) 209.
Track Removal 31, 32, 194, 207.
Train Services 79, 87, 99, 101, 109, 173, 174, 191, 203.
Tyler, Capt. 18, 19.

West Bay, 49 *et seq.*, 53, 56, 57, 59, 65, 66, 79, 85 *et seq.*, 89, 91, 95, 101 ,103, 125, 142, 145, 165, 169, 189, 191, 193, 199, 211.
West Bay Extension opening 51 *et seq.*
West Bay Land & Building Co. 49.
Westbury 7, 8, 174.
West Kent Regiment 101.
Western Region BR 175, 177 ,191.
Weymouth 16, 53, 57, 63, 66, 73, 84, 91, 145, 147, 153, 171, 174, 175, 189, 194, 211.
Wilts, Somerset & Weymouth Rly 7 *et seq.*, 16, 39, 43, 67, 163, 171, 193.
Witherstone Cutting 13, 15 *et seq.*, 26, 27, 30, 33, 44, 56, 197, 209.
World War I 79 *et seq.*
World War II 101 *et seq.*
Wylie, H.J. 9 *et seq.*,13 *et seq.*, 18, 19, 21, 27, 39.

Yeovil 7, 14, 57, 75, 89, 105, 153, 163, 169, 171, 191, 193.
Yetminster 193.